Springer Series in Supply Chain Management

Volume 28

Series Editor

Christopher S. Tang, University of California, Los Angeles, USA

Supply Chain Management (SCM), long an integral part of Operations Management, focuses on all elements of creating a product or service, and delivering that product or service, at the optimal cost and within an optimal timeframe. It spans the movement and storage of raw materials, work-in-process inventory, and finished goods from point of origin to point of consumption. To facilitate physical flows in a time-efficient and cost-effective manner, the scope of SCM includes technology-enabled information flows and financial flows.

The Springer Series in Supply Chain Management, under the guidance of founding Series Editor Christopher S. Tang, covers research of either theoretical or empirical nature, in both authored and edited volumes from leading scholars and practitioners in the field – with a specific focus on topics within the scope of SCM.

This series is Scopus-indexed.

Springer and the Series Editor welcome book ideas from authors. Potential authors who wish to submit a book proposal should contact Ms. Jialin Yan, Editor, Springer (Germany), e-mail: jialin.yan@springernature.com

Temidayo Akenroye • Marcia Mkansi
Haitao Li • Godfrey Mugurusi
Editors

Digitalizing Health Care Supply Chains in Africa

Achievements, Challenges and Impact

Springer

Editors
Temidayo Akenroye
Supply Chain Management and Analytics
University of Missouri–St. Louis
St. Louis, MO, USA

Haitao Li
Supply Chain Management and Analytics
University of Missouri–St. Louis
St. Louis, MO, USA

Marcia Mkansi
College of Economic and Management Sciences
The University of South Africa
Pretoria, South Africa

Godfrey Mugurusi
Department of Industrial Economics and Technology Management
Norwegian University of Science and Technology
Gjøvik, Norway

ISSN 2365-6395 ISSN 2365-6409 (electronic)
Springer Series in Supply Chain Management
ISBN 978-3-032-20500-1 ISBN 978-3-032-20501-8 (eBook)
https://doi.org/10.1007/978-3-032-20501-8

This Springer imprint is published by the registered company Springer Nature Switzerland AG
The registered company address is: Gewerbestrasse 11, 6330 Cham, Switzerland

Digitalizing Healthcare Supply Chains in Africa: *Achievements, Challenges and Impact*

Introduction

Healthcare supply chains are a critical component of health systems worldwide, ensuring the timely and equitable delivery of medicines, diagnostics, and health commodities to those in need. In Africa, these supply chains operate under particularly challenging conditions, characterized by fragmented processes, inadequate infrastructure, and governance deficiencies (Woodburn 2013; Modisakeng et al. 2020). These weaknesses have significant consequences, including frequent stock-outs, delays in care, and increased mortality, particularly among vulnerable populations such as women and children (Yadav 2015). The urgent need for more efficient healthcare supply chains has gained prominence in recent years, driven by increasing demand for equitable access to healthcare and the burden of both communicable and non-communicable diseases. Despite significant investments by governments and international organizations such as WHO and UNICEF, persistent inefficiencies limit the impact of these efforts (Goshorn and Usswald 2014). Furthermore, the dynamic and highly regulated nature of healthcare systems poses unique challenges, with complex interdependencies across stakeholders, processes, and technologies (Cullen and Taylor 2009). Digital transformation offers a pathway to address these systemic issues. Emerging technologies such as big data analytics, Internet of Things (IoT), blockchain, and augmented reality promise to revolutionize supply chain operations by enhancing visibility, optimizing inventory management, and fostering data-driven decision-making (Song et al. 2019; Ben-Daya et al. 2019). These tools have already demonstrated success in other industries, such as manufacturing and food systems (Klötzer and Pflaum 2017; Amentae and Gebresenbet 2021). However, their application within Africa's healthcare sector remains limited, requiring a contextual understanding of local challenges and opportunities (Shamim et al. 2017). This book, "Digitalizing Healthcare Supply Chains in Africa: Successes, Challenges, and Impact," brings together scholars and practitioners to explore the transformative potential of digital technologies in healthcare supply chains across the continent. Through a combination of case studies, thematic analyses, and

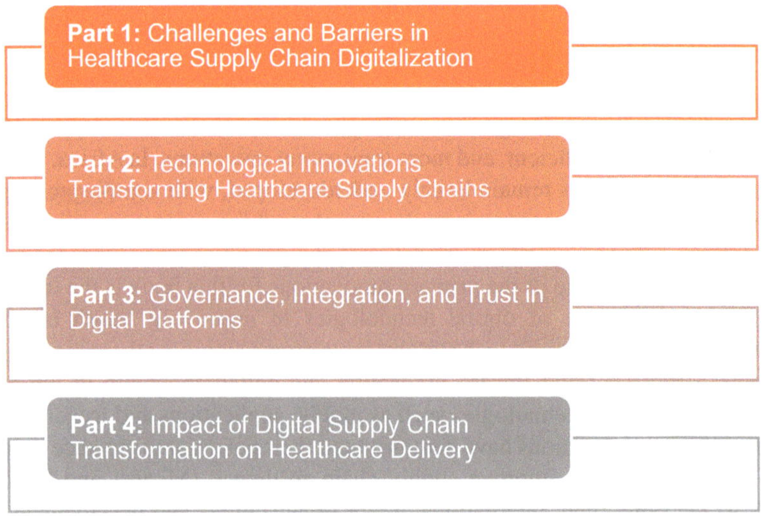

Part I: Challenges and Barriers in Healthcare Supply Chain Digitalization

The first part addresses the structural and systemic challenges that hinder digital transformation in Africa's healthcare supply chains. Through detailed discussions, the chapters reveal how political, social, and technological factors intersect to create obstacles, while also identifying pathways to overcome them. **Trout et al.** examine the maternal and child health (MCH) supply chain in South Africa, providing a compelling analysis of socio-economic stressors, such as male partner abandonment and food insecurity, that exacerbate inefficiencies. Their chapter sheds light on how fragmented data systems and limited digital infrastructure hinder the integration of mobile and digital health tools. The authors emphasize the need for collaborative efforts across sectors to establish robust data systems and foster digital readiness, offering a roadmap for improving MCH outcomes. **Asiedu et al.** expand this discussion by focusing on barriers to innovation diffusion in Uganda's public healthcare supply chains. Their research introduces the "A.R.E. Concept," which highlights the importance of adequate preparation, readiness for implementation, and efficient system management. This framework provides practical solutions for overcoming political, economic, and technological hurdles, enabling healthcare systems to better embrace digital transformation. Together, these chapters offer a nuanced perspective on the socio-economic realities and governance challenges of digitalizing healthcare supply chains. They set the stage for the exploration of innovative solutions in subsequent sections.

Part II: Technological Innovations Transforming Healthcare Supply Chains

The second part explores the promise of technological innovations and showcases how cutting-edge tools are reshaping healthcare supply chains in Africa. These chapters illustrate the transformative power of digital solutions in improving efficiency, accessibility, and decision-making. **Okoche et al.** present a case study on the use of a mobile application to coordinate malaria stock and production management in South Africa. This example demonstrates how digital tools empower small suppliers to manage inventory effectively, even in resource-constrained settings. By showcasing how the application enables real-time decision-making and operational efficiency, the chapter highlights its potential to create more agile and responsive supply chains, critical for addressing urgent health challenges like malaria. **Mkansi et al.** focus on the role of frugal artificial intelligence (AI) innovations in pediatric radiology supply chains. Their chapter examines how AI-driven tools optimize resource allocation, enhance diagnostic accuracy, and bridge healthcare disparities. By applying the Technology-Organization-Environment (TOE) framework, the authors provide actionable insights into scaling AI solutions across diverse healthcare contexts in Africa. The chapter not only highlights the benefits of AI but also addresses the socio-economic factors influencing its adoption, offering a comprehensive view of its potential. This section showcases the creative and impactful ways digital innovations are addressing logistical and operational challenges in Africa's healthcare systems. It provides readers with compelling examples of how technology is redefining supply chain management in the region.

Part III: Governance, Integration, and Trust in Digital Platforms

The third part focuses on governance, integration, and trust, which are crucial for the successful implementation of digital healthcare supply chains. These chapters explore how digital platforms enable better stakeholder collaboration, enhance transparency, and streamline supply chain operations. **Abdulkadir and Kreie** examine the effects of digital platforms on governance and visibility in Nigeria's public healthcare system. Their findings reveal how these platforms reduce medicine stockouts by fostering trust and improving coordination among stakeholders. The authors advocate for advanced capacity-building initiatives to enhance governance structures and ensure the full potential of digital platforms is realized. In a complementary chapter, **Matenda et al**. analyze Health-Guider, a file and database system designed to streamline supply chain processes. This tool simplifies tasks like appointment scheduling and prescription management while addressing integration challenges. The authors also discuss significant barriers to market access, particularly in South Africa, where restrictive policies and infrastructure gaps limit scalability. Their analysis balances the possibilities of digital tools with the challenges of implementing them in real-world settings. By focusing on governance and integration, this section emphasizes the importance of stakeholder collaboration and aligned policies. It offers practical recommendations for fostering trust and building cohesive digital healthcare supply chains.

Part IV: Impact of Digital Supply Chain Transformation on Healthcare Delivery

The final part examines the tangible impacts of digital transformation on healthcare delivery. These chapters explore how digital tools improve patient outcomes, enhance accessibility, and promote resource efficiency, offering a hopeful vision for the future. **Ogweno et al** analyze the role of mobile health (mHealth) initiatives in addressing healthcare literacy gaps in sub-Saharan Africa. Using the Stowelink Foundation as a case study, they demonstrate how digital platforms empower communities to engage in their healthcare journeys, fostering positive health behaviors and strengthening the downstream arm of healthcare supply chains. **Mkansi and Ogweno** expand on this theme by exploring the Lifesten Health application's impact on diagnosing non-communicable diseases in Rwanda. Their chapter highlights how AI-enabled mobile diagnostics extend healthcare delivery beyond traditional facilities, integrating diverse stakeholders such as pharmaceutical companies, insurers, and community forums into a cohesive ecosystem. This narrative underscores the potential of digital transformation to create equitable and patient-centered healthcare supply chains. These chapters illustrate the far-reaching benefits of digital tools, showcasing their ability to bridge gaps in healthcare delivery and improve resource efficiency. They invite readers to envision a future where technology transforms healthcare supply chains into systems that prioritize accessibility, quality, and equity.

Conclusion

The chapters in this book collectively advance the discourse on healthcare supply chain digitalization in Africa. By addressing challenges, showcasing innovations, and exploring governance and impact, the book offers a holistic understanding of the digital transformation journey. It serves as a valuable resource for academics, policymakers, and practitioners seeking to improve healthcare delivery through innovative and contextually relevant supply chain solutions. By bridging the gap between theory and practice, this volume positions Africa as a hub of innovation in healthcare supply chain digitalization, paving the way for sustainable and equitable healthcare delivery across the continent.

University of Missouri—St Louis
St. Louis, MO, USA
Temidayo Akenroye
takenroye@umsl.edu

University of South Africa
Pretoria, South Africa
Marcia Mkansi
mkansm@unisa.ac.za

University of Missouri—St Louis
St. Louis, MO, USA
Haitao Li
lihait@umsl.edu

Norwegian University of Science and Technology
Gjøvik, Norway
Godfrey Mugurusi
godfrey.mugurusi@ntnu.no

References

Akpan G, Bello I, Mohamed HF, Touray K, Kipterer J, Ngofa R, … Mkanda P (2020) The digitization of active surveillance: an insight-based evaluation of interactive visualization of active case search for polio surveillance to support decision making in Africa

Amentae TK, Gebresenbet G (2021) Digitalization and future agro-food supply chain management: a literature-based implications. Sustainability 13(21):12181

Ben-Daya M, Hassini E, Bahroun Z (2019) Internet of things and supply chain management: a literature review. Int J Prod Res 57(15–16):4719–4742

Cullen AJ, Taylor M (2009) Critical success factors for B2B e-commerce use within the UK NHS pharmaceutical supply chain. Int J Oper Prod Manage 29:1156

Dell N, Crawford J, Breit N, Chaluco T, Coelho A, McCord J, Borriello G (2013, Dec) Integrating ODK Scan into the community health worker supply chain in Mozambique. In: Proceedings of the Sixth International Conference on Information and Communication Technologies and Development: Full Papers-Vol 1, pp 228–237

Goshorn B, Usswald C (2014) Pharmaceutical supply chains in Africa–overcoming unique transport security challenges. J Transport Secur 7(4):333–337

Kene-Okafor T (2022) African health tech startups in the supply chain segment show rapid growth, spurring a $7M investment initiative. https://techcrunch.com/2022/06/22/africanhealthtech-startups-in-the-supply-chain-segment-show-rapid-growth-spurring-a-7m-investmentinitiative/

Klötzer C, Pflaum A (2017) Toward the development of a maturity model for digitalization within the manufacturing industry's supply chain

Kunnapapdeelert S, Pitchayadejanant K (2020) Hybrid SEM-neural networks for predicting electronics logistics information system adoption in Thailand healthcare supply chain. Int J Bus Perform Supply Chain Model 11(1):54–68

Mkansi M, Landman N (2021) The future of work in Africa in the era of 4IR–The South African perspective. Afr J Manage 7(suppl 1):17–30

Modisakeng C, Matlala M, Godman B, Meyer JC (2020) Medicine shortages and challenges with the procurement process among public sector hospitals in South Africa; findings and implications. BMC Health Serv Res 20(1):1–10

Shamim S, Cang S, Yu H, Li Y (2017) Examining the feasibilities of Industry 4.0 for the hospitality sector with the lens of management practice. Energies 10(4):499

Song JM, Sung J, Park T (2019) Applications of blockchain to improve supply chain traceability. Proc Comp Sci 162:119–122

Umair M, Cheema MA, Cheema O, Li H, Lu H (2021) Impact of COVID-19 on IoT adoption in healthcare, smart homes, smart buildings, smart cities, transportation and industrial IoT. Sensors 21(11):3838

Woodburn PA (2013) Analysis of challenges of medical supply chains in sub-Saharan Africa regarding inventory management and transport and distribution. London Westminster Business School

Yadav P (2015) Health product supply chains in developing countries: diagnosis of the root causes of underperformance and an agenda for reform. Health Syst Reform 1(2):142–154

Contents

Godfrey Mugurusi is an Associate Professor of Logistics and Supply Chain Management at the Norwegian University of Science & Technology (NTNU), where he also directs the Bachelor of Logistics Management program. His research focuses on digitalization and sustainability within procurement and supply chain management (PSCM), with publications in leading journals such as Journal of Purchasing & Supply Management and Operations Management Research. A former practitioner in FMCG and public procurement, he serves on advisory boards for key supply chain research initiatives across Africa.

Part I
Challenges and Barriers in Healthcare Supply Chain Digitalization

Chapter 1
Challenges and Lessons Learned to Strengthen Maternal and Child Health in South Africa and Considerations for Implementing Digital Technologies

Kate E. Trout, Gillian Bartlett-Esquilant, Chantell Witten, Eyob Teklesenbet, Julian May, and Shane Norris

1.1 Introduction

Malnutrition is a neglected and preventable aspect of maternal and child health (MCH) and is estimated to be an underlying factor in nearly 30% of children's deaths in South Africa (Department of Health 2020). Despite South Africa's efforts, through multiple programs (social grants, health services, micronutrient supplements, exclusive breastfeeding support), the population of South Africa continues to face significant mortality and a seemingly unmovable prevalence of stunting. In South Africa, the persistent burden of stunted children remains unchanged, and malnutrition among women of reproductive age is increasing. Stunting, also known as chronic malnutrition, can occur from the cumulative effects of undernutrition and infections during childhood, and notably, can occur even before birth. Stunting, severe wasting, and intrauterine growth restriction are among the most significant problems related to undernutrition, which can occur because of nutritional deficiencies and/or persistent diarrheal episodes. There is a golden interval for intervention,

K. E. Trout (✉) · E. Teklesenbet
Department of Health Sciences, University of Missouri-Columbia, Columbia, MO, USA
e-mail: kate.trout@health.missouri.edu

G. Bartlett-Esquilant
Texas A&M College of Medicine, College Station, TX, USA

C. Witten
University of the Witwatersrand, Johannesburg, South Africa

J. May
University of the Western Cape, Cape Town, South Africa

S. Norris
University of Southampton, Southampton, UK

T. Akenroye et al. (eds.), *Digitalizing Health Care Supply Chains in Africa*, Springer Series in Supply Chain Management 28,
https://doi.org/10.1007/978-3-032-20501-8_1

from pregnancy to 2 years of age, that creates an opportunity to change child growth trajectories and improve health outcomes (WHO 2008). Malnutrition during the first 2 years of life can cause a delay/decline in both physical and cognitive growth. After age 2, undernutrition will have caused irreversible damage for future development towards adulthood, making these individuals more susceptible to both infectious and chronic diseases. Immediate attention is needed to reduce childhood mortality under the age of 5, and especially in South Africa that remains an outlier despite being an upper middle-income country.

Stunting is defined as low height-for-age that is caused by chronic undernutrition, and is associated with poverty, poor maternal health and nutrition, and inappropriate feeding and care in early life. Stunting can cause several negative health outcomes such as a delay in cognitive development, hindered physical growth, and greater illness and poor health (Said-Mohamed et al. 2015). When children are stunted, it not only hampers their own physical and cognitive development, but also perpetuates a cycle of poverty as the individuals affected are less likely to achieve their full potential, to complete their education, and to escape the cycle of poverty, thus leading to continued deprivation in subsequent generations.

Nearly 30% of children under the age of 5 are nutritionally stunted in South Africa, a prevalence that has remained unchanged for more than three decades (May et al. 2020). This is particularly worrisome since the right to access sufficient food and nutrition is embedded in Sections 27 and 28 of the South African Constitution of 1996, and South Africa has consistently adopted and implemented strategies that have reduced stunting in other countries. Researchers and providers in primary care have developed guidelines on how to properly address malnutrition and child mortality (Department of Planning, Monitoring, and Evaluation of South Africa 2014). Mothers should be getting counseling on their health status and recommendations about child nutrition and where food could be found by healthcare providers. Other guidelines included exclusive breastfeeding and providing energy-dense and micronutrient-enriched foods. South Africa has been able to implement these guidelines and use community-based education to teach mothers how to prevent stunting (Department of Planning, Monitoring, and Evaluation of South Africa 2014; UNICEF 2020a, 2020b).

This places South Africa as an outlier when compared to other upper-middle-income countries regarding the ability to significantly impact preventable stunting outcomes (May and Timæus 2014; Devereux et al. 2019). Addressing stunting requires a holistic approach that considers all these complex and interrelated factors. However, the lack of Big Data in South Africa and much of Africa and Asia makes it difficult to understand the drivers and impacts of chronic malnutrition and poor maternal and child health related to stunting. Discussion has begun on how patients in South African might be able to use their phones to keep health records, thus improving digitized health data and strengthening patient-provider interactions. The idea is that patients would bring their phones when going to see a healthcare provider but would also have access to records after leaving their provider's office. Having health records on one's phone presents certain challenges. For example, if someone were to steal one's phone, the privacy of a person's records would be breached allowing others to observe sensitive information that is meant to remain private.

These types of occurrences would likely lead to mistrust and stigma within the communities, especially related to disclosing HIV status. However, mothers disclosing their HIV status can lead to improved maternal and child health by ensuring timely access to appropriate medical care and support. This disclosure also enables better planning and management of the child's health, including preventive measures against HIV transmission to reduce the risk of mother-to-child HIV transmission. Beyond HIV status, the propensity to disclose maternal and child health information in South Africa varies, influenced by factors such as cultural norms, stigma, education levels, and trust in healthcare systems. While some mothers may openly share health information to receive better care and support, others may withhold it due to concerns about stigma, privacy, or mistrust of healthcare providers. Efforts to improve health literacy, reduce stigma, and build trust in the healthcare system are crucial to encouraging more widespread and open disclosure of maternal and child health information. Further research is needed to explore how health records can be managed on phones in South Africa to digitize health data and enhance patient-provider interactions, while addressing stigma-related concerns and ensuring privacy and confidentiality.

In this chapter, we will discuss (1) the importance of engaging in community-based participatory research for directing Big Data resources for maternal and child health, and (2) the identification of the modifiable factors underlying malnutrition in South Africa that will require multi-sectoral efforts. Big Data could help South Africa monitor and use empirical data results to make supported healthcare decisions. This approach is outlined in the Nurturing Care Framework, a comprehensive plan that has been adopted by the South Africa National Department of Health, which is discussed in detail later in the chapter. Tracking variables such as the prevalence of modifiable risk factors of breastfeeding, diarrheal episodes, malnutrition, and mental health will improve maternal and child health. Big Data will also help improve and implement data-driven policies and programs by prioritizing intervenable factors by geography and time within the first 1000 days of life. The "First 1000 days" of life approach emphasizes the critical significance of the period from conception to a child's second birthday, and plays a foundational role in shaping a child's physical and cognitive development. Policies and procedures implemented from data-driven decision support will improve the public health of South Africa even while other infections and diseases such as HIV/AIDS, TB, and Covid-19 are still in high prevalence within the country.

1.1.1 Study Context

Diversity in South Africa is a defining characteristic of the nation which boasts a complex tapestry of people, cultures, languages, and ethnicities. South Africa is often referred to as the "Rainbow Nation" due to its remarkable blend of diversity.

multiple noncommunicable diseases (Chidumwa et al. 2021). This double burden of chronic and infectious diseases can complicate pregnancy and delivery, especially in women who experience hypertension, hyperglycemic disorders, and weight gain (Hoffman et al. 2021). Furthermore, South Africa women experience high rates of depression during the prenatal stage and postpartum stages of pregnancy. This factor combined with the rate of comorbidity in South Africa makes delivery very complicated, especially since South Africa lacks the resources and infrastructure to treat patients with mental illness (Pellowski et al. 2019).

South African women have a high frequency of being victims of domestic violence, with a quarter of the female population having been abused (emotionally/physically/sexually). Domestic violence tends to be underreported, due to fear of retaliation, so this rate can be assumed to be higher (Mshweshwe 2020). Abuse puts a large amount of stress and harm on pregnant women which can cause complications during and after the pregnancy. A study showed that 12% of the domestic violence in South Africa is against pregnant women contributing to depression, PTSD, substance abuse, hypertension, sexually transmitted diseases, and anxiety (Field et al. 2018). Domestic assault during pregnancy or post-delivery can lead to infant mortality because mothers who are fearful of retribution tend to forego prenatal care which can lead to low-birthweight, placenta abruption, hemorrhaging, rupturing of the uterus, and premature labor. In some facets of South Africa's culture makes some women avoid reporting the abuse they are experiencing, especially if the partner is not the only perpetrator. For example, in rural areas there are many multigenerational households, and some women face abuse from family members other than their partners. This dynamic adds to the reasoning of women not telling healthcare professionals or local authorities about their abuse. More studies need to be conducted on mothers who are experiencing abuse and mental illness during their pregnancy to hopefully lower the mortality rates of both mothers and their babies.

As discussed, chronic malnutrition in early life is still a problem in many South African regions, especially in rural areas. According to UNICEF, only 32% of mothers in South Africa exclusively breastfeed. Exclusive breastfeeding is vital in the development of a child during the first 6 months. Deaths attributed to stunting and wasting have accounted for 21%–33% of deaths in children under 5 (Nannan et al. 2022). The UNICEF data warehouse shows that the child mortality rate in South Africa has declined over the years, with a current rate of 33 deaths per 1000. The cause of death is still complex due to comorbidity rates being so high; however, we most often find that child mortality rates are caused by pregnancy and delivery complications, HIV/AIDS, neonatal illness, and chronic malnutrition (Mabaso 2013). Studies must be done to identify modifiable levers to overcome the negative impacts that poverty and inequity have on maternal and child health outcomes.

1.2.2 The Nurturing Care Framework

The Nurturing Care Framework (NCF) has been adopted by the South Africa National Department of Health as a comprehensive approach that focuses on providing integrated services that promote both survival and nurturing care through the health system (World Health Organization, United Nations Children's Fund, and World Bank Group 2018). The NCF targets middle- and low-income countries to help children not only survive but also ultimately thrive, while lowering child mortality rates throughout the world. The NCF establishes five strategic action plans to help the development of newborns and children, including: lead and invest, focus on families and their communities, strengthen services, monitor progress, and use data and innovation (Fig. 1.1).

Focusing on improving data and innovation creates opportunities to enhance practices, identify disparities, and improve healthcare outcomes. Effective and timely data gives healthcare professionals the tools to make evidence-based decisions, which lead to better outcomes in child development. When you can measure, collect, and analyze data, you can more effectively improve, manage, and control healthcare costs, access, and outcomes (Nelson et al. 2000), and stakeholders, politicians, healthcare professionals, and researchers can improve more than just child development and well-being (WHO et al. 2018). However, multidisciplinary partnerships often lack the funding and infrastructure to create the necessary multisectoral databases, where NCF can serve as a guide for new data structures and innovations. Officials and healthcare leaders must prioritize the implementation of

Fig. 1.1 The five components of nurturing care—Source: The World Health Organization, the United Nations Children's Fund, and the World Bank Group (2018) Nurturing Care for Early Childhood Development: A framework for helping children survive and thrive to transform health and human potential. Geneva: WHO

The Wits partnership is led by Professor Shane Norris who is also the Director of the DSI-NRF Centre of Excellence in Human Development (CoE-HD), one of 11 such centres established by the South African National Research Foundation to promote multi-institutional and multidisciplinary research. The University of the Western Cape and the DSI-NRF Centre of Excellence in Food Security (CoE-FS) is led by Professor Julian May, the Director of the DSI-NRF Centre of Excellence in Food Security. Over the past 10 years, the CoE-FS has explored how a sustainable food system can be achieved to realize food security for poor, vulnerable, and marginal populations. Among other projects, the CoE-FS is involved in developmental efforts that include climate smart agriculture and the development of computable general equilibrium models of food systems and data pooling projects on child malnutrition. In addition to the core functions of research and training, activities of engagement by the CoE-FS include linking thought leaders through the establishment of Communities of Practice (CoP); workshops, symposia, and conferences; demonstration plots and "proof-of-concept" projects.

As a team, we engaged in community-based participatory research (CBPR) to identify and characterize multi-dimensional and modifiable explanatory variables underlying heterogeneous MCH outcomes (mortality, malnutrition related to stunting, and mental health) across two South African provinces, Gauteng and Western Cape, using a "first 1000 days" lens. Secondarily, we assessed the feasibility of implementing digital technologies (such as mHealth applications) to augment Big Data efforts and deliver interventions. CBPR is of paramount importance in the realm of academic inquiry and social change. This collaborative approach brings together researchers and community members to jointly design, conduct, and disseminate research projects. Community-based participatory research recognizes that local communities possess invaluable insights and expertise about their own needs and challenges.

By engaging these communities as active partners in the research process, CBPR ensures that the research is not only relevant but also responsive to the community's concerns. This approach promotes a more equitable distribution of power, fosters mutual learning, and generates sustainable solutions that can directly benefit the community. Ultimately, CBPR empowers communities to take control of their own narratives, promotes social justice, and leads to more effective and meaningful research outcomes that drive positive change at the grassroots level. Through conducting key informant interviews and community focus groups, participants were encouraged to describe the complex interplay of multiple factors over the first 1000-day period to identify barriers to MCH and facilitate improvement in the intervention and policy efforts. Using the Nurturing Care Framework, we focused on identifying factors important for children to "survive and thrive" by targeting the heterogeneous MCH outcomes of mortality, malnutrition related to stunting, and mental health across the five domains: health, nutrition, responsive caregiving, security and safety, and early learning. By triangulating results from this mixed methods study, we identified key priorities to advance implementation science and Big Data for studying MCH outcomes.

We conducted key informant interviews and focus group sessions in July 2022. Informants engaged in in-depth interviews for 45 min to 1 h and included public health professionals/researchers, government stakeholders, health care professionals, and community health workers. The purpose was to collect information from a wide range of stakeholders including leaders in the field, and those who have first-hand knowledge on the topic to propose recommendations to address these priorities. Three focus group sessions were conducted in a rural agricultural community in Western Cape. Each session lasted about 2 h and included 6–11 participants who were recruited through convenience sampling. Two female caregiver (i.e., mother/grandmother) focus groups and one male caregiver (i.e., father/male partner) focus group was conducted to gather diverse perspectives. We know that men's engagement is a critical component for improving maternal and child health, yet there is a gap in involving men as part of the research processes (Ditekemena et al. 2012; Tokhi et al. 2018). Participants were (1) 18 years or older, and (2) currently caring for at least 1 child that was 2 years or younger. Each focus group was facilitated by local translators in Afrikaans and IsiXhosa trained in best practices for data collection. All interviews and focus group sessions were audio-recorded and transcribed after the sessions. We conducted thematic and content analyses of qualitative data. The information from the key informant interviews was compared with results from focus group sessions. NVivo was used for all qualitative analyses.

1.4 Results

Table 1.1 describes the characteristics of all study participants. The key informants included those in academia/research (n = 2; 28.6%), government official (n = 1; 14.3%), and community health workers (n = 3; 42.9%). Across all participant groups, the majority were unmarried. Three of the female caregivers identified as grandmothers, and the rest as mothers. All the female caregivers were unemployed, and the majority of the male caregivers (83.3%). One male caregiver identified their occupation as "self-employed," which could indicate contract labor. Over half of the female caregivers identified as colored (57.9%) predominately speaking IsiXhosa (57.9%) as their first language. Most of the male focus group identified as black African (66.7%), and all spoke IsiXhosa.

Table 1.2 describes themes impacting nutrition that focuses on the first 1000 days of life. All participants said that employment opportunities are key priorities for male and female caregivers. Key informants said that poverty and economic opportunity is the root of the malnutrition issues in South Africa. The pandemic further negatively impacted health outcomes for mothers and children. All groups stated

Table 1.1 Sociodemographic and characteristics of study participants

Sociodemographic	Key informants $N = 7$ n(%)	Female caregiver focus group $N = 19$ n(%)	Male caregiver focus group $N = 6$ n(%)
Gender			
Male	0 (0)	0 (0)	6 (100)
Female	7 (100)	19 (100)	0 (0)
Age*			
Under 20	0 (0)	1 (5.3)	0 (0)
20–29	0 (0)	7 (36.8)	0 (0)
30–39	2 (28.6)	5 (26.3)	3 (50)
40–49	4 (57.1)	2 (10.5)	2 (33.3)
50+	1 (14.3)	1 (5.3)	1 (16.7)
No answer/don't know	0 (0)	3 (15.8)	0 (0)
Marital status			
Married	3 (42.9)	4 (21.1)	0 (0)
Unmarried	4 (57.1)	15 (78.9)	6 (100)
Ethnicity			
White	2 (28.6)	1 (5.3)	0 (0)
Coloured	2 (28.6)	11 (57.9)	2 (33.3)
Black African	3 (42.9)	7 (36.8)	4 (66.7)
First language			
Dutch	1 (14.3)	0 (0)	0 (0)
English	1 (14.3)	0 (0)	0 (0)
Afrikaans	1 (14.3)	7 (36.8)	0 (0)
IsiXhosa	4 (57.1)	11 (57.9)	6 (100)
Other	0 (0)	1 (5.3)	0 (0)
Highest education			
Primary	0 (0)	1 (5.3)	0 (0)
Grades 8–10	0 (0)	7 (36.8)	1 (16.7)
Grades 10–12	4 (57.1)	6 (31.6)	3 (50)
Tertiary	3 (42.9)	1 (5.3)	2 (33.3)
No answer/none	0 (0)	4 (21.0)	0 (0)
Employment status			
Unemployed	0 (0)	19 (100)	5 (83.3)
Number of children			
1	–	5 (26.3)	1 (16.7)
2	–	6 (31.6)	2 (33.3)
3	–	5 (26.3)	1 (16.7)
4	–	2 (10.5)	2 (33.3)
5+	–	1 (5.3)	0 (0)

Table 1.2 Themes related to breastfeeding and early nutrition in the first 1000 days of life

Theme	Participants	Challenges for breastfeeding and adequate, safe nutrition
Economic opportunities	All groups	Lack of grant support and supplements for nutritious foods. Difficult to break cycles of poverty and poor health. Exacerbated by pandemic
Return to work	All groups	Returning to work was a prominent reason that mothers discontinued exclusive breastfeeding
Breastmilk storage/ Refrigeration	All groups	Lack of to store breastmilk, especially when returning to work. Informal housing lacks refrigeration and often electricity all together
Mental health issues	All groups	Mental health and lack of spousal support by male partners Stress from the pandemic Lack of economic opportunity
Domestic abuse and spouse abandonment	All groups	Domestic abuse and spousal abandonment after pregnancy were the two most common reasons that male partners negatively impacted a mother's mental health. Acknowledge the lack of support provided by male partners
House crowding	Female caregivers	House crowding and an absence of privacy
Cultural barriers	Female caregivers	Several participants mentioned that some women express and discard "bad milk" when a woman has bad thoughts or has a bad day. Female caregivers did not view water consumption as an important aspect for breastfeeding, because drink ginger beer and tea is a cultural practice for breastfeeding for milk production
Need for baby bottles	Female caregivers	Mothers often only have one baby bottle to feed formula or breastmilk. One participant reported they used an empty juice box because they did not have a bottle
Education	All groups	Lack of opportunity to receive education. Breastfeeding mothers most often get their information for their elders, which is often outdated. Porridge and water are often fed to infants as young as 2 weeks old
Water, sanitation, and hygiene	All groups	Infrequent washing and sanitization of the baby bottles between uses (e.g., every 2 weeks). Water sources remain unpredictable, and not always clean. Lack of soap, where mothers sometimes must borrow soap from neighbors. Cleaning breasts before feeding was not readily practiced. Most participants reported that water containers are covered only half of the time and infrequently washed

Note: "All groups" include key informants, female caregivers, and male caregivers that most pronounced impact was job security and food security, especially for children as a result of school closures that strained household food supply. The male caregivers said that government assistance grants were not enough to support families' needs.

> *"R350 [for the grant] did not feed the families. They called it a relief grant which was not helping at all."* Additionally, one male caregiver said, *"[the] Government had rules that said no work no pay."*

Male and female caregivers said underscored there were no protections specifically for pregnant women during lockdown during the pandemic, which included gaps in prenatal care and nutrition support. Female caregivers and all key informants said that breastfeeding was more difficult because of the mental stress of the pandemic. Conversely, two key informants also identified that, in some instances, breastfeeding improved after the pandemic because it became more difficult to afford formula. Lastly, key informants said that there was an increase in terminated pregnancies due to the pandemic, further underscoring the importance for family planning in the post-pandemic period. Key informants, and female and male caregivers identified that returning to work was a major issue for discontinuing breastfeeding, and the lack of refrigeration in low-income, informal households impacts the ability to store breastmilk and other foods. The lack of refrigeration and reliable sources of electricity make it important to consider shelf-stable foods.

One key informant said,

> There should be support for mothers who are nursing the young infants, things like maternity leave and whatever needs to be done in order to create an enabling environment for to continue breastfeeding a child.

There was a strong consensus among female caregivers that mothers would like government support to have more than one baby bottle in the household. One participant reported that she used an empty juice box to feed her baby formula because she did not have any bottles. In addition, they reported that it was difficult to heat water for bottle cleaning because of lack of electricity and load shedding power outages. There was a lack of educational opportunities cited by all participant groups. Breastfeeding mothers most often get their information for their elders, which is often outdated.

For example: Key informant said, *"They [grandmothers] are still recommending that HIV positive women feed formula only without breastfeeding."*

Female and male caregivers and key informants reported alcohol consumption and smoking is prevalent among pregnant women, which may be a symptom of poor mental health of mothers that suffer from stress. Stressors identified were male partner abandonment, domestic violence, food insecurity, economic and job insecurity, among others. We asked the community (female and male caregivers) to identify solutions that they could take to improve the situation in their communities. First, female caregivers said that educational interventions are needed to overcome barriers to maternal and child health, not just a booklet of information. Educational workshops delivered in community settings (e.g., Community Centers, places of worship) would be beneficial to support breastfeeding mothers. Male caregivers acknowledge the lack of support given to mothers by male partners and said that male-led workshops could help educate male partners on strategies to support mothers and babies.

Next, there are significant challenges related to water, sanitation, and hygiene (WASH) affecting early nutrition and health. Education and interventions should focus on sanitary practices for personal hygiene (especially during breastfeeding), and sanitizing water storage containers and baby bottles. Key informants and the community reported infrequent washing and sanitization of the baby bottles between uses (e.g., every 2 weeks) because of load shedding, no heat sources, and having to transport water. Caregivers and key informants believe that mixing formula with unsafe water is a contributing factor of infant diarrhea. Other water issues related to infrastructure were identified. Male caregivers describe unreliable safe water sources close to their home.

One male caregiver said, "*We do have water but when the taps are off and the water returns, the color of the water will change, and the water will not be clean.*"

Themes about issues with healthcare system capacity also emerged from all participants. Community-based participatory research is needed to mobilize and strengthen community partnerships, which could include increased educational opportunities about nutrition, breastfeeding, and WASH. Mothers and elder caregivers reported that it does little good to go to the clinic in the prenatal period.

One female caregiver said, *"They [nurses] only touch my belly. They don't do a scan or any tests [for prenatal care]. It does no good to go to the clinic. I don't learn anything."*

Another said, *"[We] feel like bad mothers if they can't continue to breastfeed. Healthcare workers say breastfeeding is the only option, but they aren't supported when they have challenges."*

Female caregivers indicated that nurses stress is high that can have negative impacts on mothers. One mother reported that a nurse took away her bottle instead of educating her about how to overcome breastfeeding challenges. Despite providing free care, the healthcare system is overwhelmed and lacks to capacity to increase health promotion. Another mother said that even getting an appointment is challenging.

Mothers may have to walk long distances with their children to the clinic, and said,

> If we are not waiting in line by 6 am, we may not be seen [by the healthcare professionals.

Key informants reinforced the fact that the healthcare system is overwhelmed. One key informant said,

> And then from what I've seen at the prenatal care here, there's just an overload of participants versus kind of staff and facilities. No matter how good the doctors are and she can even have good facilities, but if there's just too much of a load, it starts to overwhelm the system a little bit.

electricity and water infrastructure. Informal housing structures most often lack refrigeration to store food and/or even breastmilk, and face many challenges related to clean water and infant feeding (both breastfeeding and formula feeding). In addition, there have been significant price increases of basic foods, especially vegetables and fruits, that has been a concern as South Africa is facing an energy crisis with ongoing and prolonged electricity blackouts (also known as loadshedding). Community-based participatory research is needed to mobilize and strengthen community partnerships and resources, which could include (1) optimization of the distribution of local food supply, and (2) increased educational opportunities about early nutrition, including breastfeeding and WASH.

South Africa is in dire need of government involvement to effectively address their stunting rate, and the dual burden of malnutrition as a result. Brazil's success in narrowing health disparities was bolstered as a result of universal, free, comprehensive, and decentralized healthcare provided by the Brazilian Unified National Health System (SUS) (Castro et al. 2019). Government interventions such as these, which include community involvement and international backing from agencies like UNICEF and WHO, are critical in eradicating hunger and decreasing the child stunting rate. The government of South Africa must find a way to increase expenditures on public health in order to succeed in diminishing the child stunting rate. The government must also find a way to solicit cross-sectoral commitments to address this problem. While governments can and do play a very large role in addressing food insecurity and malnutrition, they need the support of industry, the private sector, and non-profits to succeed. By pooling the resources, innovativeness, and expertise of these different groups, meaningful progress can be made.

Finally, the lack of data networks and data bases available in South Africa is another factor directly affecting maternal and child health outcomes. After assessing the feasibility of implementing digital technologies for health outreach and improved health data environments, cell phones have low viability for geo-tracking populations and delivering Mhealth interventions. Within healthcare organizations, standardized digitized data collection methods are needed, such as an electronic health record platform. Physicians have an interest in implementing electronic-based records but have limited resources and time. Because the lack of Big Data infrastructure within healthcare organizations and low feasibility of using cellular phones as a proxy for location, longstanding cohorts, such as Birth to Twenty, provide the immediate infrastructure for implementing studying the impacts of modifiable factors along the life course and implement new interventions.

Equally problematic is the fact that the data that is available regarding maternal and child health has been siloed throughout South Africa among the various clinical and social science disciplines and have not leveraged geospatial sciences important for "place-based" approaches. These data silos contain information that is isolated and inaccessible to many or all parts of the cross-sectoral network of agencies involved in maternal and child health. Using a place-based model, the CoE-FS has established that coordination and partnering across spheres of government is possible, and that local government has both the responsibility and is capable of addressing food and nutrition security. This may require assistance from civil society organizations that have expertise in building partnerships, even when these partnerships are "difficult" and the problems requiring solutions are wicked. We have shown that universities can assist in this context when they adopt knowledge co-production practices and make use of trans-disciplinary teams. And we have identified that niche opportunities exist that can build a food system that delivers affordable, nutritious, and safe food, as well as sustainable livelihoods.

We have found that policies required for food and nutrition security have been developed, but their impact is limited due to implementation and coordination failure, often at the 'last-mile'. This refers the logistical, infrastructural, and accessibility challenges that must be addressed in order to ensure equitable access to public services for all citizens, particularly those who are most marginalized. The result is what we have termed a food and nutrition security paradox: South Africa produces sufficient food for the moment, has an adequate policy framework, generates world-quality science, but has poor food systems outcomes in almost all dimensions. Logistical challenges in South Africa's food and nutrition security include inadequate infrastructure, such as poor road networks and unreliable transportation systems, which hinder the efficient distribution of food to remote and marginalized communities. Additionally, the lack of cold chain facilities contributes to food spoilage, affecting the quality and availability of nutritious food, particularly in rural areas. To improve maternal and child health, it is essential to enhance logistical systems by investing in better transportation infrastructure and expanding cold chain networks to ensure safe and timely delivery of perishable goods.

Moreover, leveraging technology, such as mobile apps and digital platforms, can streamline supply chain management, track deliveries, and ensure that nutritional supplements and health supplies reach the most vulnerable populations. Strengthening local governance and involving community-based organizations in logistics planning can also foster more responsive and tailored solutions to meet the unique needs of different regions. Enhancing logistics and supply chain systems will improve healthcare delivery and public health efforts by ensuring consistent access to essential health supplies and nutritious food, thereby addressing critical gaps in maternal and child health services. Using convergence science allows us to identify ways in which food system planning can be improved by integrating diverse expertise from fields such as plant science, economics, dietetics, and public administration. It allows for the development of data-driven strategies that optimize resource allocation, reduce waste, and improve equitable access to nutritious and safe food.

In conclusion, currently decision-making is severely hampered as a result of the lack of integrated data and siloed approaches. Improvements in Big Data are necessary to effectively track and monitor health outcomes, policies, and regulations. Collaborations to strive for health equity should include convergence science approaches that develop new innovations across food systems, health systems, supply chains, and the economy. This data is essential for improving not only clinical decisions, but the wider view of health stakeholders that can lower the stunting rate, as well as reduce maternal and infant mortality. Government commitment will be important to funding of multi-sectoral programs, such as nutrition intake, supplementation, electricity, housing, and WASH, that have proven successful in reduced stunting (Palutturi et al. 2020). WHO/UNICEF has recommended that governments include vulnerable community members in their decision-making to create an inclusive culture and better suit the needs of the population, which can be achieved through place-based approaches, community-based participatory research, and the development of community advisory boards. Hopefully by soliciting multisectoral partnerships to help implement these many promising interventions, South Africa can make expeditious progress toward finally decreasing the rate of childhood malnutrition and stunting.

Acknowledgments Data collection supported by the DSI-NRF Centre of Excellence in Food Security at the University of the Western Cape. Travel (UID 91490) supported by MU South African Education Partnership Program. We must also thank and acknowledge the work of our local field data collectors for all the efforts in Breede Valley.

References

Aranda-Jan CB, Mohutsiwa-Dibe N, Loukanova S (2014) Systematic review on what works, what does not work and why of implementation of mobile health (mhealth) projects in Africa. BMC Public Health 14(1). https://doi.org/10.1186/1471-2458-14-188

Barron P, Pillay Y, Fernandes A et al (2016) The MomConnect mHealth initiative in South Africa: early impact on the supply side of MCH services. J Public Health Pol 37(Suppl 2):201–212. https://doi.org/10.1057/s41271-016-0015-2

Barron P, Peter J, LeFevre AE, Sebidi J, Bekker M, Allen R, Parsons AN, Benjamin P, Pillay Y (2018) Mobile health messaging service and helpdesk for south African mothers (MomConnect): history, successes and challenges. BMJ Glob Health 3(Suppl 2). https://doi.org/10.1136/bmjgh-2017-000559

Castro MC, Massuda A, Almeida G, Menezes-Filho NA, Andrade MV, de Souza Noronha KVM et al (2019) Brazil's unified health system: the first 30 years and prospects for the future. Lancet 394(10195):345–356

Centers for Disease Control and Prevention (2020) CDC in South Africa—HIV and tuberculosis (TB). Centers for Disease Control and Prevention. https://www.cdc.gov/globalhealth/countries/southafrica/default.htm#death

Chidumwa G, Maposa I, Corso B, Minicuci N, Kowal P, Micklesfield LK, Ware LJ (2021) Identifying co-occurrence and clustering of chronic diseases using latent class analysis: cross-sectional findings from SAGE South Africa wave 2. BMJ Open 11(1):e041604. https://doi.org/10.1136/bmjopen-2020-041604

Cilliers L, Flowerday S (2014) User acceptance of telemedicine by health care workers a case of the eastern Cape Province, South Africa. Electr J Inf Syst Dev Ctries 65(1):1–10. https://doi.org/10.1002/j.1681-4835.2014.tb00467.x

Davis J, Magadzire N, Hemerijckx LM, Maes T, Durno D, Kenyana N, Lwasa S, Van Rompaey A, Verburg PH, May J (2022) Precision approaches to food insecurity: a spatial analysis of urban hunger and its contextual correlates in an African city. World Dev 49:105694. https://doi.org/10.1016/j.worlddev.2021.105694

Davis J, Verberg PH, May J (2023) Diverse actor perspectives on African urban food systems: lessons from participatory food system modelling in Worcester, South Africa. Ecol Soc 28(4):26

Department of Health Republic of South Africa (December 2020) Fourth Trriennial report of the committee on morbidity and mortality in children under 5 years (CoMMiC): 2017–2020. Department of Health, Republic of South Africa

Department of Planning, Monitoring, and Evaluation of South Africa (2014) Diagnostic/implementation evaluation of nutrition interventions for children from conception to age 5. Department of Planning, Monitoring, and Evaluation of South Africa, Republic of South Africa. https://evaluations.dpme.gov.za/evaluations/441

Department of Statistics South Africa (2023) Population census 2022. https://census.statssa.gov.za/#/statsbytheme

Devereux S, Jonah C, May J (2019) How many malnourished children are there in South Africa? What can be done. Putting children first: new frontiers in the fight against poverty in Africa. CROP Int Poverty Stud 7:157–186

Ditekemena J, Koole O, Engmann C, Matendo R, Tshefu A, Ryder R, Colebunders R (2012) Determinants of male involvement in maternal and child health services in sub-Saharan Africa: a review. Reprod Health 9(1):1–8

Field S, Onah M, van Heyningen T, Honikman S (2018) Domestic and intimate partner violence among pregnant women in a low resource setting in South Africa: a facility-based, mixed methods study BMC. Womens Health 18(1). https://doi.org/10.1186/s12905-018-0612-2

Gillwald A (ed) (2023) Digitalisation for a just social compact: global south lessons from the COVID-19 pandemic. Institute of Peruvian Studies, LIRNEasia & Research ICT Africa. https://researchictafrica.net/wp/wp-content/uploads/2023/10/core-project-report_20231010.pdf

Hoffman RM, Newhouse C, Chu B, Stringer JSA, Currier JS (2021) Non-communicable diseases in pregnant and postpartum women living with HIV: implications for health throughout the life course. Curr HIV/AIDS Rep 18(1):73–86. https://doi.org/10.1007/s11904-020-00539-6

Independent Communications Authority of South Africa (ICASA) (2020) The state of the ICT sector report in South Africa. https://www.icasa.org.za/uploads/files/State-of-ICT-Sector-Report-March-2022.pdf

Losch B, May J (2023) Place-based approaches to food system resilience: emerging trends and lessons from South Africa. In: Devereux S, Bene C (eds) Resilience and food security: analysis from a food system perspective. Palgrave Macmillan

Mabaso M (2013) Overview of maternal, neonatal and child deaths in South Africa: challenges, opportunities, progress and future prospects. Int J MCH AIDS (IJMA) 2(2). https://doi.org/10.21106/ijma.23

May J, Timæus IM (2014) Inequities in under-five child nutritional status in South Africa: what progress has been made? Dev South Afr 31(6):761–774

May J, Witten C, Lake L (eds) (2020) South African child gauge 2020. Children's Institute, University of Cape Town, Cape Town

Mbunge E, Batani J, Gaobotse G, Muchemwa B (2022) Virtual healthcare services and digital health technologies deployed during coronavirus disease 2019 (COVID-19) pandemic in South Africa: a systematic review. Global Health J 6(2):102–113. https://doi.org/10.1016/j.glohj.2022.03.001

Modjadji P, Madiba S (2019) The double burden of malnutrition in a rural health and demographic surveillance system site in South Africa: a study of primary schoolchildren and their mothers. BMC Public Health 19(1). https://doi.org/10.1186/s12889-019-7412-y

Mshweshwe L (2020) Understanding domestic violence: masculinity, culture, traditions. Heliyon 6(10). https://doi.org/10.1016/j.heliyon.2020.e05334

Nannan N, Laubscher R, Nel JH, Neethling I, Dhansay MA, Turawa EB, Labadarios D, Pacella R, Bradshaw D, Pillay van-Wyk, V. (2022) Estimating the changing burden of disease attributable to childhood stunting, wasting and underweight in South Africa for 2000, 2006 and 2012. S Afr Med J 676–683. https://doi.org/10.7196/samj.2022.v112i8b.16497

Nelson EC, Splaine ME, Godfrey MM, Kahn V, Hess AM, Batalden P, Plume SK (2000) Using data to improve medical practice by measuring processes and outcomes of care. Jt Comm J Qual Improv 26(12):667–685. https://doi.org/10.1016/s1070-3241(00)26057-4

Organization WH (2008) Maternal and newborn nutrition and health. Accessed 01 August 2023. https://www.who.int/maternal_child_adolescent/events/2008/mdg5/nutrition.pdf

Palutturi S, Syam A, Asnawi A, Hamzah. (2020) Stunting in a political context: a systematic review. Enferm Clin 30:95–98. https://doi.org/10.1016/j.enfcli.2019.10.049
Pellowski JA, Bengtson AM, Barnett W, DiClemente K, Koen N, Zar HJ, Stein DJ (2019) Perinatal depression among mothers in a south African birth cohort study: trajectories from pregnancy to 18 months postpartum. J Affect Disord 259:279–287. https://doi.org/10.1016/j.jad.2019.08.052
Rabe M (2022) Telehealth in South Africa: a guide for healthcare practitioners in primary care. S Afr Fam Pract 64(1). https://doi.org/10.4102/safp.v64i1.5533
Said-Mohamed R, Micklesfield LK, Pettifor JM, Norris SA (2015) Has the prevalence of stunting in south African children changed in 40 years? A systematic review. BMC Public Health 15(1):534. https://doi.org/10.1186/s12889-015-1844-9
Taylor P (2023) Smartphone users in South Africa 2014–2023. Number of smartphone users in South Africa from 2014 to 2023. Retrieved from: https://www.statista.com/statistics/488376/forecast-of-smartphone-users-in-south-africa/#:~:text=Today%20about%2020%20to%2022,and%20on%20the%20continent%20overall
Tokhi M, Comrie-Thomson L, Davis J, Portela A, Chersich M, Luchters S (2018) Involving men to improve maternal and newborn health: a systematic review of the effectiveness of interventions. PLoS One 13(1):e0191620
Tsai AC, Venkataramani AS (2016) Syndemics and health disparities: a methodological note. AIDS Behav 20(2):423–430. https://doi.org/10.1007/s10461-015-1260-2
UNICEF (2020a, February 6) South Africa (ZAF)—demographics, health & infant mortality. UNICEF DATA. https://data.unicef.org/country/zaf/
UNICEF (2020b) What you need to know about malnutrition & feeding children. UNICEF-South Africa (2020, October 20). https://www.unicef.org/southafrica/stories/what-you-need-know-about-malnutrition-feeding-children
Wills G, Patel L, Van der Berg S, Mpeta B (2023) Household resource flows and food poverty during South Africa's lockdown: short-term policy implications for three channels of social protection. SSRN Electron J. https://doi.org/10.2139/ssrn.4331504
World Health Organization, United Nations Children's Fund, World Bank Group (2018) Nurturing care for early childhood development: a framework for helping children survive and thrive to transform health and human potential. Geneva. Licence: CC BY-NC-SA 3.0 IGO. https://www.who.int/publications/i/item/9789241514064

Dr. Kate E. Trout is an Associate Professor in Health Sciences and the Director of the Center for Convergence Science and Innovation and the Center for Health Policy at the University of Missouri, Columbia, Missouri, USA. She is a health services researcher and epidemiologist specializing in Health Information Technologies (HITs) to enhance health system access, efficiency, and quality, particularly in rural and low-resource settings. Her work bridges Public Health, Health Policy, and Health Informatics, focusing on improving health data ecosystems across the social determinants, leveraging big data and enhanced analytics to inform policy and evidence-based decision-making for transformational innovations.

Dr. Gillian Bartlett-Esquilant is Associate Dean for Graduate Studies and Professor of Primary Care and Rural Medicine at Texas A&M College of Medicine. An expert in implementation science, she focuses on translating evidence into clinical practice, particularly for vulnerable populations. Her research explores primary care, convergence science, community and clinical engagement, precision medicine implementation, and innovative educational approaches in translational biomedicine. Dr. Bartlett is a leading authority in translational biomedicine, particularly in implementation science, and fosters collaborative research and education to improve healthcare delivery and patient outcomes.

Chantell Witten holds a PhD in Nutrition from North-West University's Center of Excellence for Nutrition in South Africa, and is a researcher at the DSI-NRF Centre of Excellence in Food

Security (CoE-FS) and a registered dietitian with the Health Professionals Council of South Africa (HPCSA). She is an expert in child health, nutrition programming, and healthcare systems, with experience spanning academia, local NGOs, and international organizations such as the South African Medical Research Council, UN agencies, and Helen Keller International/Bangladesh.

Eyob Teklesenbet is a recent graduate of the University of Missouri-Columbia, where he earned his Master of Health Administration. During his time at Mizzou, Eyob served as a Graduate Research Assistant in the Department of Health Sciences, contributing to research that informed key health policy decisions and population health practices. Upon completing his degree, Eyob began an Administrative Fellowship at NYU Langone Health, where he is further developing his expertise in hospital operations and population health management.

Prof. Julian May is the Director of the DSI-NRF Centre of Excellence in Food Security at the University of the Western Cape. He holds the UNESCO Chair in Science and Education for Sustainable African Food Systems. He is an economist and has worked on options for poverty reduction, including public nutrition, land reform, social grants, information and communication technologies, and food system governance. He has published extensively and has served on international and national expert groups, including the Technical Advisory Group of the International Comparison Program, the South African Statistics Council, the Council of the Academy of Science of South Africa, and, currently, the third National Planning Commission.

Shane Norris is a Professor of Global Health at the University of Southampton and Professor at the University of the Witwatersrand, Johannesburg, South Africa, where he leads the South African Medical Research Council's Developmental Pathways for Health Research Unit. Shane's research focuses on life-course epidemiology with a specific interest in the development of intergenerational-risk for non-communicable disease. His expertise includes nutrition and body composition across the life-course and longitudinal-cohort and trial study methodologies. Shane is working with several scientists across Africa to both better understand and develop interventions that improve maternal and child health outcomes.

Chapter 2
The Barriers to Innovation Diffusion: A Public Healthcare Center Perspective in Uganda

Ernest Marfo Asiedu, Marcia Mkansi, and Oluka Pross Nagitta

2.1 Introduction

In recent years, there has been significant interest in understanding the barriers to innovation diffusion in healthcare (Dong et al. 2023; Gouya et al. 2023; Golinelli et al. 2020; Lauber and Brooks 2023; Moeenian et al. 2022; Rhodes et al. 2020). Innovations are considered essential to meet the increasing demand for specialized healthcare services (Tirado et al. 2022). However, integrating innovation into primary care within healthcare systems remains a persistent challenge. Despite differences in governmental structures and system arrangements, overcoming barriers in the innovation process is a common concern among stakeholders dedicated to designing effective healthcare services (Haring et al. 2022).

The importance of innovation lies in its ability to adapt healthcare services to meet changing expectations. A proactive, patient-centric healthcare system that aligns with evolving societal values is essential (Gouya et al. 2023). This alignment ensures that healthcare services are not only efficient but also tailored to each individual's unique needs (Blomgren et al. 2023). As the focus on patient empowerment, preventive care, and overall well-being continues to grow, societal expectations around healthcare are transforming (Farrar et al. 2020). Integrating innovation into healthcare services is essential to fulfill these evolving expectations (Barbazzeni et al. 2022).

Despite the recognized importance of innovation in healthcare, there is a notable gap in the literature regarding the specific barriers to innovation diffusion in

E. M. Asiedu (✉) · M. Mkansi
College of Economic and Management Sciences, The University of South Africa, Pretoria, South Africa

O. P. Nagitta
Uganda Management Institute, Kampala, Uganda

T. Akenroye et al. (eds.), *Digitalizing Health Care Supply Chains in Africa*, Springer Series in Supply Chain Management 28,
https://doi.org/10.1007/978-3-032-20501-8_2

developing countries, particularly in Uganda. Previous studies have primarily focused on developed nations (e.g., Blomgren et al. 2023; Moulaei et al. 2023; Norberg et al. 2023; Wang 2023), leaving a critical gap in understanding the unique challenges faced by developing countries (Nannyonga and Singull 2020; Wafula et al. 2023). This gap highlights the need for targeted research to identify and address the barriers that hinder innovation in Uganda's public healthcare system.

While innovation in Uganda's public healthcare centers holds great promise, there has been little attention paid to the barriers that can hinder the spread of these innovative ideas within its public healthcare system. Therefore, this study aims to explore the barriers preventing innovation from freely spreading in Uganda's public healthcare system. Understanding these barriers is crucial for developing methods that facilitate successful implementation.

This study is significant because it addresses a critical gap in the existing literature and provides valuable insights into the specific barriers to innovation diffusion in Uganda's public healthcare system. By identifying these barriers, the study contributes to the development of strategies that can enhance the adoption and implementation of innovative healthcare solutions. This, in turn, can lead to improved healthcare outcomes, increased efficiency, and better patient care in Uganda.

The remainder of this study is divided into five sections. The literature review is followed by the methodology, presentation of findings, discussion, and ultimately, conclusions and recommendations.

2.2 Literature Review

2.2.1 Barriers to Innovation Diffusion

This section sheds light on the pressing issues that require innovative solutions and explores the reasons behind both the desire for and barriers to innovation within public healthcare facilities. The regulatory environment and policy framework significantly influence how innovation spreads (Horgan et al. 2019). Supportive policies that incentivize innovation can accelerate adoption, while unclear or burdensome laws may create obstacles (Rhodes et al. 2020). The challenge arises when policy contexts lag behind the rapid pace of technological progress, hindering the potential benefits of innovations (Hu et al. 2020). Given the growing population and evolving healthcare needs, innovation is essential (Shrestha et al. 2022). Traditional healthcare methods are strained by the increasing burden of communicable and non-communicable diseases, as well as population aging (Jimenez Carrillo et al. 2020). Innovations are necessary to meet the demand for specialized healthcare services (Tirado et al. 2022).

Uganda, like other countries, faces the unpredictability of disease epidemics (Abila et al. 2020). Rapid responses to emerging infectious illnesses underscore the need for innovation (Moin et al. 2022). From swift diagnoses to effective data surveillance systems, innovation serves as a crucial first line of defense during health emergencies (Moeenian et al. 2022). Financial constraints directly impact healthcare funding in Uganda, a common challenge in underdeveloped nations (Kyamanywa and Redding 2021). To optimize resource utilization, reduce costs, and ensure robust healthcare services despite budget limitations, innovation remains essential (Pioch et al. 2023).

The pursuit of healthcare equity benefits significantly from innovation. However, access to healthcare services often remains limited for marginalized and rural populations. Innovators must create solutions that go beyond geographical barriers, ensuring healthcare reaches even the remotest corners of the country, leaving no community behind (Blattner et al. 2023). Uganda's healthcare system must align with international standards, as the global healthcare landscape evolves in tandem with technological advancements (Stoumpos et al. 2023). Integrating digital health technologies, telemedicine, and data analytics is crucial for Uganda to maintain its position at the forefront of efficient and contemporary healthcare (Kok et al. 2023). The shift from a disease-centered to a patient-centered paradigm of treatment relies heavily on innovation. Innovations have the potential to revolutionize various aspects of healthcare, including personalized medicine, improved patient engagement, and customized treatment plans (Al Muammar et al. 2018). This transformation reflects evolving societal expectations, emphasizing preventive care, patient empowerment, and holistic well-being (Hickmann et al. 2022).

The primary barrier lies in the lack of funding available to public health facilities. Budgetary constraints often hinder the adoption of novel strategies and the acquisition of state-of-the-art equipment (Safarani et al. 2018). The high initial costs associated with implementing new technologies, such as telemedicine infrastructure or electronic health records, can further strain already limited resources, impeding the widespread adoption of creative solutions (Ajami and Bagheri-Tadi 2013).

Another significant barrier is the reluctance of healthcare personnel to adapt to new technologies and procedures. Established practices and routines are deeply ingrained, making it challenging for healthcare workers to accept and adjust to innovations (Dyb et al. 2021). Concerns about increased workload, unfamiliarity with technology, and potential disruptions to existing processes contribute to this resistance (Waldman et al. 2022). Successful innovation often requires improving digital literacy among medical professionals (Campanozzi et al. 2023).

However, a lack of thorough training and experience with digital technologies might make it difficult for innovations to be successfully adopted (Olaye and Seixas 2023). Bridging the digital literacy gap is essential to enable healthcare professionals to effectively incorporate new technology into their daily work (Boo and Oh 2023). Connectivity issues and inadequate infrastructure pose significant challenges, especially in underprivileged or remote areas. Reliable internet access is crucial for telemedicine, digital health apps, and other technological advancements (Golinelli et al. 2020), but implementation can be hindered by infrastructure limitations (Ihekoronye and Osemene 2022).

2.3 Methodology

This section outlines the methodology used for the empirical research conducted in this study, as depicted in Fig. 2.1.

Based on Fig. 2.1, the study utilized a multiple case-study approach, allowing researchers to investigate variations and commonalities among individual cases. As a result, this approach facilitates data generalization by considering the outcomes observed in each case, as well as identifying patterns and relationships across cases (Creswell and Poth 2018; Yin 2018). In light of this, the study selected this research design to achieve a comprehensive understanding and offer novel insights into the barriers to innovation diffusion from a public healthcare perspective, using data from Uganda.

2.3.1 Sampling and Data Collection Procedure

The study used three general hospitals for the case study. Each general hospital constitutes a case, and all three constitute of multiple cases within the bounded system, as explained by Creswell and Poth (2018). The study selected the hospitals from two different regions, namely Northern, and Eastern, out of the four regions in

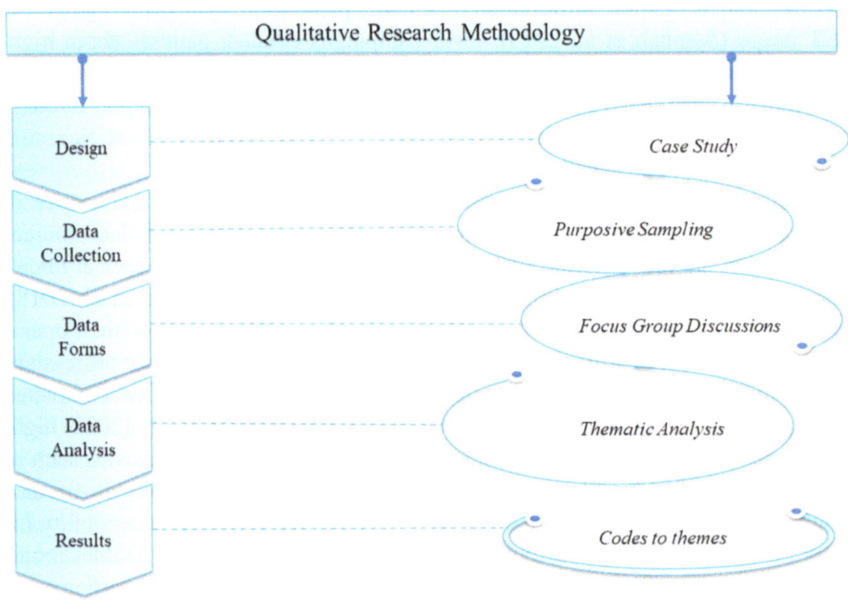

Fig. 2.1 Qualitative research methodological model. *Source:* Adopted from Asiedu (2024)

Table 2.1 Demographic profile

Hospital codes	DTMC members codes	Gender	Position	Years of experience
#K	K1	Male	District medicine management supervisor	10 years
	K2	Male	Pharmacist	12 years
	K3	Male	IT officer	8 years
	K4	Male	Hospital dispenser	9 years
	K5	Female	Assistant inventory management	6 years
	K6	Female	Hospital procurement officer	7 years
#M	M1	Female	Hospital superintendent	10 years
	M2	Male	Store officer 1	13 years
	M3	Female	Store officer 2	9 years
	M4	Female	Technician	10 years
	M5	Female	Pharmacist	7 years
#N	N1	Male	Pharmacist	12 years
	N2	Male	Store officer 1	10 years
	N3	Female	Store officer 2	7 years
	N4	Female	Hospital superintendent	6 years

Uganda. The rationale for choosing these hospitals lies in their government ownership, established systems for managing drug supply and distribution, and supervision by the Ministry of Health. The study employed purposive sampling to deliberately select fifteen (15) members of the Drug Therapeutic Management Committee (DTMC), as shown in Table 2.1, based on their experience and availability.

Within each case, the study chose these DTMC members from the departments of IT, Stores, Pharmacy, and Administration, all of whom are responsible for utilizing the hospital systems to manage drug supply and distribution. Furthermore, these committee members received extensive endorsements from their respective hospitals, primarily due to their substantial expertise in the subject area. Their roles encompass a minimum of 6–13 years of experience which is suitable to fulfil the research objective, as indicated in Table 2.1. The study used the focus group discussion method (FGD) to collect data from DTMC members. Participants were informed that all responses would be kept confidential to the extent possible, as they gave their consent for the session to be tape recorded.

2.3.2 *Data Analysis*

The study employed thematic analysis as the method to analyze the FGD dataset. Furthermore, the study adhered to the qualitative analysis steps outlined by Creswell (2014) and employed a "winnow" strategy to eliminate less relevant data (Guest et al. 2012). Subsequently, the study utilized Atlas.ti to extract quotations from participants' narratives, assign codes, create categories, and develop themes in alignment with the research objectives. To maintain both ethical standards and ensure that their identities remain confidential, the study assigned pseudonyms (codes #K, #M, #N, and K1-K6, M1-M5, N1-N4) to hospitals and DTMC members as shown in Table 2.1. Furthermore, the study mapped sub-codes (categories) and themes across cases using Asiedu's (2020) Model-Cage concept, highlighting both differences and similarities.

2.4 Presentation of Findings

This section presents the barriers to innovation diffusion from a public healthcare perspective, using data from Uganda.

2.4.1 *Case Analysis*

In this section, we present the analysis findings from each case dataset. For each case, we summarize the mapping results across participants in Tables 2.2, 2.3, 2.4 and discuss them as follows:

CASE 1 Table 2.2 presents the four themes that emerged subsequent to categorizing the codes created from the participants' narratives in Case One. These themes are explained as follows:

The first theme that emerged was the lack of political will regarding technology adoption feasibility and the acquisition of state-of-the-art systems (see Table 2.2). This theme is characterized by the fact that the Health Authority holds the sole prerogative to procure health systems without a comprehensive understanding of the existing challenges, as alluded to by **K1**:

> The Ministry of Health designed the RAAS solution to facilitate the supply chain. It has all the components for ordering and provides financial reports, consumption data, and reporting rates. However, it still has some gaps. **[District Medicine Management Supervisor]**

The most concerning aspect is that these health systems are both inefficient and inadequate, as they are designed for specific purposes. Consequently, this situation has led to frustration among health staff, who find that these systems do not serve

Table 2.2 The barriers to innovation diffusion from the perspective of public healthcare centers in Uganda from **Case 1**

Thematic Analysis' findings on the barriers to innovation diffusion from the perspective of healthcare centers in Uganda			**CASE 1**
Aggregated themes	Themes	Category (sub-codes)	Codes
The barriers to innovation diffusion from the perspective of public healthcare centers in Uganda	Lack of political will to do technology adoption feasibility and purchase state-of-the-art systems	Acquisition of health systems without full knowledge of the prevailing challenges	*Systems acquisition is the sole prerogative of the health authority*
			Health authority acquisition of systems without full knowledge of the prevailing challenges
			Health staff awaiting opportunity to share their frustrations with the authority
			Lack of health authority awareness of existing manual process
		Acquisition of incomprehensive health systems	*Provision of inefficient system*
			Acquisition of new system for specific function
			Lack of comprehensive system
	Difficulties in embracing new technologies and disruptions	Reluctance of healthcare personnel's adaptation to change	*Tedious approval process*
			Inefficient administrative process
			Cumbersome systems usages
			Cumbersome stock ordering process
			Solely use of HODs for approval
		Poor connection and inadequate infrastructure	*Power outage*
			Technology disruptions
			Frequent system downtimes
			Unreliable backup system

(*continued*)

Table 2.2 (continued)

Thematic Analysis' findings on the barriers to innovation diffusion from the perspective of healthcare centers in Uganda			**CASE 1**
Aggregated themes	Themes	Category (sub-codes)	Codes
	Lack of systems' integration	Lack of communication between the existing systems	*Existing systems are not integrated across different units within the same hospital*
			Existing systems are not integrated across different hospitals
			Inability to access data from other hospitals
		Inability to use systems as communication channels	*Orders are sent* via *emails*
			SMS is used to communicate report on stock
	Lack of systems' inventory management automation	Manual tracking and reporting processes	*Excel is used to report stock*
			Delivery analysis is done with excel
			Analyze budget utilization
			Monitor budget inflation rates
		Manual stock delivery and receipt process	*Stock delivery is tracked manually using excel*
			Manual receipt of supplies
		Manual record-keeping process	*Excel is used to keep records*
			Printing orders
			Use hardcopies

their intended purposes. They eagerly await an opportunity to express their concerns to the health authority, as strongly uttered by **K1**:

> When it comes to the aspect of receiving, we are still using the paper-based method. Although the system has implemented the aspect of receiving, it has not yet completed the build. However, even before the advent of technology, we had a manual system in place at the hospital. I hope that the minister will visit us here to gain an understanding of how we manage the facility from administration up to this point. **[District Medicine Management Supervisor]**

The second theme involved difficulties in embracing new technologies and dealing with disruptions as shown in Table 2.2. The reluctance of healthcare personnel to adapt to change stems from the cumbersome nature of using health systems,

Table 2.3 The barriers to innovation diffusion from the perspective of public healthcare centers in Uganda from **Case 2**

Thematic analysis' findings on the barriers to innovation diffusion from the perspective of healthcare centers in Uganda			**CASE 2**
Aggregated themes	Themes	Category (sub-codes)	Codes
The barriers to innovation diffusion from the perspective of public healthcare centers in Uganda	Lack of political will to do technology adoption feasibility and purchase state-of-the-art systems	Acquisition and monitoring of health systems is sole prerogative of health authority	*Systems acquisition is the sole prerogative of health authority*
			Systems remain the responsibility of government
			Cost of systems is only known to health authority
			Health authority has the sole prerogative of system monitoring
			Systems acquisition is based on public funding
		Acquisition of incomprehensive health systems	*Existence of two systems with different purposes*
			A system for stock ordering
			A system for capturing data
	Technologies accessibility and performance inefficiencies	Poor connection and inadequate infrastructure	*Internet connectivity issues*
			Power outages
			System instability
			Technology limitations
		Onsite system performance inefficiencies	*Operational stress*
			Tedious approval process
			Inefficient procedures and processes for stock ordering
			Stock request approval resides to only HoD
			Operations verification issues
		Offsite system's accessibility inability	*Onsite system accessible only*
			Inability to access system outside work environment via *mobile device*
			Inconvenience and frustration
			Creation of staff inconvenience

(*continued*)

which are characterized by inefficient administrative processes. The technology disruption is attributed to poor connections and inadequate infrastructure, resulting from power outages, frequent system downtimes, and an unreliable backup system. This is explained by **K2** and **K3.** For instance, **K3** passionately indicated that:

> With RAAS, at some point, like when the system goes down, the machine is always disturbed, depending on the power issue. From here, we used to have a backup even when the power was not available, so we could still serve, but it is no longer the case. **[IT Officer]**

The third theme pertains to the lack of systems integration. Currently, the existing systems are not seamlessly integrated across different units within the same hospital or even across different hospitals. Consequently, health staff at one hospital cannot access drug availability data from other hospitals. Regrettably, the systems designed for managing drug supply and distribution cannot serve as internal communication channels; instead, they rely on SMS for stock reporting (see Table 2.3). This is largely elaborated by **K1**:

> Currently, the systems are not interconnected. I will say that as a country, we have numerous systems in place, but they're not linked, so effective communication together is one challenge. You receive the order from the CSSP, then you come back into RAAS, and then you begin transcribing. ...We have structured it in such a way that every month we compile stock status. We have an Excel sheet that we developed with my colleagues here, and whenever the month ends, we send SMS notifications to the facilities so that the delivery can be tracked at the district and hospital levels **[District Medicine Management Supervisor].**

The final theme focuses on the lack of automated inventory management systems. Currently, tracking and reporting of drug supply and distribution are manually performed using Excel. Additionally, stock delivery and receipt of supplies also rely on manual Excel processes. Lastly, stock record-keeping is manually conducted, including the printing of orders and hardcopies (see Table 2.3). This is again explained in the **K1** narrative:

> We always print the orders and provide them with hard copies. The order roll is the one that is in PDF form, serving as the soft copy. Now, when the orders are delivered, we conduct a delivery analysis. We examine our budget inflation rates and also assess our order rates. Additionally, we review an Excel sheet that I created to guide us on how we utilize our budget. **[District Medicine Management Supervisor]**

CASE 2 Table 2.3 outlines the five themes that emerged during the categorization of codes derived from participants' narratives in Case 2. These themes are elucidated as follows:

The first theme identified in this case pertains to the lack of political will regarding the feasibility of technology adoption and the acquisition of state-of-the-art systems, as previously observed in Case 1. The procurement of health systems relies on public funding and falls under the responsibility of the government. Monitoring these systems remains the sole prerogative of the Health Authority. However, the existing systems are incomprehensive, serving different purposes: one for stock ordering and another for capturing data (see Table 2.3), as explained by **M2** and **M3** respectively:

> The heads of different departments have access to order medications. The system is supplied by the Ministry of Health. The cost associated with the system and maintenance is absorbed by the Ministry of Health. **[Store Officer 1]**
>
> We have two systems now. The first one is used to monitor distributions and capture data within the facility, and it is managed by the Ministry of Health. The second one is the one we have been talking about, which is used for ordering, and it is managed by the National Medical Store**. [Store Officer 2]**

From Table 2.3, the second theme that emerged from this case relates to technological accessibility and performance inefficiencies. The persistent experience of internet connectivity issues, power outages, and system instability contributes to the challenges of poor connection and inadequate infrastructure in the context of Case 2, as alluded to by **M2**:

> The issue of internet connectivity is also a challenge, as it goes off and on. Sometimes, patients have to wait for the internet to come back so that their information can be entered. Initially, there were some issues because the person entering the data was slow, the internet was slow, and sometimes the power was also a challenge. When the power is not on, someone needs to go back and enter the data in the books. Unfortunately, we lost a lot of data from the computers because if somebody saw how many patients there were today and it wasn't entered in the system, we had to go back tomorrow and enter the work because tomorrow's work is slow. **[Store officer 1]**

Additionally, there are on-site system performance inefficiencies, including inefficient procedures and processes for stock ordering, as well as issues with operations verification. Furthermore, the inability to access the existing system outside the work environment via mobile devices creates inconvenience and frustration, adding operational stress for health personnel (see Table 2.3), as coincidentally asserted by both **M3** and **M4:**

> When you are at home and something happens, the only way to access the information is when you are physically in the hospital. There is no way to access the system from a mobile device. **[Store officer 1, Technician]**

Additionally, there are on-site system performance inefficiencies, including inefficient procedures and processes for stock ordering, as well as issues with operations verification. Furthermore, the inability to access the existing system outside the work environment via mobile devices creates inconvenience and frustration, adding operational stress for health personnel (see Table 2.3), as coincidentally asserted by both **M3** and **M4:**

> When you are at home and something happens, the only way to access the information is when you are physically in the hospital. There is no way to access the system from a mobile device. **[Store officer 1, Technician]**

The third theme pertains to the lack of systems integration, as previously observed in Case 1. Currently, the existing two systems are not integrated, and there is also an inability to obtain drug information across different hospitals. Consequently, communication across different hospitals and between the Health Authority and suppliers is facilitated via WhatsApp (see Table 2.3). These assertions are mainly made by **M3**, **M2,** and **M4** respectively:

> We have two systems now. The first one is used to monitor distributions and capture data within the facility, and it is managed by the Ministry of Health. The second one is the one we have been talking about, which is used for ordering, and it is managed by the National Medical Store. **[Store Officer 2]**
>
> We have formed WhatsApp groups called "admin" that are managed by the drug inspector. These groups have all the names of the workers in the district. For example, if we want a particular drug, we tell them that we need it. Whoever has it in the centres will say, "For me, have you come?" Then, we make orders and come and look at the supplies. We are also able to redistribute supplies. For example, at the hospital, we have a lot of patients. When our supplies are done, we are able to go out and look for other supplies from nearby centres. Even in the wards, I have seen that the pediatrician has formed groups. **[Store Officer 1]**
>
> The drug inspectors communicate with different groups only through WhatsApp. **[Technician]**

The fourth theme focuses on the challenges of embracing new technologies. Healthcare personnel exhibit reluctance in adapting to and fully embracing digitalization, as presented in Table 2.3. This is evident in their slow uptake of system usage. The underlying cause is a lack of computer skills, stemming from inadequate training and limited experience with digital technologies within these hospitals, as clearly explained by **M2** and **M4** respectively:

> Some people have issues with computer skills, so they are slow to learn. When the internet is on and off, we lose information. Also, most of the IT staff don't know how to deal with these issues. **[Store Officer 1]**
>
> There are a lot of discrepancies, particularly when it comes to drugs, therapeutics, and mixed prescriptions. As far as my involvement is concerned at the departmental level, that is OPD, it has been almost three years since MOH trained us in certain criteria with the management of medicine and therapeutics, particularly when it comes to direct prescriptions because we are in high demand. **[Technician]**

From Table 2.3, the final theme focuses on the negative impact of technological disruptions on the quality of health delivery. Currently, patient records are manually entered into books in the midst of system connectivity challenges. These laborious manual entries overwhelm healthcare employees, leading to extended patient waiting times, discrepancies in records, and data loss. This is predominantly asserted in the **M2** narratives:

> When there is an electricity issue or the internet goes off, the system saves the logs. However, the rest of the patients will have to be entered manually in the files. When the system comes back, you have to recapture the data into the system. …What we need is a stable internet connection. When the internet is unreliable, we lose information. Also, most of the IT staff don't know how to address these issues. **[Store Officer 1]**

CASE 3 Table 2.4 delineates the three themes that emerged during the categorization of codes derived from participants' narratives in Case 3. These themes are elaborated thereof.

The first theme is technological accessibility and performance inefficiencies, as previously observed in Case 2. There are on-site system performance inefficiencies involving ineffective administrative processes, causing experienced delays. Similarly, health personnel's inability to access the system outside the work environment via mobile devices causes inconvenience among them, as highlighted by **N1**, **N2**, and **N3** (see Table 2.4). For instance, **N3** stated that:

> My system is the one where you have to walk in and see what is happening in the department. You go to the store to know what is happening there, and that is it. **[Store Officer 2]**

The lack of system integration is the second theme that emerged from this case, as previously observed in preceding cases. Currently, the existing two systems are not integrated across different units within the same hospital and across different hospitals. This makes it a challenge to obtain drug information across different hospitals, as indicated by **N2** and **N3** (see Table 2.4). But this is strongly underscored by **N2**:

> We lack a system that allows us to see when other hospitals have stock or when our store is running out of that stock. However, there is a system called RAAS that we use to send monthly updates. Not everyone can view it, but it can show you which region has more of a specific ARV. You can then talk to the responsible person to lobby for you so that you can get it to another district. **[Store Officer 1]**

The final theme that emerged from this case is the lack of automation in inventory management systems. Currently, the available systems are unable to track stock shelf life and stock expiration. Moreover, stock record-keeping is done manually by scanning hardcopies of orders and inputting them into the systems, using paperwork such as dispensing logbooks (see Table 2.4). This is predominantly explained by **N1**:

> The challenges that we experience are paperwork and delays. This is because when you transport it, someone has to approve those plans and then issue them. If there were software, I could just sit down and click it. The transactions we conduct with patients are manual. When a patient arrives, we record their details and send them to the lab from the prescriber's office. The lab then sends the details back to the prescriber, who then sends them to the pharmacy. At the pharmacy, we enter the prescriptions in the dispensing logbooks. **[Pharmacist]**

2.4.2 Cross Case Analysis

This section presents the findings from the FGD dataset across the cases. The study adapted the Model-Cage concept by Asiedu (2020) to illustrate differences and similarities of the themes across all the cases, as well as the sub-codes (categories) within the themes across all the cases. These findings are discussed below.

From Figs. 2.2 and 2.3, the findings suggest that emerging themes and their corresponding categorized sub-codes predominantly occurred between two or among the three cases. As evidently illustrated in Figs. 2.2 and 2.3, there was a lack of system integration across all three cases. Additionally, the lack of political will to adopt feasible technology and invest in state-of-the-art systems, along with difficulties in embracing new technologies and disruptions, emerged in Case 1 and Case 2. Similarly, systems' inventory management automation was lacking in Case 1 and Case 3. Also, there were technology accessibility and performance inefficiencies in Case 2 and Case 3.

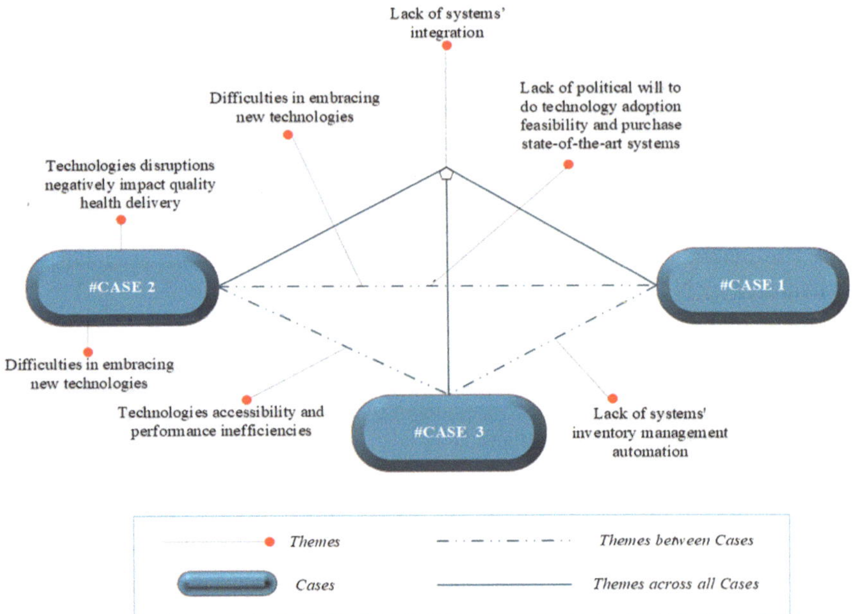

Fig. 2.2 Model-Cage for emerging themes across all cases. *Source:* Authors' own construct (2024), adapted from Asiedu's (2020) Model-Cage

2.5 Discussions

This section discusses the findings of the barriers to innovation diffusion from a public healthcare perspective, using data from Uganda.

To begin, the study revealed the existence of Healthcare Supply Chain Systems that are used to manage drug supply and distribution in Uganda's public healthcare centers. However, these systems are not digitally enabled. This finding confirms the assertion that innovations are indispensable in healthcare services (Shrestha et al. 2022; Tirado et al. 2022).

The findings also confirm an assertion by Rhodes et al. (2020) that the potential benefits of innovations are hindered by some obstacles. These obstacles that are hindering innovation diffusion within Uganda's public healthcare facilities, as broadly presented above, have culminated in the proposal of a Framework, as shown in Fig. 2.4 and are briefly presented below.

- *Lack of political will regarding the feasibility of technology adoption and the acquisition of state-of-the-art systems* arises because the government and its health authority acquire Healthcare Supply Chain Systems: one for stock ordering and another for capturing data. Unfortunately, these systems are not digitally enabled and the acquisition was also done without full knowledge of the prevailing challenges at the health facilities.

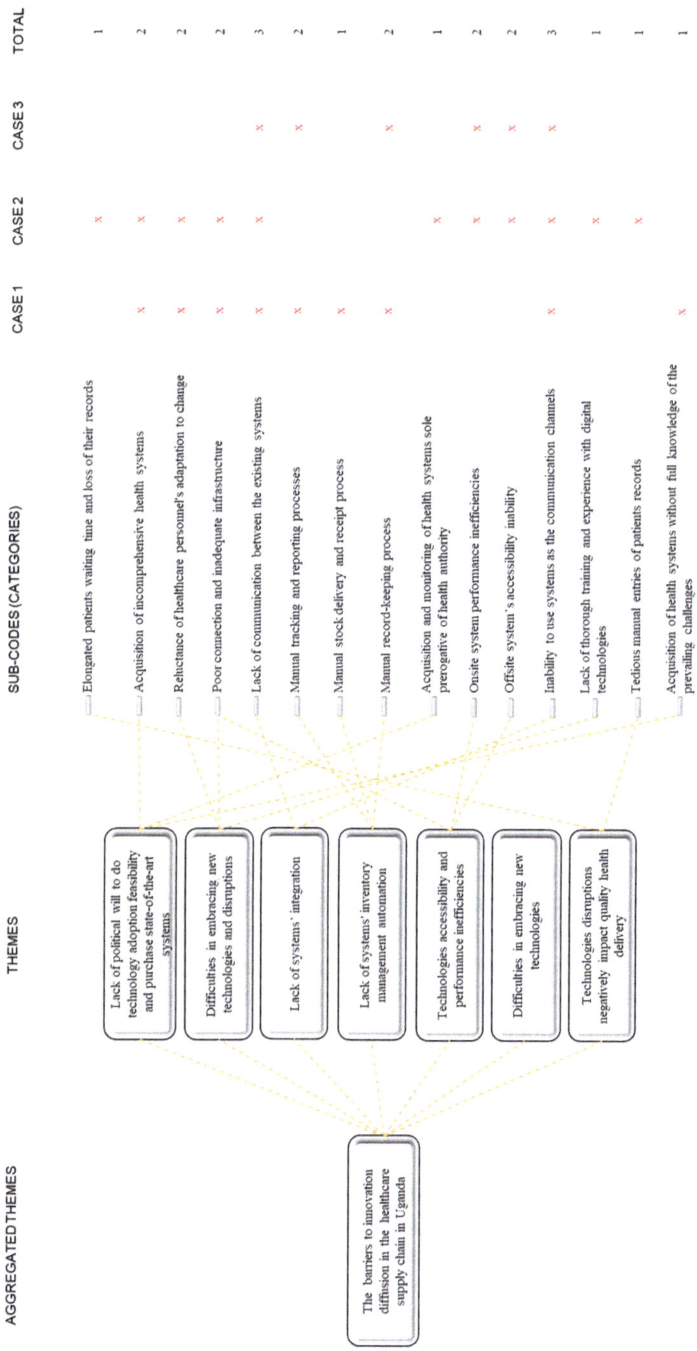

Fig. 2.3 Model-Cage for emerging themes and the categorization of sub-codes across all cases. *Source:* Authors' own construct (2024), adapted from Asiedu's (2020) Model

Also, the "A.R.E. Concept" postulates readiness for system implementation. This is characterized by adequately training healthcare personnel with computer skills prior to system implementation, enabling them to adopt digital technologies. Additionally, there should be adequate infrastructure, including secured internet connectivity, reliable power sources, and backup systems.

Lastly, the "A.R.E. Concept" suggests that there should be efficient system management. The system should be constantly monitored to ensure effective feedback mechanisms that facilitate rapid information exchange and redistribution of medicines at all health centers, aiming to improve patients' healthcare. Additionally, there should be proper user rights to control medicine requests, approval, and reporting. Efforts should be made to reduce technological disruptions, such as ensuring a reliable power supply, especially in rural areas. This includes exploring solar-powered systems to minimize patient waiting times and avoid discrepancies in patients' records and data loss.

In a nutshell, findings from our study provide practical insights into the obstacles associated with the adoption and implementation of new technologies intended to transform health supply chains in Uganda through our proposed Framework "The Barriers to Innovation Diffusion: A Framework from the Healthcare Center Perspective." Additionally, our study proposes the "A.R.E. Concept" as the panacea to manage the absurdities entrenched in the quest to embrace digital technology in the health supply chain for sustainable care to patients by ensuring prompt supply of medications, especially in the context of Uganda. The general implication is that these findings serve as a guide and draw the attention of the policy and decision-makers such as governments, and health ministries, the need of investing in Digital-Enabled Health Supply Chain Systems at the various healthcare centers to enhance resource efficiency, build resilience, and take proactive measures to safeguard the lives of patients.

References

Abila DB, Ainembabazi P, Wabing H (2020) COVID-19 pandemic and the widening gap to access cancer services in Uganda. J Pan-Afr Med 35(2):140. https://doi.org/10.11604/pamj.supp.2020.35.140.25029

Addotey-Delove M, Scott RE, Mars M (2023) Healthcare workers' perspectives of mHealth adoption factors in the developing world: scoping review. Int J Environ Res Public Health 20(2):1244. https://doi.org/10.3390/ijerph20021244

Ajami S, Bagheri-Tadi T (2013) Barriers for adopting electronic health records (EHRs) by physicians. Acta Inform Med 21(2):129–134. https://doi.org/10.5455/aim.2013.21.129-134

Al Muammar AM, Ahmed Z, Aldahmash AM (2018) Paradigm shift in healthcare through technology and patient-centreedness. Int Arch Public Health Comm Med 2:015. https://doi.org/10.23937/iaphcm-2017/1710015

Alenazi TH, BinDhim NF, Alenazi MH, Tamim H, Almagrabi RS, Aljohani SM, Basyouni HM, Almubark RA, Althumiri NA, Alqahtani SA (2020) Prevalence and predictors of anxiety among healthcare workers in Saudi Arabia during the COVID-19 pandemic. J Infect Public Health 13(11):1645–1651. https://doi.org/10.1016/j.jiph.2020.09.001

Althabhawi NM, Zainol ZA (2022) The patent eligibility of 3D bioprinting: towards a new version of living inventions' patentability. Biomolecules 12(1):124. https://doi.org/10.3390/biom12010124

Alzahrani A, Gay V, Alturki R (2022) The evaluation of the usability in mobile applications. Proceedings of the 40th International Business Information Management Association (IBIMA), 23–24 November 2022, Seville, Spain

Asiedu EM (2020) An inclusion of value leaks into earned value analysis as a measure of project management. Doctoral thesis, The University of South Africa. UNISA Institutional Repository. http://hdl.handle.net/10500/27241

Asiedu EM (2024) Incidents and impacts on revenue in the telecommunications sector: a multiple case-study approach. J Telecommun Digital Econ 12. https://doi.org/10.18080/jtde.v12n1.852

Aufa BA, Nurfikri A, Mardiati W, Sancoko S, Yuliyanto H, Nurmansyah MI, Arumsari I, Koire II (2023) Feasibility, acceptance and factors related to the implementation of telemedicine in rural areas: a scoping review protocol. J Digital Health 8(9):20552076231171236. https://doi.org/10.1177/20552076231171236

Barbazzeni B, Haider S, Friebe M (2022) Engaging through awareness: purpose-driven framework development to evaluate and develop future business strategies with exponential technologies toward healthcare democratization. J Public Health Med 25(10):851380. https://doi.org/10.3389/fpubh.2022.851380

Bassoumah B, Adam AM, Adokiya MN (2021) Challenges to the utilization of community-based health planning and services: the views of stakeholders in Yendi municipality, Ghana. BMC Health Serv Res 21:1223. https://doi.org/10.1186/s12913-021-07249-8

Beldek T, Konyalıoğlu AK, Akdağ HC (2020) Supply chain Management in Healthcare: a literature review. In: Durakbasa N, Gençyılmaz M (eds) Proceedings of the international symposium for production research 2019. ISPR 2019. Lecture notes in mechanical engineering. Springer, Cham. https://doi.org/10.1007/978-3-030-31343-2_50

Blattner K, Clay L, Nixon G, Richard L, Miller R, Crengle S, Anton R, Stokes T (2023) The place of rural hospitals in New Zealand's health system: an exploratory qualitative study. Rural Remote Health 23:7583. https://doi.org/10.22605/RRH7583

Blomgren J, Jappinen S, Perhoniemi R (2023) Identifying user profiles of healthcare, social and employment services in a working-age population: a cluster analysis with linked individual-level register data from Finland. PLoS One 18(11):e0293622. https://doi.org/10.1371/journal.pone.0293622

Boo S, Oh H (2023) Perceptions of registered nurses on facilitators and barriers of implementing the AI-IoT-based healthcare pilot project for older adults during the COVID-19 pandemic in South Korea. J Public Health Front 10(11):1234626. https://doi.org/10.3389/fpubh.2023.1234626

Brell R (2019) Informal online opinions: medico-legal considerations in new and social media. Aust J Gen Pract 48(1–2):13–16. https://doi.org/10.31128/AJGP-09-18-4712

Campanozzi LL, Gibelli F, Bailo P, Nittari G, Sirignano A, Ricci G (2023) The role of digital literacy in achieving health equity in the third millennium society: a literature review. J Front Public Health 11:1109323. https://doi.org/10.3389/fpubh.2023.1109323

Creswell JW (2014) Research design: qualitative, quantitative and mixed methods approaches, 4th edn. Sage Publications Ltd, London

Creswell JW, Poth CN (2018) Qualitative inquiry and research design: choosing among five approaches. SAGE

Dong Y, Mun SK, Wang Y (2023) A blockchain-enabled sharing platform for personal health records. Heliyon 8(7):e18061. https://doi.org/10.1016/j.heliyon.2023.e18061

Dyb K, Berntsen GR, Kvam L (2021) Adopt, adapt, or abandon technology-supported person-centred care initiatives: healthcare providers' beliefs matter. BMC Health Serv Res 21:240. https://doi.org/10.1186/s12913-021-06262-1

Farrar MA, Carey KA, Paguinto SG, Kasparian NA, De Abreu Lourenço R (2020) "The whole game is changing and you've got Hope": Australian perspectives on treatment decision making in spinal muscular atrophy. Patient 13(4):389–400. https://doi.org/10.1007/s40271-020-00415-w

Shrestha A, Alawa J, Ashworth H, Essar MY (2022) Innovation is needed in creating electronic health records for humanitarian crises and displaced populations. Front Digit Health 4:939168. https://doi.org/10.3389/fdgth.2022.939168
Stoumpos AI, Kitsios F, Talias MA (2023) Digital transformation in healthcare: technology acceptance and its applications. Int J Environ Res Public Health 20(4):3407. https://doi.org/10.3390/ijerph20043407
Tirado V, Engberg S, Holmblad IS (2022) "One-time interventions, it doesn't lead to much"—healthcare provider views to improving sexual and reproductive health services for young migrants in Sweden. BMC Health Serv Res 22:668. https://doi.org/10.1186/s12913-022-07945-z
Ventola CL (2014) Mobile devices and apps for health care professionals: uses and benefits. P T 39(5):356–364
Wafula ST, Namakula LN, Ninsiima LR, Ssekamatte NK, Walekhwa AW, Mugume IB (2023) Barriers and opportunities for improving management of snakebites: perspectives of healthcare workers in northern Uganda. PLoS One 18(9):e0291032. https://doi.org/10.1371/journal.pone.0291032
Waldman J, McPaul A, Jahoda A (2022) A comparison of the content and nature of worries of autistic and neurotypical young people as they transition from school. J Natl Centre Biotechnol Inform 27(3):667–678. https://doi.org/10.1177/13623613221111313
Wang H (2023) Reflection and foresight on personal information protection and optimization in public health emergencies in China-from the perspective of personal information collection during the period of China's dynamic-zero COVID-19 prevention and control policy. Int J Environ Res Public Health 20(2):1290. https://doi.org/10.3390/ijerph20021290
Yibin D, Seong K, Mun YW (2023) A blockchain-enabled sharing platform for personal health records. Open Access J 9(7):e18061. https://doi.org/10.1016/j.heliyon.2023.e18061
Yin RK (2018) Case study research and applications: designs and methods, 6th edn. SAGE
Yunos NE, Sharkawi HM, Hii KC, Hu TH, Mohamad DSA, Roslim N, Masron T, Singh B, Divis PCS (2022) Spatio-temporal distribution and hotspots of plasmodium knowlesi infections in Sarawak, Malaysian Borneo. J Sci Rep 11(1):4080. https://doi.org/10.1038/s41598-021-83204-1

Dr. Ernest Marfo Asiedu is a certified project management professional affiliated with PMI since 2013, with over 10 years of project management experience in the telecom industry across Africa. His career in the telecom industry has encompassed various managerial roles. Beyond this industrial experience, he also serves as a research fellow at the University of South Africa. He is deeply involved in data analysis training, conducting workshops on both qualitative and quantitative data analysis for researchers and doctoral students. His research interests revolve around uncovering the inherent absurdities within management practices and developing innovative frameworks and models to address them.

Prof. Marcia Mkansi is the College Head of Research, Post-graduate Studies, Innovation, and Commercialisation, a Professor of Operations and Supply Chain Management and the former Head of the Department of Operations Management at the College of Economic & Management Sciences, University of South Africa. She serves as a non-executive director for Hellmann Worldwide Logistics, and an advisory board member of the Africa Resource Centre (ARC), a Bill and Melinda Gates Foundation (BMGF)-funded non-governmental organization, set up to be a resource to the public health sector in African governments. Her university-industry alliances include, but are not limited to, Kuehne Foundation, The Innovation Hub, and SAP skills Africa. She is a nominee for the Top Women Standard Bank and UN women projects, and a finalist under the research, innovation, and creative economy category of the National Science and Technology Forum (NSTF)—South32 awards.

Dr. Oluka Pross Nagitta is a member of the Educational Programmes Committee, African Institute for Supply Chain Research, and the Institute of Public Procurement Professionals of Uganda. In the past six years, she was a Chairperson of the Contracts Committee at Uganda Management Institute and has also trained various people in Public Procurement and Supply Chain Management from various universities in Uganda. Currently she is working at Uganda Management Institute as a lecturer, and her teaching and research interests are in public procurement and Supply Chain Management. Pross was part of the team that carried out procurement audits in Uganda, Tanzania, and Malawi. Pross has also worked as a Consultant in Sierra Leone, under the UNICEF-funded project, which mapped the medicine supply chain. She has researched widely in public procurement and presented papers at international conferences.

Chapter 3
The Impact of Mobile Application Innovation on Coordination of Malaria Stock and Production Management: A Supplier Case Study in South Africa

John Michael Maxel Okoche, Marcia Mkansi, Tshililo Ramovha, Oluka Pross Nagitta, and Temidayo Akenroye

3.1 Introduction

In Africa, availability of medicines underscores attainment of the third Goal of the United Nations Sustainable Development Goals that aims at ensuring health and wellbeing for all people. Specifically, one of the targets is that by 2030, the population of all countries should have access to crucial, quality, safe, and affordable essential medicines and vaccines. Nonetheless, its achievement poses a formidable challenge, more so in developing countries (Khuluza and Heide 2017) where coordination of the supply chain is wanting (Nanyunja et al. 2011), at least with inconsequential solutions to the dilemma of the availability of medicines (Leung et al. 2016; Yadav 2015). The coordination dilemma has significant implications on the availability of Artemisinin-based Combination Therapies (ACTS) meant for the treatment of simple malaria in several countries within sub-Saharan Africa (Khera and Mukherjee 2019; Watsierah and Ouma 2014). The World Health Organization

J. M. M. Okoche (✉)
Department of Operations Management, University of South Africa, Pretoria, South Africa
e-mail: okochjm@unisa.ac.za

M. Mkansi
College of Economic and Management Sciences, The University of South Africa, Pretoria, South Africa

T. Ramovha
University of Limpopo, Johannesburg, South Africa

O. P. Nagitta
Uganda Management Institute, Kampala, Uganda

T. Akenroye
Supply Chain Management and Analytics, University of Missouri–St. Louis, St. Louis, MO, USA

T. Akenroye et al. (eds.), *Digitalizing Health Care Supply Chains in Africa*, Springer Series in Supply Chain Management 28,
https://doi.org/10.1007/978-3-032-20501-8_3

(2022) reported that Sub-Saharan Africa accounted 95 percent of world death globally.

According to several scholars (Nagitta and Mkansi 2023; Nagitta et al. 2019; Stanley et al. 2009), lack of Information and Communication Technology (ICT) such as decision support systems amplified the problem of multi-embedded supply chain. Khurana et al. (2013) underscored the need for development of appropriate applications for integration of end-end processes for Malaria Medicines was critical towards addressing the challenge of medication. Although mobile applications are available in some areas, they do not cover the end-to-end processes of the supply chain coordination of ACT drugs (Mpimbaza et al. 2015). Khurana et al. (2013) underscored the need for development of appropriate applications for integration of end-end processes for Malaria Medicines was critical towards addressing the challenge of medication. Furthermore, the applications which were available the market such as Pilldrop, iWander app, and Remote Area Medical, never addressed a multi-embedded challenge in healthcare supply chain coordination.

Hence, Nagitta and Mkansi (2019) established a theoretical model for a multi-embedded supply chain incorporating the micro, market, and macro dimensions for the availability of ACTs in Africa. In order to strengthen the health care system in developing countries especially Africa, Mkansi and Ramovha (2023), extended the latter study by developing a mobile application for coordinating industry, academic, and corporations' in order to contribute towards a shared agenda for transformation of healthcare system. Using the design science methodology, the mobile application incorporates quantitative computer programming approach by use of the Internet of Things (IoT) model, barcode technology, and Xamarin technology and the Microsoft dot net (NET) Framework (Mkansi and Ramovha 2023). The mobile application (App) innovation addresses a multi-embedded supply chain coordination which is the root cause for common problem of understocking, overstocking, and non-availability of malaria medication. The application was meant to support in reduction of high cost for medication developing countries. Experimental research resulted in a functional mobile application responding to the needs of the multi-embedded supply chain coordination problem related to ACTs.

The mobile application equips small manufacturers and public healthcare centres with the technology to improve efficiency. Since its development, the application has been utilised by a small-scale manufacturer of malaria products in Pretoria (South Africa) to help strengthen and improve internal supply chain processes of stock management, production, productivity, and cost reduction and waste management. However, the extent of impact to the small manufacturer's internal supply chain remain unexplored. In this study our goal and purpose is to extend this discussion by first identifying the mechanisms by which the mobile application impacts on the internal supply chain coordination for the small manufacturers in South Africa. Mahotra and Majchrzak (2024) noted that the growth of crowdsourcing remains basic despite the huge technological advancements, hence the need for cross-disciplinary knowledge sharing.

This gap demands exploration of the stakeholders involved in the internal supply chain coordination in small manufacturers in South Africa. This was critical in understanding the impact of the mobile application on coordination of the malaria stock and production management. Tomašev et al. (2020) emphasised the need for better collaborations between AI researchers and domain experts for social good applications. The goal was to explore and assess the impact of mobile application on the Internal Supply Chain Coordination. The study established that mobile application was critical for improvement of manufacturing, production, productivity, and cost reduction. Our study established that the mobile application is critical in streamlining internal supply chain performance in manufacturing. Developing countries experience challenges in supply chain coordination: Challenges limited funding (Alexander et al. 2020; Eggers 2020; Lee and Persson 2016), technology advancement (Mbuyisa and Leonard 2017; Manyika et al. 2016), shortage of raw materials (Desai and Looze 2020; Bartik et al. 2020; Alexander 2020), shortage of power (Herbane 2010; Bohn et al. 2020; Desai and Looze 2020), and meeting quality standards (Tene et al. 2018; Engidaw 2022).

However, the use of the mobile application (App) innovation would benefit not just South Africa but developing countries with similar constraints. The main contributions of this study are three-fold. First, the paper provides a comprehensive practical insight for improvement of internal supply chain coordination management using the mobile application. The mobile application improves internal supply chain coordination by strengthening manufacturing, production output, productivity, and reducing production costs. Second, theoretical contribution by closing the loop which was not clear on the extent to which internal supply chains contributes market level stakeholders. This is critical expansion of knowledge by providing internal mechanisms for improvement of supply chains by directly and indirectly contributing to attainment of global and African Union agenda 2063 and Un Priority (African Union 2022). Finally, the paper provides insights on how academia can transform research into innovation for strengthening and improving supply chain coordination.

The paper itself is organised as follows. Introduction in Sect. 3.1. The literature is presented in Sect. 3.2. Then in Sect. 3.3, we show the methods used. The results are then covered in Sect. 3.4, after which the implications of the study are shown in Sect. 3.5 and Limitations of the study in Sect. 3.6.

3.1.1 The Mobile Application

The mobile application the "UNISA ACT", was developed on the basis of core features and architecture deduced through healthcare supply chain problem relevance, and incorporated inventory management and distribution principles for design as a process, to produce mobile application as design artefact. Using a waterfall methodology, the application was produced with the unified User Interface (UI). The application is hosted in a Xamarin shell fly out. According to Mkansi and Ramovha

(2023), the unified User Interface (UI) uses responsive web design principles to provide an optimal viewing and interaction experience for any screen size, device, or orientation (Fig. 3.1).

The application is critical for use by the micro, macro, and market stakeholders. The micro-environment stakeholders to be supported by application are the various health care centres; the district hospitals, referral hospitals, district medical offices, and health centres receive malaria drugs from either private pharmacies, national medical stores, or donors. The micro-level stakeholders can place orders for the drugs, tracking orders, dispensing drugs, understanding current within the facility and keeping required stock level to meet customer requirements. The macro level stakeholders' UN system, governments, international organisations, civil society organisations, donors, and malaria working groups can view and access the holistic

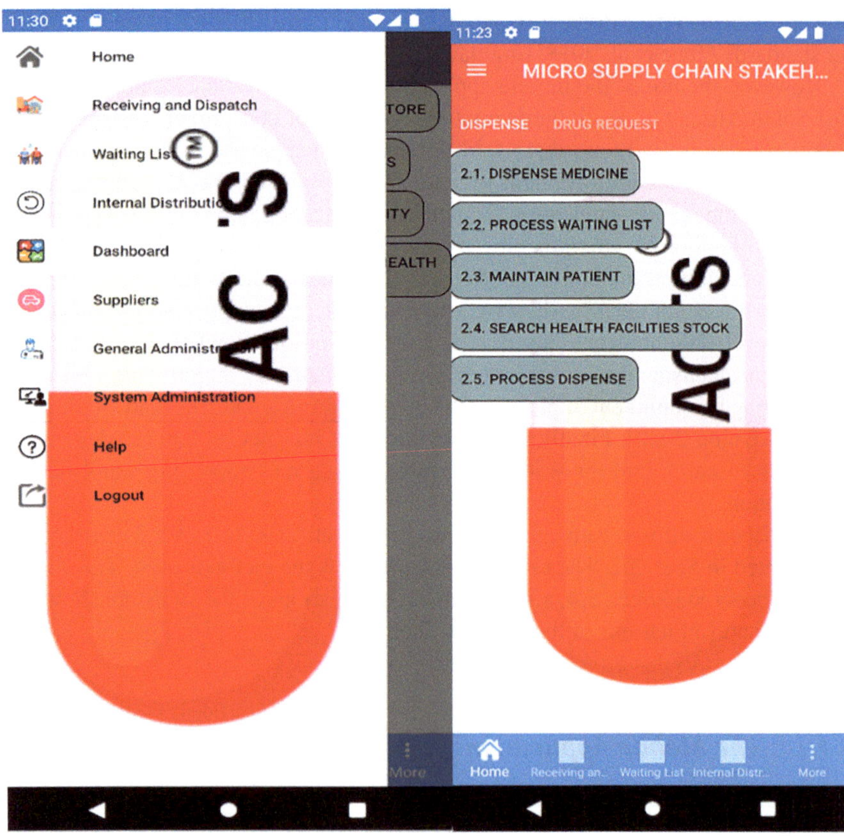

Fig. 3.1 Mobile application ACT mobile app high level. Source: Mkansi M, Ramovha T (2023) A mobile application innovation for public healthcare supply chain coordination. In: Yang XS, Sherratt RS, Dey N, Joshi A. (eds) Proceedings of eighth international congress on information and communication technology. ICICT 2023 (Lecture notes in networks and systems), vol 694. Springer, Singapore. https://doi.org/10.1007/978-981-99-3091-3_5

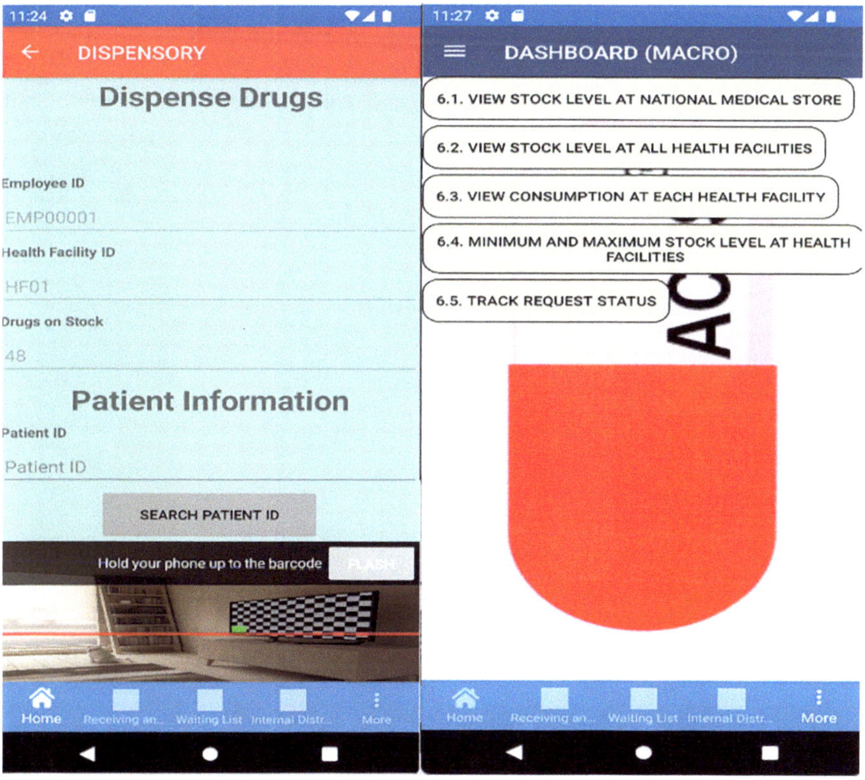

Fig. 3.1 (continued)

operation of the system. The market level stakeholders consist of local pharmaceutical companies and distributors, domestic public and private suppliers, international public and private suppliers, private for-profit wholesalers, and private not for profit providers. The system provides the market level stakeholders with appropriate information for good market conditions. The innovation uses the application layer in IoT to provide for the dashboard to allow the different stakeholders to view and analyse stock status, view the demand for the products. At network level, the sensors had to provide for interface to scan for the requirements at different levels.

This chapter explores the impact of this mobile application at a market level and is limited to a single internal supply chain case of small manufacturer of malaria products. The mobile application plays a critical role in coordination of the entire supply chain, therefore critical for improvement of the entire supply chains by broadening the value of this technology adoption to a wider spectrum. In our study, the exploration was mainly on the internal supply chain but the application is significant as it has mechanisms for coordination of the micro and macro health environment. First, the micro-environment stakeholders to be supported by application are the various health care centres; the district hospitals, referral hospitals, district

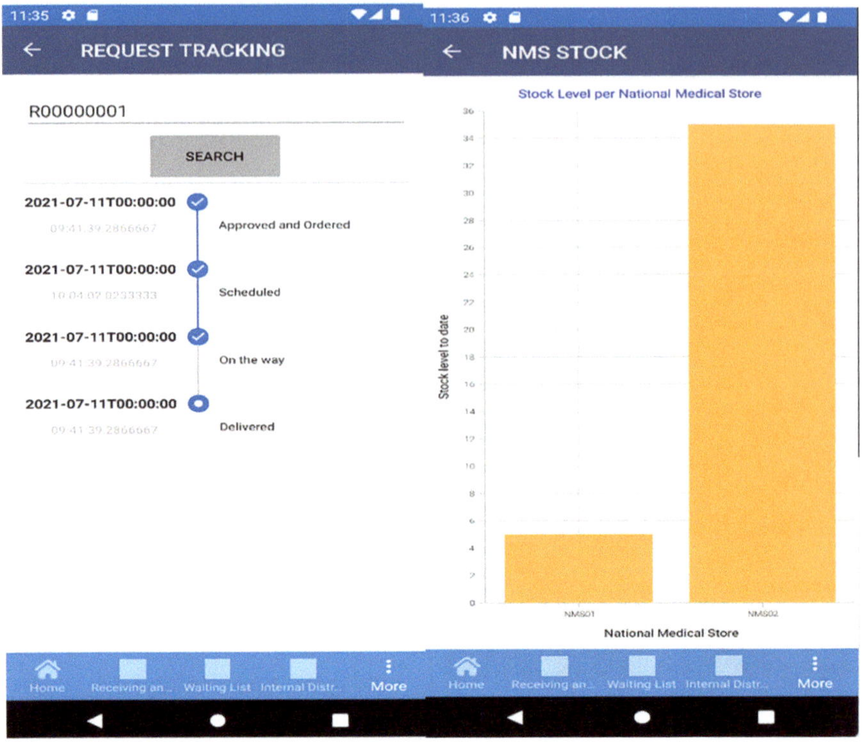

Fig. 3.1 (continued)

medical offices, and health centres receive malaria drugs from either private pharmacies, national medical stores, or donors. Finally, the macro-stakeholders and macro level stakeholders will benefit from improvement of the internal supply chains provided by the mobile application.

The following section provides a critical review of the literature for contextualisation of the coordination mechanisms of coordination of Artemisinin-based Combination of Therapies (ACTS).

3.2 Literature Review

A comprehensive review of the literature discusses the critical aspects' contextualisation for coordination of Artemisinin-based Combination of Therapies, (ACTS): inventory and production management, challenges in developing countries, and Mobile application coordination of Malaria stock.

3.2.1 *Inventory and Production Management of Healthcare*

Academic literature is nuanced with approaches used by supply chain for inventory and production management of healthcare. Internal supply chain refers to the chain of activities integrated with a holistic performance of activities across departmental boundaries within the company (Soares et al. 2017). Abdallah et al. (2021) highlight the necessary steps for internal quality, internal supply chain as quality leadership, customer focus, IT-enabled organisation, supply chain integration, quality management, customer quality involvement, information sharing, cooperation, and continuous improvement. An effective supply chain provides mechanisms for coordination and integration of the entire system (Yadav 2015). Sharma and Kumar (2017), argues that despite the critical need todevelopment an effective internal supply chain, firms are often reluctant to share information, resulting in poor coordination and limited integration. Oluka et al. (2021) state that appropriate coordination mechanism is helpful in development of a seamless organisation effective in planning, tracking, and estimating the lead times based on real-time data. Singh (2011) argues that information sharing supports in strengthening coordination and integration in the supply chain. Kabra et al. (2015) state that integrated and coordinated supply chains exhibit a great level of collaboration among members.

Additionally, Simatupang and Sridharan (2018) argue that coordination harnesses collaboration which is characterised by a higher-level interest, representing an affective, volitional, shared interest process. Tjosvold and Weicker (1993) argue that collective effort requires coordination and integration. In order to harness coordination for investment by the company, it is required to harness coordination which improves collective understanding, shared vision, resources, and common focus (Bhattacharya et al. 2015). The firm's ability to harness internal collaboration provides a competitive advantage as a result of internal supply chain development (Tamym et al. 2020), included building internal alliances for delivery of services (Choi et al. 2018). Development of appropriate coordination mechanisms is necessary for the successful availability of malarial drugs (Oluka et al. 2021). Datta and Christopher (2011) highlight that coordination in the supply chain provides opportunity for streamlining market demands, customer preferences, and coordination of activities. Supply chain coordination usually improves accuracy, timeliness, adequacy, credible information, and complete information within the organisation (Pujara and Kant 2015).

Coordination is critical for information sharing reducing supply chain costs, demand variability, and improves responsiveness (Awwad et al. 2018). Coordination helps the organisations ability to respond to environmental changes quickly and efficiently (Shokouhyar et al. 2020), which is crucial for an organisation's success and competitiveness (Shokoohyar et al. 2022). Organisations which fail to strengthen internal coordination and integration end up losing market share (Rossini et al. 2022). Management of internal supply chains has become critical in addressing challenges in manufacturing. Mobile applications have become critical in strengthening integration, coordination, and supply chain environment (Yuan and Cao 2022;

Dagestani and Qing 2022; He et al. 2022; Palea et al. 2023). The digital technology improves supply chain management (Yuan and Cao 2022; Dagestani and Qing 2022; He et al. 2022; Calzolari et al. 2022; Palea et al. 2023). The applications provide mechanism for integrating the operations in the organisation (Yuan and Cao 2022). Palea et al (2023) argued that digital technology strengthens coordination in the supply chain improving industry manufacturing. These have proved critical towards improvement in the supply chain environment, systematically strengthening manufacturing (Nicholson et al. 2023). Hasibuan et al. (2018)) observed that digital technology improves supply chain environment for effective manufacturing firms.

A well-coordinated supply chain system enables an organisation to manage its resources efficiently and view various aspects of its operations (Supply Chain Council 2022), with a network of collaborating entities; suppliers, manufacturers, distributors, and retailers (Akkucuk 2020) with an objective of efficient utilisation of resources (Hasibuan et al. 2018). Mathur et al. (2018) argue that organisation performance together with appropriate manufacturing requires improvement in effectiveness and efficiency. Furthermore, Skowron-Grabowska et al. (2022) argue that applications are critical in improvement of supply chain reliability. Reliable supply chains help by consistently meeting customer demands and delivering products and services on time, in the right quantities, and at expected levels of quality. Internal supply chain management is critical in increasing productivity and production in manufacturing firms (Nicholson et al. 2023; Chen et al. 2023; Li et al. 2023). Coordination in the supply chain improves stakeholder participation in the manufacturing process (Nicholson et al. 2023). Chen et al. (2023) also argued that mobile applications increase productivity by harnessing communication, connectivity, and digital information-sharing services improving decision making. Li et al. (2023) established that digital technology by use of dashboards harnesses timeliness in production.

3.2.2 Challenges in Developing Economies

African, small-scale industries have diverse challenges: limited funding (Alexander et al. 2020; Eggers 2020; Lee and Persson 2016), technology advancement (Mbuyisa and Leonard 2017; Manyika et al. 2016), shortage of raw materials (Desai and Looze 2020; Bartik et al. 2020; Alexander 2020), shortage of power (Herbane 2010; Bohn et al. 2020; Desai and Looze 2020), and meeting quality standards (Tene et al. 2018; Engidaw 2022). Small-scale industries in Africa don't have adequate short-term and long-term financing (Alexander et al. 2020). According to Eggers (2020), the small-scale industries don't have access to cheap source of credit. The challenge of acquisition of limited credit forces small-scale manufacturers to rely on family and friends as a source of capital (George et al. 2016). Capital from family and friends is relatively cheap but can have shadow costs that may not make it ideal, especially for business growth (Lee and Persson 2016).

The small-scale manufacturers are also constrained by access to advanced technology (Manyika et al. 2016; Mbuyisa and Leonard 2017); due to high costs attributed to new technology. Manyika et al. (2016) highlight that a majority of the small-scale enterprises in Africa still use traditional and outdate technology undermining business performance. A growing body of evidence suggests that digitalisation could revolutionise the way small and micro businesses operate (Mbuyisa and Leonard 2017). Shortage of raw materials as a result of limited working capital is a major challenge affecting small-scale manufacturers in Africa. Desai and Looze (2020) established that access to raw materials has proved problematic for the small-scale manufacturing industries. Similarly, Bartik et al. (2020) noted that shortage of raw materials had affected manufacturing in Africa. The lack of materials was because of limited working capital impacting the access to required raw materials (Alexander 2020).

Small-scale industries continue facing a major challenge of power shortage due to increased demand for electricity (Herbane 2010). The power shortage undermines the ability of the manufacturers to operate at full capacity (Bohn et al. 2020). Furthermore, the small-scale industries are not in position to purchase their own source of electricity (Desai and Looze 2020). Small-scale industries in Africa have also found it difficult to meet the global quality standards. African business entities have found it difficult to compete internationally due to inability to meet normative requirements at international level (Engidaw 2022); the firms don't have funds for research in order to improve upon the quality (Alexander et al. 2020; Eggers 2020). Emergent literature highlights importance of strengthening supply chain management in order to address the challenges faced by small-scale industries (Quang et al. 2016).

3.2.3 Coordination of Malaria Stock Using Mobile Applications

A comprehensive of academic literature reveals four coordination mechanisms for improvement using mobile applications: transformation of manufacturer, technology innovation, improvement of productivity, and reduction of production costs. The first cohorts of scholars argue that mobile applications address challenges for the small-scale manufacturing by transforming manufacturing (Benner and Tushman 2003). The applications harness industry effectiveness (Mathur et al. 2018), efficiency (Supply Chain Council 2022; Hasibuan et al. 2022), reliability (Skowron-Grabowska et al. 2022), and relevance (Queiroz et al. 2022). Mathur et al. (2018) in their study established that use of mobile applications for strengthening internal supply chains improves effectiveness in manufacturing. The applications improve supply chains by streamlining coordination, collaboration with the organisation (Supply Chain Council 2022). Akkucuk (2020) highlights that applications integrate operations effectively by managing resources using collaboration and resources efficiently. The network of collaborating entities within the organisation streamlines efficient utilisation of resources (Hasibuan et al. 2018). Furthermore, the platforms provided strengthen relevance and reliability of the company operations (Queiroz et al. 2022.

Mobile applications improve company performance by ensuring that operations are relevant for the needs required. In addition, Skowron-Grabowska et al. (2022), established that the applications play a critical role of ensuring that manufacturing is consistent and reliable in meeting customer demands and requirements. A well-coordinated supply chain system enables an organisation to manage its resources efficiently and view various aspects of its operations (Mathur et al. 2022). Mobile applications systematically transform manufacturing by strengthening coordination and integration, therefore harnessing effectiveness, efficiency, relevance, and reliability (Supply Chain Council 2022). Secondly, technology innovation is critical in improving production in the manufacturing (Benner and Tushman 2003). Companies can improve the operations using the mobile applications for increasing the company output during the production process (Nicholson et al. 2023; Skowron-Grabowska et al. 2022; Chen et al. 2023; Li et al. 2023). Nicholson et al. (2023) argue that the mobile applications create a good environment for free flow of vital information, therefore improving production capabilities of the manufacturer. Furthermore, the applications' flexibility provides a backbone for quality control management (Skowron-Grabowska et al. 2022).

Manufacturers, therefore, by use of mobile applications increase the quality of the products and services by use of innovation technology. Li et al. (2023) argue that manufacturing by use of modern technology improves partnerships and collaboration which are responsible for improved production. Manufacturing companies are now using mobile applications for strengthening employee participation enabling them to collect, access, and share critical manufacturing data and achieve continuous improvement (Ak and Patatoukas 2016). Zhu et al. (2021) argue that the technology has proved useful for manufacturers in integrating the different departments improving company production. The power of mobile applications lies in their ability to work right down on the production line, where the actual manufacturing process takes place.

The third cohort of scholars argue that mobile applications play a critical role in improving productivity by manufacturing companies (Benner and Tushman 2003). The applications harness industry effectiveness (Nicholson et al. 2023; Frank et al. 2019; Ebert and Duarte 2018). The company productivity is strengthened by improving mechanisms used for stock management (Nicholson et al. 2023). Appropriate stock management systematically improves the company productivity by enabling seamless information flow (Oluka et al. 2021). The mobile application removes the traditional borders which undermine increased productivity. In addition, the mobile application is also critical in reducing wastage which is responsible for company productivity. Ebert and Duarte (2018) established that mobile applications manufacturers usually reduce waste by use of mobile applications. This is in agreement with Frank et al. (2019) who also highlighted that mobile applications reduce unnecessary waste during the production process by use of appropriate raw materials. The next level of improved productivity by use of application by the mobile applications helped in monitoring employee performance (Li et al. (2023). Technology can facilitate monitoring employee performance. Zhu et al. (2021) argue that manufacturers use mobile devices to connect employees to collect, access, and share critical manufacturing data and achieve continuous improvement.

Finally, the next cohort of academic literature emphasises the role of mobile application technology in reducing production costs (Frank et al. 2019; Ebert and Duarte 2018; Cai et al. 2010; Cai et al. 2010). Frank et al. (2019) argued that mobile applications reduce costs by reducing waste in the manufacturing processes. The mobile application innovation technology reduces operation costs by integration, reducing waste, and the cost of production (Ebert and Duarte 2018). Cai et al. (2010) established that digital technology is responsible for cost reduction. Digital innovation improves supply chain by removing bureaucracy which results in high costs of production (Gurbaxani and Dunkle (2019). The applications reduce cost by converging capabilities using telecommunication infrastructures, which is the result of extensive technical innovation (Goerzig and Bauernhansl 2018). Russel (2019) reiterates that mobile applications are critical in dealing with a big challenge of expensive and costly services (Rose et al. 2015; Fenny et al. 2018). Although mobile applications are available in some areas, they do not cover the end-to-end processes of the supply chain coordination of ACT drugs (Mpimbaza et al. 2015).

Khurana et al. (2013) underscored the need for development of appropriate applications for integration of end-to- end processes for Malaria Medicines, which is critical towards addressing the challenge of medication (supported by our critical mapping in Table 3.1). Furthermore, the applications which were available in the market, such as Pilldrop, iWander app, and Remote Area Medical, never addressed a multi-embedded challenge in healthcare supply chain coordination. In order to strengthen the health care system in developing countries especially Africa, the mobile application was designed to strengthen supply chain coordination. However, the extent to increased production, productivity and transformation of manufacturing remains unexplored. Our study addresses the latter gap.

3.3 Methodology

3.3.1 Research Design

We used exploratory case study research design with a qualitative approach. A single case study was used for evaluating the impact of the mobile application innovation on the coordination of malaria stock and production management. Yin (2003) argues that case study research design is critical in capturing the context and lived realities of the participants in relation to mobile application. Finally, the study design was flexible in qualitatively exploration of the perspectives of the participants in understanding of the impact of the mobile application (Creswell and Creswell 2017). The case study research design is critical in gaining insights of a particular study as it

Table 3.1 Showing the critical benefits of the mobile applications in addressing manufacturing challenges

			Performance measures												
Categorisation	Year and author	Application	Effectiveness	Efficiency	Reliability	Relevance	Outputs	Participation	Quality control	Integration	Coordination	Stock management	Waste management	Timely production	Bureaucracy
Transformative manufacturing	Mathur et al. (2018)	Improves effectiveness in manufacturing	x												
	Supply Chain Council (2022)	Improved efficiency in manufacturing		x											
	Hasibuan et al. (2018)	Efficient resource utilisation		x											
	Skowron-Grabowska et al. (2022)	Improved reliability in manufacturing			x										
	Queiroz et al. (2022)	Improves relevance and reliability in manufacturing				x									
Production	Chen et al. (2023)	Production outputs by appropriate scheduling production					x								
	Nicholson et al. (2023)	Internal stakeholder participation						x							
	Skowron-Grabowska et al. (2022)	Improves quality control during the production							x						
	Li et al. (2023)	Integration of operations facilitating collaboration and partnerships								x					

		Strengthen coordination									x				
Productivity	Nicholson et al. (2023)	Improvement in stock management										x			
	Frank et al. (2019)	Streamline waste management											x		
	Ebert and Duarte (2018)	Waste management by using of appropriate raw materials											x		
	Li et al. (2023)	Digital technology harnesses timely production												x	
Cost reduction	Cai et al. (2010)	Cost reduction													
	Frank et al. (2019)	Cost reduction by waste management											x		
	Ebert and Duarte (2018)	Cost reduction by integration										x			
	Gurbaxani and Dunkle (2019)	Cost reduction by removing bureaucracy													x

provides the researcher with an opportunity to critically examine a single case in time as opposed to several cases. The impact of the mobile application on either of the segments of the supply chain i.e. micro, market, and macro remained unexplored.

A single case study was used for exploration of the impact of the mobile application on the market segment case of small business manufacturer of malaria products in Gauteng province of South Africa. In particular, our study focussed on how the mobile application improves internal supply chain process in terms of coordination, production, productivity, waste, and stock management. The company which was used as a case study is a bio-technology company which specialises in the manufacture of slow-release fibres in Pretoria Gauteng Province. The company mainly manufactures slow-release fibres from polypropylene copolymer. The fibres which are manufactured usually engineered for storing high amount of liquid within their matrix and slowly release small amounts over a long period of time. The technology which is used by the small-scale manufacturer aimed at slowly releasing high value actives in order to prolong effectiveness and cost reduction for the practical applications.

The manufacturer produces long lasting insect repellent textile-based products which are washable for at least 8 months. Furthermore, repellent fibre combines cotton, wool, polyester, and polyamide for the final repellent textile-based products. The manufacturer operates under Nanomaterials Industry Development Facility (NIDF) manufacturing insect repellent hiking socks, natural repellent creams, repellent spray, and repellent bans. Small business and manufacturers have challenges in coordination, reduction of waste, productivity, efficiency, effectiveness, reliability, and competitiveness. Impact assessment of the application is critical towards improvement in the operations. Furthermore, this is critical in building capacity which is limited capacity of Africa in responding to humanitarian crisis induced by outbreaks as seen in Covid19 case. Supply chains are mainly internal and external, but the major focus is internal supply chain management. This impact study is essential for strengthening and improvement in operations of the small health care manufacturers in Africa.

3.3.2 Sample and Data Collection

The major purpose of our study was to assess the impact of the mobile application for internal supply chain process in small-scale manufacturers in Africa. We conducted nine focus group discussions covering the designer of the application and staff in the small-scale manufacturer with in-depth and rich information about operations of the manufacturer. The participants' perspectives were interviewed to help in assessing the impact of the mobile application in the performance of the internal supply chain mechanisms of the small-scale manufacturer. Recognising that interviewees participated in the pilot and utilisation of the mobile application in the operations of the manufacturer. We conducted nine focus group discussions with the developer of the application and staff in the small-scale manufacturer. This was critical in framing and structuring the impact of the mobile application on the internal supply chain of the company.

We purposively selected interviewees with a critical understanding of the mobile application to support in understanding the impact of the mobile application (Suri 2011). In particular, Participants with in-depth insight on the impact of the application to their business' supply chain stock management processes. The interviews and focus group discussions were recorded in the Microsoft teams and were transcribed to facilitate the process of interpretation. The interview protocol focused on understanding the impact of the mobile application on the internal supply chain of the small-scale manufacturer in South Africa. Follow-up questions were used to clarify responses. In line with Creswell and Creswell (2017), the study used anonymity for harnessing ethical considerations during the study. The views of the respondents were critical in understanding the impact of the mobile application on the internal supply chain of the small-scale manufacturer in South Africa.

3.3.3 Data Analysis

The focus group discussions were recorded in the micro-soft teams or laptop audio instruments and were later transcribed, coded, and analysed using MAXQDA (a computer-aided qualitative data analysis software). The transcripts were uploaded to the software and subsequently open coding, followed by inputting coding groups or themes (also known as axial coding). The perspectives of the respondents in view of the impact of the mobile application on the internal supply chain were captured. Open coding was undertaken using the MAXQDA. In this context, words and phrases reflect the narrative of the participants who were involved in development and use of the mobile application formed the evaluation of the application. After the open coding process, by use of the software hierarchical axial coding was used to identify and connect multiple codes to map out the impact of the mobile application (Babbie 2017). The coded themes from hierarchical axial coding were combined as significant inputs for thematic development and the iterative process between themes that emerged from the data and the literature for impact of digital applications on the internal supply chain management. Polit and Beck (2012) guided the process for applicability or transferability with background description, the outline of the methodology, and the preservation of transcripts. The audio record and transcripts of the perspectives of participants were appropriate and relevant for convergence and support of the constructs discussed by Yin (2018).

3.4 Results

This study used the MAXQDA software for analysis of interviews and Focus Group Discussions (FGDs) for assessing the impact of the mobile application on the internal supply chain of the small-scale manufacturer in South Africa. The findings

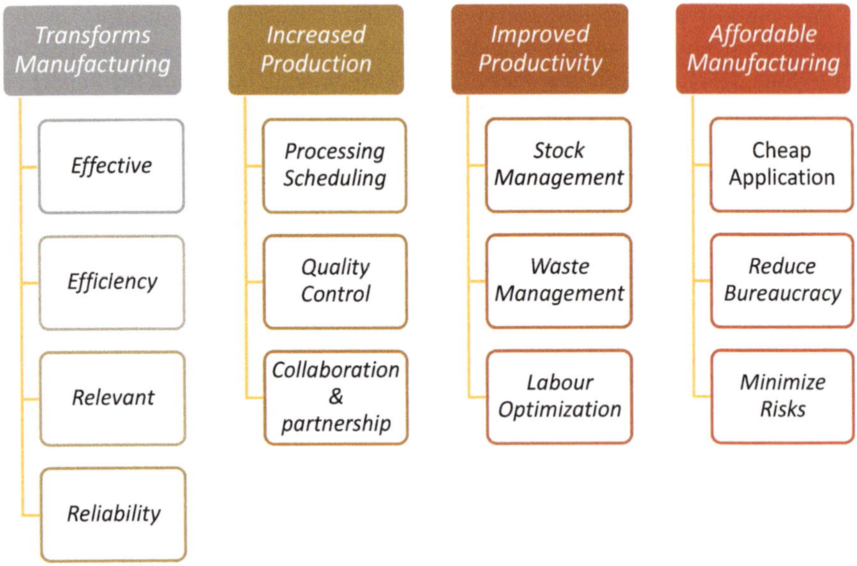

Fig. 3.2 Impact of mobile application

revealed the impact of the mobile application by transforming manufacturing, increasing production and affordable manufacturing.

Figure 3.2 provides critical opportunity for strengthening of the internal supply chain therefore transformation of manufacturing, increased production, and affordable manufacturing.

3.4.1 Transformation of Small-Scale Manufacturing

The innovation is critical in the transformation of small-scale manufacturing in Africa by harnessing effectiveness, efficiency, relevance, and reliable manufacturing. The application's ability to streamline manufacturing is critical for improvement in manufacturing in developing countries riddled with ineffectiveness, inefficiency, irrelevance, and unreliable manufacturing mechanisms. First, the application is critical towards strengthening effectiveness in the production by the small manufacturers in Africa. The application has improved the operations of the small manufacturing by systematically adopting to modern techniques of production. Production and productivity have been improved by adoption of manufacturing techniques like lean manufacturing and just-in time systematically transforms manufacturing in small manufacturing plants. The application by use of dash boards schedules production process by helping the different personnel in manufacturing process to schedule. One of the discussants during the impact assessment opined that the mobile application is critical for improvement of effectiveness in manufacturing in company. In his own words the discussant who opined that:

> "the application is useful in ensuring that manufacturing is effective as the processes are automated therefore, helping attainment of desired objectives. Timely information is very important for small scale manufacturers which is one of the features of the application being position to relay accurate and timely information for all the stakeholders. This is very important in delivery of timely and harnessing effectiveness in the manufacturing." By use of dashboards and remote sensors stakeholders are in position to input information and acquire resources required for effective performance.

Secondly, the innovation has proved critical for improvement of efficiency in the small-scale manufacturing firm. The application harnesses efficiency by streamlining processes which were previously done manually by use of smart phones and computers across the entire production system. One of the discussants during the discussion emphasised the ability of the mobile application to improve efficiency as it streamlines operations of all the stakeholders. The Chief Executive Officer argued that the mobile application streamlines operations by integrating activities in the same platform which strengthens efficiency in manufacturing.

> In his own words the discussant highlighted that: "the mobile application helps in integrating the operations of all the stakeholders which can be viewed in dashboards. This is very important in strengthening and making operations more efficient in the same platform." Different actors in the supply chain view the different dashboards and access useful information to undertake respective obligations therefore improving efficiency.

Thirdly, the mobile application transforms the manufacturing units by adoption and use of local and relevant technology which is applicable to the manufacturing conditions in Africa. The mobile application is simple, relevant, and cheap technology adopted for local conditions in Africa. One of the discussants during the impact assessment highlighted that the mobile application is cheap and relevant for developing countries. In his own words the discussant highlighted that:

> the application is adoptable to both to desktops, laptops and mobile telephones making it convenient for both the small and big companies to use.

The design requirements which were developed was on the basis of the local requirements for developing countries. This is critical in ensuring that the application meets the requirements for Africa where mobile phones are across the entire society. Finally, the mobile application improves the reliability in manufacturing as the requirements of the health products have to be provided in a timely and reliable manner for saving life. Health sector manufacturing transformation requires improvements in relevance reliability of healthcare system. One of the discussants during the discussions argued that the mobile application can be reliable in supporting the manufacturing system as it provides real-time information for the users across the entire value chain of the manufacturing system. In his own words the discussant who argued that:

> the mobile application by use of dash boards automatically relays accurate information during the manufacturing process as opposed to the manual system. The automation helped in

> reliable information which I required by all employees. Effective manufacturing requires reliable information across the manufacturing process.

The mobile application uses remote sensors for inputting customer demands and requirements for the next intermittent processes in the manufacturing system. Actions by the different employees in the manufacturing system are guided by reliable information which are accessible on the platform. The innovation helps under-resourced health care systems to acquire right information and maintain good relationships with customers and meeting their expectations.

3.4.2 Increased Production

First, mobile application has proved useful for scheduling the production processing in the manufacture of insect repellent hiking socks, natural repellent creams, repellent spray, and repellent bans. One of the respondents demonstrated how systematically, the mobile application by use of barcodes sequences the production. The use of the very barcode ensures that production is sequenced and moves from one step to the next correct step sequentially. The new process must begin immediately after the first process has been undertaken. The next process by detecting the code automatically follows the right sequence to conduct the correct process. The manufacturer by use of bar codes has systematically been in position to align the processes during manufacturing. The mobile application has proved critical towards strengthening the production process in the small-scale manufacturing. The insight from the respondents demonstrated the processing by the mobile application and stated that:

> After you have completed the fibre. You'll scroll down and start the process of rewinding. You see the very same barcode that you have put under recipe B11. So, you don't need to, re-enter the barcode. So, the system will know that you have completed the fibre now it activates button of, is it rewind that we are talking about. Furthermore, there will be a report that says mixed step 1. Step 1 complete.

The capabilities of the application will improve the ability of the manufacturers to produce more and meet the market demands in the communities. Furthermore, the platform integrates the small-scale manufacturers with all the critical stakeholders that require the products in the same platform. Secondly, the mobile application has proved useful for strengthening of quality control and systematically driving the small-scale manufacturer for certification under the international standards for quality control under ISO certification. One of the respondents underscored the importance of the system by stating that the application is proving useful for quality control under ISO 9000 series. In his own words the CEO argued that:

> This programme is very important for us because we intend to get ISO 9000 series certification and I think one of their requirements is the tracking of the work floor from raw materials up to the final product. So, this programme we are going to implement with all the zeal that we have because it forms part of our quality control with. Furthermore, we have to adopt the ISO 9000 project, and ISO 9000 project needs the completion of adoption of

> mobile application before we start ISO project. I can't go to ISO 9000 without finishing this one first.

The application is proving critical towards the transformation of the manufacturing in the small-scale manufacturing industry. Furthermore, quality is crucial towards competition in manufacturing and meeting the expectations of the customers. Finally, the mobile application provides the opportunity for collaboration of all the stakeholders in the production process right from the start to the end of the product. The manufacturer who participated in the impact assessment argued that the application is critical for improvement of collaboration the production. In his own words the participant argued that:

> the application provides an opportunity for the employees in our firm to participate effectively in the production process. This is critical in making meaningful contributions by all the players involved in value addition right from the start to the end of the value chain. This is critical for strengthening collaboration and partnerships in the production of quality products. Collaborative manufacturing increases productivity and production in our company.

This is critical in building synergies for collaborations and partnerships to productivity and production by emerging manufacturing plants in Africa. Partnerships and collaboration by all the key players deliver benefits for society and greater public. In the long run, the manufacturing industry will be in position to grow and transform due to strengthened interdependences among the key players in Industry and different departments in the manufacturing plant.

3.4.3 Improved Productivity

First, the mobile application is critical for improvement in stock management by the small-scale manufacturer. The innovation has improved stock management by automatically tracking employee performance, therefore significantly strengthening stock management. One of the senior managers in the small-scale manufacturing argued that the application has helped them to translate from physical manufacturing to automation by reduction of waste management as a result of productivity by effectively using labour. In his own words the participant argued that:

the mobile application helps in stock management which is a big challenge to small manufacturers. The mobile application helps in monitoring stock status report and consumption levels which is critical for increased productivity. You see waste stock management, add stock with results, add waste stock.

Secondly, the mobile application has proved useful for waste management for the small-scale manufacturer. The innovation has streamlined waste management by tracking the employee performance effectively as opposed to the previous traditional systems. One of the respondents during the impact assessment highlighted that the mobile application will be critical in reduction of waste as it provides manufacturers with mechanisms for tracking wastages. In his own words the discussant highlighted that:

> the application reduces wastage which normally occurs in raw materials, processing and production of poor products leading losses. The application facilitates measurement of how oil and other raw materials used against the number of outputs. This has proved useful in waste management by our firm.

The mobile application, therefore, streamlines waste by tracking raw materials and improving production processes, therefore reducing wastage. The modification in the application has wastage controls which is critical for cost reduction.

Thirdly, the mobile application has proved useful for better optimisation of labour for the small-scale manufacturer. The innovation has optimised labour utilisation by tracking the employee performance effectively as opposed to the previous traditional systems. One of the senior managers in the small-scale manufacturing argued that the application has helped them to translate from physical manufacturing to automation by reduction of waste management as a result of productivity by effectively using labour. In his own words the participant argued that:

> initially monitoring staff performance was undertaken manually but now employees have to wear and we were using manual stock take, at the end of the day people have to wear, wear, and wear whatever is left. But the problem is, you stopped the machine at 03:15 you have to clean it and all that, 03:30 people are already anxious the bus is leaving at 03:45, so you know people are anxious to quickly leave and go to the bus stop to wait for their bus or else they will be in trouble. So we realized that this manual system does not work but if we use this system as we have designed, this automated system, this a very good way to do it because it captures the data as they move so you know exactly what's left and what's not left.

The application is proving critical towards the transformation of the manufacturing in the small-scale manufacturing industry. Furthermore, quality is crucial towards competition in manufacturing and meeting the expectations of the customers.

3.4.4 Cost Reduction

In Africa, manufacturing is very costly despite availability of raw materials. This is as a result of poor technology. The mobile application innovation technology reduces operation costs by integration, reduction of duplication, and removal of waste across the supply chain. Furthermore, the platform provides a transparent and accountable system for healthcare services. First, the application is cost effective and applicable to the small-scale industries in Africa. The affordability of the technology suitable to conditions in Africa is an exemplary role of how academic segment is contributing towards transformation of Africa and the health care system. One of the discussants highlighted the cost implication of the technology being critical for use by small-scale manufacturing firm. In his own words the production manager stated that the application is relatively cheaper in comparison to innovation technology available in the market for example Sage is very expensive for our firm. This is appealing and substantially help us in the production and meeting our customer requirements.

Secondly, the application reduces costs appropriately for order and stock management. The operators are in position to appropriately monitoring stock orders. One of the respondents during the impact assessment highlighted that the mobile application will be critical in reduction of waste as it provides manufacturers with mechanisms for tracking wastages. In his own words the discussant highlighted that:

the application reduces wastage which normally occurs in raw materials, processing and production of poor products leading losses. The application facilitates measurement of how oil and other raw materials used against the number of outputs. This has proved useful in waste management by our firm.

The mobile application, therefore, streamlines waste by tracking raw materials and improving production processes, therefore reducing wastage. The modification in the application has wastage controls which is critical for cost reduction. Thirdly, the application can play a role of reducing bureaucracy which normally increases costs. The application provides mechanisms for verification online without necessarily going through so much bureaucracy. One of the discussants during the impact assessment highlighted that the mobile application eliminates bureaucracy by provision of the platform and use of barcodes for inputting information for reduction of costs. The chief Executive Officer in his own words stated that:

I think I have a meeting in the Morning where we can generate QR codes for all the raw materials that we have and then what you do is get that, print it, print the stickers and then we put the codes on the different processes, therefore improving the scheduling of the operations during the manufacturing right from the start to the end. This will help us reduce the bureaucracies we normally face during our production. We can start with the trials and from what I see we need smart phones so probably we need to purchase maybe I don't know 2 smart phones.

This is critical in the reduction of costs for the different stakeholders who are in different geographical locations. The employees from different locations and value chains can easily interact using the platform. Finally, use of the mobile application reduces costs by minimising risks during the manufacturing process. The discussions during the impact assessment highlighted the importance of the mobile application in streamlining communication and availability of information for all the stakeholders in the supply chain, therefore minimising risks. In his own words, the industry player argued that:

the mobile application improves the operation as it reduces risks to loses which increase costs of production. The application by use of dashboards provides critical information to the employees involved in the production process right from the start of the production to the final part of production. The information is critical for planning and reduction of risks significantly reducing the costs of production.

At best, the application harnesses mechanisms for cost reduction by minimisation of wastes, risks, and bureaucracy during the manufacturing by the manufacturer.

3.5 Discussions

The study undertook an assessment of the impact of the mobile application innovation on the internal supply chain in small-scale manufacturer in South Africa. In this chapter, we provide a synthesis of the underlying impact of the application in the context of developing countries. The study established that the mobile application impacted by transformation of manufacturing, increased production, and reduced the costs of production. First, our study established that the mobile application facilitates transformation manufacturing in Africa. The findings are similar to previous studies that examined the influence of digital applications on the operations of manufacturing (Mathur et al. 2018; Queiroz et al. 2022; Skowron-Grabowska et al. 2022). Specifically, we established that digital applications transform manufacturing by strengthening effectiveness, efficiency, relevance, and reliability.

Similarly, Mathur et al. (2018) established that mobile applications improve effectiveness in manufacturing. The ability to achieve the desired results in organisations is harnessed by digital technology. Our study established that small-scale manufacturing is strengthened and improved by streamlining manufacturing effectiveness, efficiency, relevance, and reliability. In view of efficiency, the mobile applications provide a platform for efficient utilisation of resources. Supply Chain Council (2022) argued that platforms facilitate establishment of well-coordinated supply chain system, enabling an organisation to manage its resources efficiently and view various aspects of its operations (Supply Chain Council 2022), with a network of collaborating entities; suppliers, manufacturers, distributors, and retailers (Akkucuk 2020) with an objective of efficient utilisation of resources (Hasibuan et al. 2018). The mobile application enhances effectiveness by integrating the critical players in the healthcare supply chain. Mathur et al. (2018) argue that an organisation's performance together with appropriate manufacturing requires improvement in effectivenesss and efficiency.

Furthermore, Queiroz et al. (2022) highlight that relevance and reliability are critical drivers of good organisation performance. Reliability in the system depends on the ability of the supply chain to consistently meet customer demands and delivering products and services on time, in the right quantities, and at expected levels of quality (Skowron-Grabowska et al. 2022). A well-coordinated supply chain system enables an organisation to manage its resources efficiently and view various aspects of its operations (Supply Chain Council 2022), with a network of collaborating entities; suppliers, manufacturers, distributors, and retailers (Akkucuk 2020) with an objective of efficient utilisation of resources (Hasibuan et al. 2018). Secondly, the study established that the mobile application increased production by the small-scale manufacturing in Africa. As regards to increasing production, and in line with earlier research (Nicholson et al. 2023; Skowron-Grabowska et al. 2022; Chen et al. 2023; Li et al. 2023), this study supports the role of the mobile application in production capabilities.

Our study established that the mobile application increases production outputs by appropriate scheduling production. The application provides a uniform environment where the stakeholders participate collectively during the manufacturing process (Nicholson et al. 2023) enabling free flow of vital information for production. Mobile applications streamline processing removing traditional barriers and borders within the firm and increasing production output by manufacturing firms. The study also established that the mobile application increased production by strengthening quality control. The findings complement Skowron-Grabowska et al. (2022) who also argued that digital applications improve quality control during the production. Mechanism involved in quality control follow through the process orientation and required improvements during the processing. ISO 9000 series certification requires tracking of the work flow from the start to the end.

Our study also established that the innovation improved production by improving collaboration and partnerships within the manufacturing firm. The findings confirm early findings by Li et al. (2023), who also established that digital technology helps the firm to integrate operations facilitating collaboration and partnerships. The different employees involved in the production process participate in the production obtaining required information on time. Progressive manufacturing companies are already using mobile devices to connect employees to collect, access, and share critical manufacturing data and achieve continuous improvement (Ak and Patatoukas 2016; Zhu et al. 2021). The power of mobile applications lies in their ability to work right down on the production line, where the actual manufacturing process takes place.

Thirdly, innovation harnesses productivity by the small-scale manufacturing in Africa. This is supported by earlier studies (Nicholson et al. 2023; Frank et al. 2019; Ebert and Duarte 2018), this study supports the role of the mobile application improving the manufacturers productivity. Our findings highlight that the mobile application impacted the stock management capacity of the manufacturer. The application provides an appropriate mechanism for stock management, significantly improving productivity (Nicholson et al. 2023) and enabling free flow of vital information for productivity. Furthermore, the mobile applications have removed all borders and broken barriers previously undermining productivity. The study also established that the mobile application streamlined waste management, therefore improving productivity. Our study findings are in agreement with previous scholars who established that waste management can appropriately be managed using mobile applications (Frank et al. 2019). Ebert and Duarte (2018) highlighted that mobile applications reduce unnecessary waste during the production process by use of appropriate raw materials.

Our study also established that use of mobile application technology was critical in optimisation of labour. Li et al. (2023) also established that use of mobile application technology improves the ability of the manufacturer to effectively supervise and monitor employee performance. Employee productivity is improved as the supervisors are in position to effectively supervise the employee performance by using outputs. Technology can facilitate monitoring employee performance. Zhu et al. (2021) argue that manufacturers use mobile devices to connect employees to collect, access, and share critical manufacturing data and achieve continuous improvement.

Finally, it was established that the mobile application impacted the costs of production by making production more affordable. The innovation systematically reduced costs through integration, reduction of duplication, and removal of waste across the supply chain. Furthermore, the platform provides a transparent and accountable system for the manufacturer. Frank et al. (2019) also asserted that digital technology platforms reduce waste in the manufacturing. The mobile application innovation technology reduces operation costs by integration, reducing waste, and the cost of production (Ebert and Duarte 2018). The use of mobile application platforms helps in cutting down processes which lead costly power consumption and different challenges. This is critical in transformation of manufacturing in the health sector. The integration in processing reduces costs as the approach reduces duplication. Traditional manufacturing without use of advanced technology exposes manufacturers to high costs.

Similarly, Cai et al. (2010) established that digital technology is responsible for cost reduction. Gurbaxani and Dunkle (2019) also argued that digital technology results in cost-effectiveness in manufacturing due to removal of bureaucracy. Manufacturers view the platforms and execute tasks without delays, therefore reducing costs in the production. The convergence in a variety of capabilities results in cost reduction in handsets and associated telecommunication infrastructures are the result of extensive technical innovation (Goerzig and Bauernhansl 2018). The integration is critical in reduction of production costs making production cost effective in manufacturing, systematically improving health services. Using online platforms (Russel 2019), the mobile applications are critical in dealing with a big challenge of expensive and costly services (Rose et al. 2015; Fenny et al. 2018). The mechanisms provided by the mobile application innovation technology reduces operation costs by integration, reduction of duplication, and removal of waste across the supply chain. Platforms enable employees to collect more accurate data, share it across the organisation rapidly, analyse, and use for improved manufacturing. Better, faster information flow harnesses team work, predicts problems by use of equipment, material supplies, and saves money for the company.

3.5.1 Practical Contribution and implications

In practice, this paper provides practical insights for internal supply chain coordination as it improves mechanism: manufacturing, production, productivity, and reduced costs in Health Care Supply Chains. The practical contribution lies in presenting a comprehensive framework for integrated coordination of manufacturing plants in Africa. Moreover, it offers practical insights for streamlining manufacturing processes by streamlining coordination and operations in manufacturing plant. First, the mobile application provides a practical mechanism for improved coordination by transforming manufacturing in the development country context. At best, the mobile application provides a relevant, reliable, efficient, and effective mechanism for transforming manufacturing of the drugs in the developing country context. Small-scale manufacturers in Africa are faced with different challenges in terms of relevance, effectiveness, and reliability of manufacturing. The mobile application provides an innovative approach for transformation of manufacturing.

Secondly, in practice the paper provides appropriate mechanism for increasing manufacturing production output. This is critical in the transformation of small manufacturing in Africa which continuously faces low production outputs. Specifically, the mobile application increases production, by improving processing scheduling, quality control, and collaboration and partnerships. The study has a practical implication to firms faced with limitations in production outputs in developing countries. Firms can systematically improve the production outputs by strengthening process scheduling, quality control, collaboration, and partnerships with suppliers and stakeholders involved in the health sector. Thirdly, the paper provides the practical implication to practitioners seeking to improve productivity within the internal supply chain. Specifically, the mobile application improves internal supply chain productivity by streamlining stock management, waste management, and optimisation of labour. This is critical for small manufacturing plants which have continued to experience low productivity due to wastage, poor stock management, and inadequate capacity for labour optimisation.

Finally, the application provides innovative mechanisms for cost reduction in the internal supply chain in manufacturing. The new innovation provides a cheaper option with appropriate mechanisms for cost reduction. Specifically, the mobile application reduces costs by use of a cheap mobile application, reduced bureaucracy, and risk minimisation. The application provides an appropriate avenue for meeting financial challenges for small-scale manufacturers in Africa. The mobile application is affordable, therefore practically helpful in addressing financial challenges faced by developing countries.

3.5.2 Methodological Contribution

The methodology and approach use for the study contributes to the use of qualitative research methodology for assessment of the impact of the design science using a case study research design. Using focus group discussions and key informant interviews for the impact of the mobile application, the UNISA ACT app was assessed by conducting focus group discussion with a small manufacturer which had started using the mobile application. The methodology employed demonstrates how qualitative compliments design science. The mobile application under impact assessment was designed using computer experience, and the impact assessment is explored qualitatively. We demonstrate a closed loop between qualitative and computer design, highlighting design thinking and user integration in practice. Furthermore, the input from this study is important for continuous development for artefacts which have been developed.

3.5.3 Theoretical Contribution

The study provides insight on the contribution of the mobile application innovation on the market coordination dimension in relation to availability of the medicine for the market as a result of improved internal supply chain mechanisms by the small-scale manufacturers. Mechanisms for strengthening of small-scale manufacturers by transforming manufacturing, productivity, and production have been critically established. This is critical for improvement of market level equilibrium by inducing health technology equilibrium, increasing access and availability of medicine, improving supply chain coordination of Acts, harnessing affordability of medicine, and transformation of the health system and economy. The loop which was previously not clear on the extent to which the internal supply chain contributes to the market level stakeholders consisting of local pharmaceutical companies and distributors, domestic public and private suppliers, international public and private suppliers, private for profit wholesalers, and private not for profit providers.

In addition, this study expands the knowledge generation theory to support the improvement of the operation of internal supply chains in developing countries. This has been achieved by identifying challenges, weaknesses, and limitations of the internal supply chains in manufacturing in less developed countries. In context, improved internal supply chains by strengthening manufacturing, production, productivity, and reducing costs is critical for firm performance in developing countries. Finally, gaining a contextual understanding of developing countries supply chains with appropriate improvement mechanisms is essential for advancing coordination of internal supply chains in developing countries.

3.6 Limitations of the Study

Our study focus was mainly internal supply chain coordination for small manufacturing of pharmaceutical plants in South Africa. Our study is bound to have theoretical, contextual, and theoretical limitations. First, our study's focus was on the internal supply chain coordination of the pharmaceutical plant in South Africa. Despite the merits of our study, supply chain coordination is a holistic theoretical concept which is underpinned by the system's theory, highlighting that a system consists of sub-systems which contribute to the entire performance of the entire system and sub-systems. Theoretically, excluding other sub-systems of supply chain coordination limits our understanding of how the mobile application contributes to coordination mechanism across the entire supply chains, including internal, micro, macro, and external supply chains. Therefore, we recommend future studies to adopt an approach that will allow a holistic theoretical examination of supply chain's coordination examining system with subs-systems.

Secondly, contextual limitation, our study mainly focused on a single case which was used for exploration of mobile application on the market segment for small-scale manufacturer of malaria products in Gauteng. This was critical in the development of appropriate mechanisms for improvement of internal supply chains in South Africa and developing countries. Contextually, the study has limitations in pharmaceutical companies with different processing mechanisms. Future studies could explore the mobile application to better understand the unique contexts across different countries in which pharmaceutical companies operates in multi-embedded value chains. This can strengthen the unique attributes and development of theories.

Finally, our study used a qualitative single case study methodology for exploration of internal supply chain coordination for exploration of the impact of the mobile application on the market segment case of small business manufacturer of malaria products in Gauteng province of South Africa. Single case studies and interpretive philosophical founded studies have limitations on generalisation of findings. Future studies could explore use of multiple case studies and integration positivism for confirmation of theory and practice. Eisenhardt (2017) provides a justification of use of multiple case studies in the development of theory for internal supply chains. In addition, future research could also integrate interpretive and positivist philosophical underpinning for confirming theory development. Use of mixed methods could strengthen the concepts developed in our study.

References

Abdallah AB, Alfar NA, Alhyari S (2021) The effect of supply chain quality management on supply chain performance: the indirect roles of supply chain agility and innovation. Int J Phys Distrib Logist

African Union (2022). Goals & priority areas of agenda 2063. https://au.int/en/agenda2063/goals. Accessed 24 November 2023.

Akkucuk U (2020) SCOR model and the green supply chain. In: Waste management: concepts, methodologies, tools, and applications. IGI Global, pp 366–382

Awwad M, Kulkarni P, Bapna R, Marathe A (2018, September) Big data analytics in supply chain: a literature review. In: Proceedings of the international conference on industrial engineering and operations management, vol vol. 2018, pp 418–425

Babbie E. (2017) The basics of social research (7th ed.). Cengage Learning: Boston.

Bartik AW, Bertrand M, Cullen ZB, Glaeser EL, Luca M, Stanton CT (2020) How are small businesses adjusting to COVID-19? Early evidence from a survey. NBER Working Paper No. w26989.

Bhattacharya S, Mukhopadhyay D, Giri S (2015) Framework for study of supplier relationships in Indian automotive supply chains. J Supply Chain Manag Syst 4(3):47–63

Cai S, Jun M, Yang Z (2010) Implementing supply chain information integration in China: the role of institutional forces and trust. J Oper Manag 28(3):257–268

Chen Y, Xu S, Lyulyov O, Pimonenko T (2023) China's digital economy development: incentives and challenges. Technol Econ Dev Econ 29(2):518–538

Choi T, Wallace SW, Wang Y (2018) Big data analytics in operations management. Prod Oper Manag 27(10):1868–1883

Datta PP, Christopher MG (2011) Information sharing and coordination mechanisms for managing uncertainty in supply chains: a simulation study. Int J Prod Res 49(3):765–803

Desai S, Looze J (2020) Business owner perceptions of COVID-19 effects on the business: preliminary findings. Trends in Entrepreneurship, No. 10. Kauffman Foundation

Ebert C, Duarte CHC (2018) Digital transformation. IEEE Softw 35(4):16–21
Eggers F (2020) Masters of disasters? Challenges and opportunities for SMEs in times of crisis. J Bus Res 116:199–208
Frank AG, Mendes GHS, Ayala NF, Ghezzi A (2019) Servitization and industry 4.0 convergence in the digital transformation of product firms: a business model innovation perspective. Technol Forecast Soc Chang 141:341–351
George G, Kotha R, Parikh P, Alnuaimi T, Bahaj AS (2016) Social structure, reasonable gain, and entrepreneurship in Africa. Strateg Manag J 37(6):1118–1131. https://doi.org/10.1002/SMJ.2381
Goerzig D, Bauernhansl T (2018) Corporate architectures for the digital transformation in small and medium-sized corporates. Procedia CIRP 67:540–545
Gurbaxani V, Dunkle D (2019) Gearing up for successful digital transformation. MIS Q Exec 18(3):209–220
Hasibuan A, Arfah M, Parinduri L, Hernawati T, Harahap B, Sibuea SR, Sulaiman OK (2018) Performance analysis of supply chain management with supply chain operation reference model [Paper presentation]. Journal of Physics: Conference Series, Prima, Indonesia
Herbane B (2010) Small business research: time for a crisis-based view. Int Small Bus J 28(1):43–64
Kabra G, Ramesh A, Arshinder K (2015) Identification and prioritization of coordination barriers in humanitarian supply chain management. Int J Disaster Risk Reduct 13:128–138
Khurana S, Chhillar N, Kumar V, Gautam S (2013) Inventory control techniques in medical stores of a tertiary care neuropsychiatry hospital in Delhi. Health 5(1):8–13
Lee S, Persson P (2016) Financing form family and friends. Rev Financ Stud 29(9):2341–2386
Li X, Wang H, Yang C (2023) Driving mechanism of digital economy based on regulation algorithm for development of low-carbon industries. Sustain Energy Technol Assess 55:102909
Manyika J, Lund S, White O, Berry C (2016) Digital finance for all: powering inclusive growth in emerging economies. Available at: http://www.mckinsey.com/mgi
Mahotra A, Majchrzak A (2024) Digital innovations in crowdsourcing using AI tools. Technovation, 133:102997.
Mathur B, Gupta S, Meena ML, Dangayach G (2018) Healthcare supply chain management: literature review and some issues. J Adv Manag Res 15(1):265–287
Mbuyisa B, Leonard A (2017) The role of ICT use in SMEs towards poverty reduction: a systematic literature review. J Int Dev 29(2):159–197
Mkansi M, Ramovha T (2023) A mobile application innovation for public healthcare supply chain, Proceedings of eighth international congress on information and communication technology: ICICT 2023, London, Volume 2, pp. 51.
Mpimbaza A, Miles M, Sserwanga A, Kigozi R, Wanzira H, Rubahika D, Nasr S, Kapella BK, Yoon SS, Chang M, Yeka A (2015) Comparison of routine health management information system versus enhanced inpatient malaria surveillance for estimating the burden of malaria among children admitted to four hospitals in Uganda. Am J Trop Med Hyg 92(1):18–21
Nagitta, PO, Mkansi M (2019) Exploring the supply chain coordination dimensions for artemisinin-based combination therapies in uganda. Int J Supply Chain Manag 8(4):134–151
Nagitta OP, Kajjumba GW, Mkansi M (2019) Exploring the supply chain coordination dimensions for Artemisinin-based combination therapies in Uganda.
Nagitta, PO, Mkansi M (2023) Macro environment determinants affecting the availability of Artemisinin-based Combination Therapies in Uganda. Int J Pharm Healthc Mark 17(1):97–114
Nicholson JR, Howells III TF, Wasshausen DB (2023) Measuring the US digital economy. Advances in business statistics, methods and data collection, pp 105–124
Polit, DF., Beck, CT. (2012). Nursing research: Generating and assessing evidence for nursing practice (9th ed.). Philadelphia, PA: Wolters Kluwer Health, Lippincott Williams & Wilkins.
Pujara AA, Kant R (2015) Supply chain information sharing. Int J Inf Syst Supply Chain Manag 8(1):22–38

Quang HT, Sampaio P, Carvalho MS, Fernandes ACB, An DT, Vilhenac E (2016) An extensive structural model of supply chain quality management and firm performance. Int J Qual Reliab Manag 33:444–464
Queiroz M, Wamba S, Jabbour C, Machado M (2022) Supply chain resilience in the UK during the coronavirus pandemic: a resource orchestration perspective. Int J Prod Econ 245:108405
Rose J, Persson JS, Heeager LT, Irani Z (2015) Managing e-government: value positions and relationships. Inf Syst J 25(5):531–571
Rossini M, Powell DJ, Kundu K (2022) Lean supply chain management and Industry 4.0: a systematic literature review. Int J Lean Six Sigma, ahead-of-print. https://doi.org/10.1108/IJLSS-05-2021-0092
Sharma A, Kumar R. (2017) Sharing of information in supply chain management, vol 6.
Shokoohyar S, Shokouhyar S, Hakimioun S (2022) Explicating the effects of big data analytics capabilities on supply chain resilience dimensions: dynamic capabilities approach and complex adaptive system perspective. Int J Logist Syst Manage 43(4):451–483
Shokouhyar S, Seddigh MR, Panahifar F (2020) Impact of big data analytics capabilities on supply chain sustainability: a case study of Iran. World J Sci Technol Sustain Dev 17(1):33–57
Simatupang TM, Sridharan R (2018) Complementarities in supply chain collaboration. Ind Eng Manag Syst 17(1):30–42
Singh RK (2011) Developing the framework for coordination in supply chain of SMEs. Bus Process Manag J 17(4):619–638
Skowron-Grabowska B, Wincewicz-Bosy M, Dymyt M, Sadowski A, Dymyt T, Wąsowska K (2022) Healthcare supply chain reliability: the case of medical air transport. Int J Environ Res Public Health 19(7):4336
Soares A, Soltani E, Liao YY (2017) The influence of supply chain quality management practices on quality performance: an empirical investigation. Supply Chain Manag Int J. https://doi.org/10.1108/SCM-08-2016-0286
Tamym L, El Oaudghiri MD, Benyoucef L, Moh ANS (2020) Big data for supply chain management in Industry4.0 context: a comprehensive survey. In: 13ème conference internationale de modelisation, optimisation et simulation (MOSIM2020), 12–14 Nov, AGADIR, Morocco
Tene TV, Yuriev A, Boiral O (2018) Adopting IDO management standards in Africa: barriers and cultural challenges. In: Boiral O, Allur E (eds) Three decades of dissemination of ISO 9001 and two of ISO 14001: looking back and ahead. Springer International Publishing, pp 59–82
Tjosvold D, Weicker D (1993) Cooperative and competitive networking by entrepreneurs: a critical incident study. J Small Bus Manag 31(1):11
Tomašev N, Cornebise J, Hutter F, Mohamed S, Picciariello A, Connelly B, ... Clopath C (2020) AI for social good: unlocking the opportunity for positive impact. Nature Communications, 11(1), 2468.
World Health Organization (2022) World Malaria Report 2021. World Health Organization. www.who.int/news-room/fact-sheets/detail/malaria
Yadav P (2015) Health product supply chains in developing countries: diagnosis of the root causes of underperformance and an agenda for reform. Health Syst Reform 1(2):142–154
Yin RK (2018) Case study research and applications: Design and methods (6th ed.). Sage, CA: Los Angeles.

Dr. John Michael Maxel Okoche is a Researcher in the Department of Operations Management, College of Economics and Management Science, University of South Africa, Muckleneuk Campus Pretoria, South Africa. His research interests cover Supply Chain, Crowdsourcing, International Business, Artificial Intelligence, Entrepreneurship, and International logistics. He is a Director of Smishels International Consulting Group and has undertaken management consultancies in East Africa and South African Regions.

Prof. Marcia Mkansi is the College Head of Research, Post-graduate Studies, Innovation, and Commercialisation, a Professor of Operations and Supply Chain Management and the former Head of the Department of Operations Management at the College of Economic & Management Sciences, University of South Africa. She serves as a non-executive director for Hellmann Worldwide Logistics, and an advisory board member of the Africa Resource Centre (ARC), a Bill and Melinda Gates Foundation (BMGF)-funded non-governmental organization, set up to be a resource to the public health sector in African governments. Her university-industry alliances include, but are not limited to, Kuehne Foundation, The Innovation Hub, and SAP skills Africa. She was a nominee for the Top Women Standard Bank and UN women projects, and a finalist under the research, innovation, and creative economy category of the National Science and Technology Forum (NSTF)—South32 awards.

Tshililo Ramovha is an experienced IT professional specialising in software development, systems analysis, DevOps, solution architecture, and project management. He is currently pursuing a PhD in Computer Science at UNISA and holds a Master's in Information Technology (2022). With over 18 years of experience, he serves as Manager of Business Systems Administration at the University of Limpopo since 2010. Previously, he worked as a System Analyst and Software Developer at TTH Business Consulting. Tshililo is TOGAF 9, COBIT 5, and Prince2 Project Management certified. His research includes "A Mobile Application Innovation for Public Healthcare Supply Chain Coordination", published in ICICT 2023, London.

Dr. Oluka Pross Nagitta is a member of the Educational Programmes Committee, African Institute for Supply Chain Research, and the Institute of Public Procurement Professionals of Uganda. In the past 6 years, she was a Chairperson of the Contracts Committee at Uganda Management Institute and has also trained various people in Public Procurement and Supply Chain Management from various universities in Uganda. Currently she is working at Uganda Management Institute as a lecturer, and her teaching and research interests are in public procurement and Supply Chain Management. Pross was part of the team that carried out procurement audits in Uganda, Tanzania, and Malawi. Pross has also worked as a Consultant in Sierra Leone, under the UNICEF-funded project, which mapped the medicine supply chain. She has researched widely in public procurement and presented papers at international conferences.

Temidayo Akenroye is an Associate Professor of Supply Chain & Analytics at the University of Missouri–St. Louis. He holds a PhD in Supply Chain Management from the University of Salford, UK, and an MS in Sustainability Leadership from the University of Cambridge. His research and expertise focus on using supply chain management to address sustainable development challenges such as healthcare, food security, and global sustainability. Widely published, he is a sought-after commentator on global supply chain issues.

Chapter 4
Frugal Artificial Intelligence (AI) Innovations in Paediatric Radiology Supply Chain: Diffusion and Impact in Africa

Marcia Mkansi, Frank Ranganai Matenda, Godfrey Mugurusi, and Aaron L. Nsakanda

4.1 Introduction

Paediatric radiology and imaging are an integral part of paediatric healthcare and treatment planning. However, access to paediatric radiology and imaging resources remains a remarkable challenge in low-income and middle-income countries' healthcare supply chains, especially in Africa (Abdel-Wahab et al. 2024; Anazodo et al. 2023; Molyneux 2020). Access is restricted due to limited financial resources, scarce infrastructure, unreliable access to cutting-edge technologies, and a shortage of specialised healthcare experts. These challenges result in delayed diagnoses, unsuitable treatments, high morbidity, and preventable mortalities. Frija et al. (2021) propounded that, in the medical setting, imaging denotes diverse technologies implementing ionising (computed tomography, plain X-rays, nuclear medicine) and non-ionising radiation (magnetic resonance imaging, ultrasound) to diagnose, monitor, or treat medical conditions. Paediatric radiology is a specialised arm of radiology that focuses on the imaging and diagnosis of diseases in infants, children, and adolescents (Ahmed et al. 2024). In other words, paediatric radiology is an arm of specialised healthcare supply chain that focuses in diagnosing and treating diseases and injuries of children using imaging techniques.

M. Mkansi (✉) · F. R. Matenda
College of Economic and Management Sciences, The University of South Africa, Pretoria, South Africa
e-mail: mkansm@unisa.ac.za

G. Mugurusi
Department of Industrial Economics and Technology Management, Norwegian University of Science and Technology, Gjøvik, Norway

A. L. Nsakanda
Sprott School of Business, Carleton University in Ottawa, Ottawa, ON, Canada

T. Akenroye et al. (eds.), *Digitalizing Health Care Supply Chains in Africa*, Springer Series in Supply Chain Management 28,
https://doi.org/10.1007/978-3-032-20501-8_4

In practice, patient care is influenced by the healthcare supply chain, among other things (Kasula 2023). The author (Kasula 2023) further postulated that "healthcare supply chain management encompasses a spectrum of interconnected processes involved in sourcing, procurement, distribution, and management of medical supplies, pharmaceuticals, equipment, and services". From a supply chain lens, paediatric radiology represents a critical part of the value chain that could be at the upstream or downstream parts of the healthcare chain providing goods and services such as X-rays, computed tomography, ultrasound, magnetic resonance imaging, and positron emission tomography. However, radiologists are finding it difficult to uphold high interpretation precision while capitalising on efficiency exam volumes and quantities of images per study increase (Rubin 2000). A method to address these challenges in paediatric radiology is to integrate AI in the healthcare supply chain.

AI has the ability to change many facets of health care landscape. It disrupts the manner in which traditional health care practices are being done. Since the launch of AI in radiology, the expectation has been that AI will enhance the health care and cut costs (van Leeuwen et al. 2022). For instance, AI has demonstrated amazing abilities in automating image analysis, augmenting diagnostic precision, and permitting remote consultations. In the healthcare supply chains, AI innovations have appeared as a glimmer of hope, vowing to deal with the existing challenges and augment the dexterity and sensitivity of healthcare logistics (Kasula 2023). AI innovations can further enhance the efficacy of supply chains by permitting real-time predictive maintenance, data analysis, and adaptive decision-making, thereby transfiguring the manner in which resources are managed and apportioned within healthcare facilities (Kasula 2023). Balasubramanian et al. (2023) opined that the COVID-19 plague uncovered weaknesses in international healthcare systems and high pointed the necessity for innovative, technology-driven solution like AI.

Nevertheless, it should be noted that AI is just a tool, not the objective. Conventional AI innovations usually need significant financial investments, healthy infrastructure, and non-stop access to high-quality data (Aagaard and Tucci 2024; Gholizadeh et al. 2024; Cowls et al. 2023), resources that are limited in numerous African settings. This is where frugal AI comes as a game-changer. Frugal AI denotes to scalable, cost-efficient, and context-sensitive technological innovations that can function under resource-restricted environments (see, for instance, Qin 2024; Martínez-Arellano and Ratchev 2024; Albert 2019). Basically, frugal AI innovations are designed to deal with the specific needs of low- and middle-income regions since they developed to operate efficiently with minimal computational power. Interestingly, in paediatric radiology, AI innovations can streamline workflows, offer diagnostic support and extend the reach of radiological services to underserved populations or economically constrained markets.

Against this background, this chapter examines the diffusion and impact of frugal AI innovations within paediatric radiology supply chains across Africa. Technology diffusion denotes the process by which technology spreads among institutions in the market, via competition or collaboration, influencing market entry and exit tactics. The study seeks to offer actionable insights into the integration of frugal AI into healthcare systems. In Africa, there is a shortage of trained radiologists (Karera et al. 2024; Trauernicht et al. 2022; Rabinowitz and Pretorius 2005), mainly due to underfunding of the healthcare sector and inadequate training ability, among other reasons (Rosman et al. 2019). This puts Africa at a precarious position especially when compared to other continents.

Through this lens, the study contributes to a growing body of knowledge on leveraging technology to address systemic healthcare challenges in Africa. By focusing on paediatric radiology, it underscores the importance of child health as a fundamental pillar of societal well-being and sustainable development. The findings aim to provide a roadmap for policymakers, technologists, and healthcare providers to harness frugal AI innovations in creating more resilient and inclusive healthcare systems for children across the continent.

The chapter is organised as follows. Section 4.2 presents the review of literature, and Sect. 4.3 looks at data and methodology. In Sect. 4.4, study results are outlined. Section 4.5 concludes the study and outlines the implications and opportunities for further research.

4.2 Literature Review

In healthcare, supply chain management is vital in promoting the continuous flow of resources essential for efficient patient care delivery (Kasula 2023). The author (Kasula 2023) further opined that supply chain management's role in healthcare has advanced past simple inventory control and logistics and, nowadays, it is vital for optimising operational efficiency, promoting timely access to important medical resources, and eventually, augmenting patient care results (Kasula 2023). This indicates that healthcare supply chain management is important more than before since it influences treatment efficacy, patient safety, and accessibility of healthcare service. Even though healthcare supply chain management is indispensable, it is endowed with a multiplicity of challenges which include challenges in demand prediction, inventory management, compliance with regulations, and product expiration and recalls management. To address these challenges, cutting-edge technologies such as AI have been adopted and have revolutionised healthcare supply chains. Dogru and Keskin (2020) propounded that healthcare is one of the disciplines that AI has a huge value potential. The industry, including supply chain operations, has seen unmatched progress in AI applications (e.g., Sugar.IQ—a diabetes management application, and Migraine.AI—a personalised migraine management application) in the last two decades (Dogru and Keskin 2020). Supply chains have massively profited from the adoption of AI technologies (Dogru and Keskin 2020).

Even though AI is indispensable, its adoption in the healthcare sector, where it may offer the most significant value, is low (Bughin et al. 2017). Dogru and Keskin (2020) stated that some of the main challenges in implementing AI in healthcare include the following: (i) machine learning algorithms need a wide amount of personal data for performance and customisation of health services; (ii) designing an efficient and effective user interface; (iii) the use of AI for practical purposes need a wider collaborative and interdisciplinary teamwork; and (iv) customisation and potential bias. Acemoglu and Restrepo (2018) indicated that AI is increasingly replacing labour, producing a strong "displacement effect" in economies. In the same vein, Dogru and Keskin (2020) propounded that current developments in AI in diagnostic radiology image analysis is expected to have a displacement effect on radiologists. Further, AI applications presently function in the grey legal area that is not being well regulated (Dogru and Keskin 2020; Whittaker et al. 2018).

In practice, there are concerns against utilising AI in the healthcare sector (Dogru and Keskin 2020). Specifically, there are major mistrust issues when it comes to AI application. Patients fear that AI can violate their privacy, while practitioners are doubtful when it comes to the precision of automated verdicts. This mistrust concerning the use of AI partly emanates from the asymmetric environment that victimises the patients through unbecoming medical manners and data breaches but not able to penalise institutions that design or implement them to provide healthcare amenities (Dogru and Keskin 2020). Panch et al. (2018) proposed that, to enhance trust, researchers and developers should prove to clinical decision-makers that the suggested machine learning algorithms are able to produce required health results through executing practical clinical trials. Also, patients should be enlightened that after they part with their personal data, they will receive enhanced health services (Dogru and Keskin 2020). Researches and government regulations can assist in the protection of clients from possible dangers and guarantee that institutions that design and implement AI are held accountable (Dogru and Keskin 2020). Promoting accountability can enhance public trust concerning AI, which can benefit supply chains that depend on AI to improve the effectiveness of their operations (Dogru and Keskin 2020).

There is a swelling interest in digitalising the supply chains in African healthcare sectors. Interestingly, investments in digital technologies have been on the increase. However, the challenges and concerns against utilising AI can affect the diffusion and impact of frugal AI innovations within paediatric radiology supply chains across Africa. This is problematic since in Africa the radiologist staffing standing seems worse than in well-resourced areas (Rosman et al. 2019). Several studies across African economies have indicated that there is a general shortage of radiologists which affects the quality of healthcare delivery. Moreover, even though a multiplicity of studies concerning AI innovations in healthcare have been done, few studies have paid great attention to AI innovation in radiology. Healthcare supply chain research inspired by the prevalence of AI in radiology stresses issues of ethics, possible opportunities, and challenges in application (Siala and Wang 2022; Morley et al. 2020), but very little attention and evidence on frugal AI innovations by the specialists for the specialists. Earlier research on the topic has been restricted and disjointed, resulting in an incomplete comprehension of the subject matter. In reality, there's growing interest and appetite for empirical case studies on the diffusion and impact of frugal AI innovations in healthcare supply chain (Sarkar and Mateus 2022; Bhatti et al. 2017).

4.3 Methodology

Drawing from the Technology-Organization-Environment (TOE) framework for innovation diffusion, this chapter qualitatively explores the case of Africa-based frugal AI innovations in paediatric radiology. Qualitative case studies are rooted in real-world problems immersed in participant environments (Yin 2017). Data is gathered through participant(s) narratives of experience, behaviour, and perceptions (Widner et al. 2022; Yin 2017). This chapter considered a single case study, amongst the diversity of case study approaches (such as embedded, holistic, and cross case studies), which focuses on a single unit of analysis (Gerring 2016; Yin 2003), in this case the chief executive officer (CEO) of a specialised organisation that offers radiological products and services. There are limited African paediatric radiologists that are both specialists and innovators of frugal AI, with a significant measure of international impact, hence we selected a single case study as the foci of our study. Advocates of a holistic case study approach emphasise greatly its strength in unearthing rare instantiation and patterns of themes that emerge within a specific context and impossible to quantify. The digital healthcare entrepreneur and paediatric radiologist provides weight of such a rare and extreme case study.

A team of three conducted a semi-structured interview to collect data from the CEO who is both an innovator and a specialised paediatric radiologist. Interview data was supplemented by data and information from web-documents, media reports, news, videos, World Health Organisation (WHO) endorsement report, and testimonial insights of other practitioners on the company's digital platform. The data was analysed through conventional content analysis since it is implemented when the existing research on a particular issue is restricted. Conventional content analysis involves coding schemes categories that are derived directly from text data (Kleinheksel et al. 2020; Hsieh and Shannon 2005). A systematic review of the transcripts revealed a case narrative necessary for depicting the company's products, diffusion approach, impact, and paediatric radiology supply chain and outputs. In addition to open coding, we further engaged axial coding to our data. Open coding helped us break the ice to explore different aspects of data insights, whilst axial coding helped us identify themes and connect insights into meaningful patterns to the inner layers of frugal innovations vis-à-vis TOE framework for innovation diffusion. The latter and former coding approach are greatly endorsed by Babbie (2015). The links between frugal innovations and TOE framework are depicted in Fig. 4.1.

The TOE framework is developed to comprehend the factors that affect the adoption and implementation of technology in organisations. It involves of three key components: technology, organisation, and environment. Technology denotes the systems, tools, and processes that organisations may pick to adopt and its key features incorporate its complexity, compatibility with current systems, and perceived relative advantage over other choices. Organisation refers to internal organisational factors like structure, size, culture, and available resources. Environment embraces

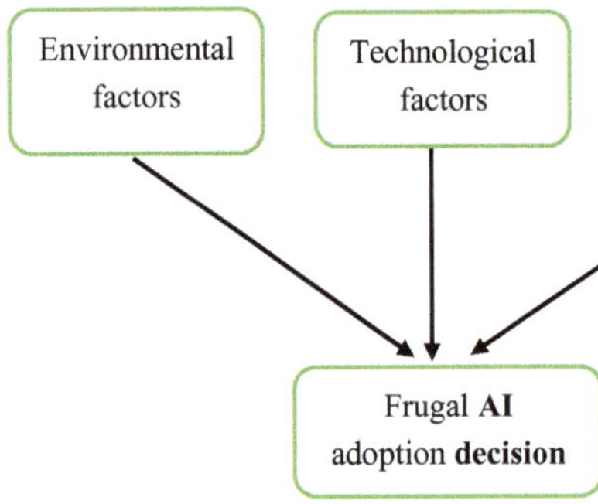

Fig. 4.1 Technology-Organisation-Environment framework

external factors that influence the organisation, like market conditions, regulatory requirements, and competitive dynamics.

4.3.1 Case Description

The case under study (i.e., the institution) commenced its operations in the year 2019 by three healthcare innovators and grew to 13 employees by the time of data collection in 2023. Although we focused on a single company perspective, its distinctive approach as an African creator of frugal AI innovation in paediatric radiology, encompassing entrepreneurship, healthcare supply chain, and paediatric specialisation provides valuable insights. This perspective, particularly of offering paediatric radiology products to radiologists in African and global markets, highlights the diffusion and impact of frugal innovations in this specialised field. The company boosts a suite of four frugal AI in paediatric radiology products, with some embedded in a turnkey service from teleradiology, computer-aided training, radiology AI innovation (for chest, ultrasound and mammography) to radiology AI assurance, and quality tools. The impact of the company to industry have been acknowledged by key national and international institutions such as WHO and MassChallenge Switzerland.

4.4 Findings

The findings of this study are presented for each of the TOE contexts included.

4.4.1 Technological Construct of TOE Framework

The technological infrastructure of the case study is a suite of frugal AI innovations in paediatric radiology products, with some embedded in a turnkey service from teleradiology, computer-aided training, radiology AI innovation (for chest, ultrasound and mammography) to radiology AI assurance, and quality tools and computer-aided training tool. The following sub-headings were derived from conventional content analysis:

AI Tools (Radiology AI for Chest, Ultrasound and for Mammography)—Technological

The following views accompanied the responses on the AI tools used in radiology:

> We started off with just the AI tools and we've got a suite of products there. So, we have a radiology AI for chest, ultrasound and for mammography and essentially what it does it's a clinical decision support. So, if you look around AI solutions you wouldn't find that many solutions that are focused on imaging and healthcare in children right, and that's because you know the children's healthcare is unique. **CEO**
>
> Academic institutions, radiology schools including other subspecialty schools, schools for radiographers, physiotherapists can use CAT as an educational course to upskill specialists in training. In addition, the company provides access to qualified teleradiology services with highly experienced, board-certified senior radiologists in South Africa, including certified paediatric radiologists. **Website**

The frugality aspects of the innovations are observed from their peculiar capabilities of addressing scarcity of infrastructure and limited human capital by optimising limited resources to save time, reduce costs, maximise outputs, whilst maintaining service quality, scalability, and sustainability of healthcare paediatric value chain. Against the frugal capabilities, the company transforms intra healthcare services and extra industry's conventional operations to manifest agile healthcare supply chain rife with varying degrees of ease of use, compatibility consistent with the needs of paediatric radiologists, perceived relative advantage, and perceived importance of compliance.

Agile Healthcare Supply Chain Operations, Quick Decisions Referral—Compatibility

Insights on the compatibility and compliance of innovations emerge in the following sentiments:

> The typical scenario is you'll have a chest X-ray, you'll complete your chest X-ray and you'll be told either to come in an hour or come in a few weeks for your report...with our AI, if you're seeing a caseload of 200 patients, you imagine a patient going and having a chest X-ray and immediately within 12 milliseconds they're able to get what is wrong in their chest and the referring doctor is able to say, okay, this is an emergency I can triage you

> or isolate you. Now this is like in milliseconds you get a response, it goes immediately to your referring doctor and then they can decide. So, it's life changing but it still it's decision support. It is not a stand-alone product, and we never sell a product that is going to replace doctors right. I'm a radiologist, I'm there to assist and augment. **CEO**

This finding shows that frugal AI innovations are compatible with the organisational business processes. The alignment between organisational business processes and frugal AI innovations is vital for frugal AI innovations diffusion.

Time Savings and Quality—Perceived Relative Advantage

The following sentiments accompanied the responses on the perceived relative advantage of frugal AI innovations:

> So, it assists a radiologist or a medical doctor to diagnose faster, to diagnose more accurately and to triage cases that require urgent attention. If you build a product that is pertaining to a radiologist and you have a technology background and experience, it's going to be good and robust in terms of the technology and suit every aspect of an AI? **CEO**

The participant emphasises the issue of time savings, accuracy that helps to improve healthcare service, which transforms conventional operation in terms of speed, quality, and time. The latter are core principles of the service delivery and enacted in the conception of on time, right quantity, and place of the supply chain greater purpose. Looked at differently, the responses highlight the perceived advantage of the class of paediatric innovations, which is a critical factor of adoption and ultimately diffusion; whilst removing perceived barriers of resource scarcity (i.e., human capital) and perceived risks of misdiagnosis.

Efficiency of Human and Technical Support and Cost Savings—Perceived Ease of Use, Reduced Barriers, and Complexity

The participant placed more emphasis on efficiency of human resources, upskilling, and the amplified technical support that produce high quality results and interpretations with less data, enabling paediatric radiologists to utilise the support system with less effort, thus creating less complexity, whilst improving the attitude of users. Consequently, leading to repeat use, adoption, diffusion, and impact of the system to children, healthcare service, and specialists.

Insights on the perceived ease of use, reduced barriers, and complexity emerge in the following sentiments:

> So, you require less data, but you need the expertise of a radiologist. The previous other solutions look at quantity whereas we are looking at quality. In terms of quality X-rays, we're feeding the AI or the algorithms with quality because it's able to now interpret X-ray and from saying that's Tuberculosis (TB) to annotated details showing on an X-ray, i.e., TB because I see these signs on an X-ray. **CEO**

> Using our tool which is called Computer Aided Training (CAT), our education tool/educational course to upskill specialists in training and consultants, radiologist can work with AI, but at the same time they're learning about paediatric imaging. So, it's in a gamified way, it's an education tool and what's the indirect effect of CAT? It will improve adoption because once you start working with AI, you realise it's easy. **CEO**

Change Management—Perceived Barrier and Risk

The following sentiments reflect insight on the perceived barrier and risk:

> Something we realised during this, which is the biggest barrier, was that doctors are afraid that AI is going to replace them. Specifically, in Africa or I would say South Africa, there is still that mindset and that culture. So, we thought how do we change this narrative? What do we need to do? And it is education. It's enhancing you; you're becoming better and you're becoming faster. Indirectly, you are adopting but you're also upskilling. So, that's our second product CAT. **CEO**

Notably, perceived barrier and risk highlight tension, which if not properly managed, can affect diffusion and impact. In prior analysis, it's clear that the class of frugal innovations provides ways of reducing barriers to infrastructure and limited human capital. However, in the subsequent quote, the participant highlighted perceived barriers and risk to diffusion. In particular, relating to change management by paediatrics radiologist. The company and its CEO use education as a mitigating factor, which appears to increase interest and potentially accelerate adoption, diffusion, and impact.

4.4.2 Organisational Construct of TOE Framework

The findings here are presented according to the crucial dimensions of organisation context for technology adoption.

Slack Resources, Firm Size and Scope, and Financial Readiness—Impact of Internet Protocol (IP) Consumption

The AI-based paediatric radiology company self-funded its business and had to contend with financial barriers vis-à-vis international competitors. Limited financial resources constrained the company's ability to scale up and gave competitors an advantage of a market share and visibility. The participant highlighted frustration over the market's cultural orientation that is not towards local innovation due to perceived quality and prestige of products. Although the case under study had investment promise, the lack of surplus of thereof hinders its ability to buffer against environmental and/or humanitarian shocks. Looked at differently, the participant reinforced the notion that organisations with a surplus of resources (referred as slack resources in the TOE framework) can outperform their rivals. Unfortunately, for the case understudy, creating trade imbalance that resulted in trade deficit. The following views reflect the aforementioned findings:

> The one thing that intimidated us, and I would say that has been one of the barriers is that we funded the company ourselves. In the beginning, we had these competitors who came from the United States of America (USA) that were raising over 20 million US dollars. We were a company that was founded in Africa and self-funded. Why do we always have to feel afraid in Africa and go for a company that's based in the US and United Kingdom (UK)? Only because they're from the US or UK. They may not have a fantastic product. So, I think supporting our own solutions is the best… March 2020 COVID hit and South Africa was impacted, Netcare is one of the biggest healthcare groups that invested in us. So, all those opportunities that were lined up for us unfortunately had to be diverted towards dealing with the crisis. That was the big setback. CEO

Proactive Technical Orientation—Diversification of Products and Business Model

A silent observation of short-term adaptation strategy from the lack of surplus resources and limited financial capital by the paediatric radiologist narrative highlights the advantage of investors' network. As a radiologist with networks to hospitals and potential health group investors, the company's management optimised the relationship and humanitarian crisis to its advantage. When the prospective investor diverted its funds from the start-up company due to COVID-19 humanitarian crisis, the frugal AI innovators adapted their diffusion approach from the investor and transaction base model to free open platform that accelerated its market penetration and product validity in Intensive Care Units (ICUs) and casualties' arm of the healthcare service supply chain. On the other hand, a proactive technical orientation is observed in its pivot strategy from X-ray solutions to COVID-19 pneumonia AI solution. Thus, leading to accelerated market penetration, increased validation, and credibility of products. Pivoting to free offerings placed the case under study at a prime position for investors and transactions-based financial models.

The following sights reflect the above-mentioned findings:

> The positive was that we have a chest X-ray solution for pneumonia and our AI was tested on ICU X-rays and then here's COVID pneumonia. As a radiologist, I know what COVID-19 pneumonia looks like. We retrain the product, and you know by the end of April 2020, we had a COVID-19 pneumonia AI solution that we shared generally to South Africa. We opened up the platform freely available to general practitioners. One of the first sites that we piloted our solution used it in their ICUs and their casualties to triage solution. So, COVID-19 may have devastated the rest of the world but in terms of technology like ours, we were able to pivot, build a better solution. Where it impacted us was where we lost an investor that was going to open up opportunities. However, they did come through later on, so we were able to actually create a product for COVID-19. So, we were able to grow during COVID-19. **CEO**

Management Support—Corporate Expatriation and Globalisation of Operations

In lieu of the market's reaction towards frugal innovations vs. international products, the management's long-term strategy was to relocate its legal domicile (also known as corporate expatriation) to the UK for investors' confidence and better market opportunities. This highlights a double-edged sword for African startups and healthcare supply chain. On one hand, it's an opportunity for corporate expatriation to maintain a global appeal by African markets. On the other hand, it is a loss since migration of African innovators to international markets for global investors appeal and better regulation impacts local economies development from taxes, erosion of local expertise, outflow of wealth, job creation, and talent retention.

The following viewpoints reflect the aforementioned findings:

> We haven't left Africa, yes, our Headquarters (HQ) is in is in the UK, but it's always been our vision to democratise access to diagnostic healthcare in Africa. So, whilst we're not headquartered in Africa our focus is still very much on Africa. It's just we're doing it now from the UK because we feel that gives us access to more investment and capital as well as stability in terms of investors. But in terms of operations, we're still very focused in Africa. **CEO**

4.4.3 Environmental Construct of TOE Framework

From the case study, several themes pertaining to the environmental construct are prominent and are presented here.

Regularity and Market Structure—Corporate Inversion, Transnational Corporations, Globalisation of Healthcare Supply Chain Operations

The critical insight that emerged from the case study includes corporate inversion, transnational corporations, and globalisation of healthcare supply chain operations. Although interrelated, the latter concepts emphasise, to a particular degree, different aspects of frugal AI innovations' diffusion and impact. Together they elucidate, on one hand, organic primary models underpinning the diffusion, operations, success, and impact of frugal AI innovations in paediatric radiology healthcare supply chain from the environmental construct of the TOE framework. On the other hand, the frugal AI innovation in paediatric radiology and its transition to foreign markets mediated by regulatory framework and South Africa's prominent adoption of international IPs highlights both a positive and negative organisational and environmental impact to healthcare supply chain.

From the positive perspective, the participant highlighted corporate inversion induced by the need for FDA regulation, which led to transfer of legal domicile, even though the market focus is Africa. This provides the African frugal innovator superior competitive edge, global status of its operation, transnationality of its operations as it appeals to multiple countries and attracts investment opportunities far much better than its previous legal domicile in Africa. The negative aspects are the outflow of wealth and erosion of expertise, which ultimately limit generation of African-based frugal AI intellectual property, as the actors are removed from the context of operations which inspired and could continue to elevate the innovations. Consequently, African healthcare supply chain evolution continue to play catch-up.

The following views reflect the aforementioned findings:

> The unfortunate thing is that Africa doesn't have their own regulatory, I would say certification. They follow the UK (this European) or the American regulation that is the Food and Drug Administration (FDA). That is a sad thing as well, right because we started off as a South African company headquartered initially in South Africa and then we moved to the UK and that's where our HQ is. We were trying to sell our solution to places in South Africa and other African countries and they were buying solutions from Europe or America. For us, as an African company, I think that's sad and that we don't support each other... If you have a regulatory certification recognised like either by the FDA or a CE mark that gives you huge advantage cause, then you can market and commercialise your product. However, it does limit some innovators because, let's face it, if you have the capital, you can get an FDA or a CE mark very quickly because you can just outsource it to a consulting company that helps you get it... it's a barrier for companies that want to get into the AI space, and that again gives you a competitive edge if you want to market it. **CEO**
>
> First ever African-founded company to receive FDA clearance for an AI device. **Website**

Professional Trade and Association—Credibility and Trust, Market Impact, Global Adoption

Furthermore, the TOE framework acknowledges the weight of professional trade and association to innovation adoption. In the case under study, the authors observed reports that allude to WHO endorsement of computer-aided detection (CAD), which constitutes one of their product offerings. The latter adds global authority and credibility of the frugal AI innovations as WHO only endorses products that meet rigorous scientific standards that align with global health priorities. In most cases, the endorsement serves as a catalyst for diffusion, adoption, and impact in a global healthcare supply chain arena, which unlocks funding opportunities, trust, market demand, competitive edge necessary for success. It also highlights ethical approvals of the products, which is critical for sustainable development goals for health and well-being.

The following opinions reflect the aforesaid findings

> WHO has updated its recommendations for TB screening to now include the use of CAD applications in chest radiography, according to officials who discussed the update during a presentation on March 23 organised by the International Society of Radiology. **Media reports**

4.5 Discussion

Numerous interesting findings were discovered from our empirical study. These findings are discussed for each of the TOE contexts encompassed in this study, i.e., technological context, organisational context, and environmental context.

4.5.1 Technological Construct Insight for Diffusion and Impact

Within the technological context, it was discovered that frugal AI innovations address the challenges of scarcity of infrastructure and restricted human capital by optimising constrained resources to save time, reduce costs, maximise outputs, whilst upholding service quality, scalability, and sustainability of healthcare paediatric value chain. Under the same line of reasoning, the accuracy of frugal innovations assists in the enhancement of healthcare service delivery, which changes conventional operations and augments the efficiency of human resources in terms of speed, quality, and time, among other issues. Numerous studies have validated these stated benefits of frugal innovations in healthcare systems (Sarkar and Mateus 2022; Bianchi et al. 2017; Verma 2017).

Frugal AI innovations also alter healthcare services and the conventional operations of the industry, resulting in agile healthcare supply chain associated with fluctuating degrees of ease of use, compatibility coherent with the requirements of paediatric radiologists, perceived relative advantage, and perceived importance of compliance. In the same vein, Dranove and Garthwaite (2022) and Choy et al. (2018) postulated that AI is altering production across all sectors of the economy, including healthcare. However, it should be noted AI has the potential to both complement and substitute traditional labour inputs (Dranove and Garthwaite 2022). Basically, the results highlight the perceived advantage of the class of paediatric innovations, which is a critical factor of adoption and ultimately diffusion; whilst removing perceived barriers of resource scarcity (i.e., human capital) and perceived risks of misdiagnosis.

The study discovered that frugal AI innovations need to be compatible with the organisational business processes to promote their adoption and diffusion. This is validated by Stjepić et al. (2021) who indicated that new technology should be compatible with the existing technology. Further, it has been highlighted that upskilling and improved technical support that produce high quality results and interpretations with less data are required to allow paediatric radiologists to implement the support systems with less effort, thereby creating less complexity, whilst improving the attitude of users. This results in repeat use, adoption, diffusion, and more impact of the innovations to the healthcare supply chain. Rao (2023) postulated that even though the incorporation of AI can enhance and improve patient results and decrease the workload of healthcare experts, there is a requirement for substantial upskilling and of healthcare workers. Even though it is widely documented that frugal innovations provide ways of reducing barriers to infrastructure and limited human capital, the study exposed that perceived barrier and risks to diffusion need to be managed to enhance diffusion and impact. These barriers and risks can be eliminated through education that can amplify the interest and possibly accelerate adoption, diffusion, and impact.

4.5.2 Organisational and Environmental Constructs for Diffusion and Impact

The study argues that organisational and environmental factors of the TOE framework constitute a make or break of frugal innovation diffusion and impact to healthcare supply chain in Africa. As for the organisational context, it has been discovered that, in addition to international competition, African AI-based paediatric radiology companies have to fund themselves since they face financial barriers which prevent them from growing, thereby giving competitors an advantage of a market share and visibility. The lack of surplus resources hinders the companies' ability to buffer against environmental and/or humanitarian shocks. In the same vein, Chakravarty propounded that lack of innovation funding is a challenge in South Africa, especially at the early stages of product development. The authors further articulated that, even when funding there, a deterrent comes from the extremely bureaucratic processes around its access. The study also discovered that the market's cultural orientation is not towards local innovation due to perceived quality and prestige of products. Investors prefer to invest in international companies instead of local companies. This is not surprising since the perception that international brands provide superior quality and prestige compared to local products is predominant among customers in several African countries (see, for instance, Yeboah-Banin and Quaye 2021 and references therein). This customer bias can impact investor behaviour, possibly resulting in a preference for international companies over local ones.

The study discovered that companies with networks to hospitals and potential health group investors can benefit from these relationships, especially in crisis periods. Also, to enhance technology diffusion, the frugal AI innovators can alter their diffusion approach from the investor and transactions-based model to free open platform that can accelerate their market penetration and product validity. That is to say they can pivot on free offerings to position themselves at prime positions for investors and transactions-based financial models. Basically, companies can adopt a proactive technical orientation to accelerate their market penetration, increase validation and credibility of products. Although African firms can relocate to developed countries like the US and UK for investors' confidence, better market opportunities, better regulation, and global appeal, it is a loss since migration of African innovators to international markets negatively affects the growth and development of local economies.

Within the environmental context, the important views that emerged from the analysis incorporate corporate inversion, transnational corporations, and globalisation of healthcare supply chain operations. These concepts highlight diverse facets of frugal AI innovations diffusion and impact. On one hand, they explain organic primary models behind the diffusion, operations, success, and impact of frugal AI innovations in paediatric radiology healthcare supply chain from the environmental construct of the TOE framework. On the other hand, they show frugal AI innovation in paediatric radiology and its transition to foreign markets facilitated by regulatory frameworks. Klein et al. (2014) (and references therein) validated the issue of regulatory frameworks. The transition of frugal innovations to foreign markets highpoints both positive and negative organisational and environmental impacts to healthcare supply chain. For instance, from the positive side, corporate inversion persuaded by the need for better regulation (although the market focus is Africa) provides African frugal innovators with superior competitive edge, global status of its operation, transnationality of its operations as it appeals to many multiple countries and attracts investment opportunities that are much better than their previous legal domicile in Africa. However, corporate inversion results in the outflow of wealth and erosion of expertise, which ultimately limit generation of African-based frugal AI intellectual property. Overreliance on foreign IP, as local creators are discouraged in pursuing frugal innovations, breeds unintended vulnerability and geopolitical tensions in cases of healthcare shocks i.e., humanitarian shocks.

Consequently, African healthcare supply chain evolution continue to play catch-up. Culturally, corporate expatriation, corporate inversion, and transnationality of frugal AI innovations in healthcare lead to loss of identity, whereby foreign innovations overshadow local traditions, eroding cultural uniqueness and frugal innovations. Subsequently, African healthcare system experience prolonged dependence on foreign innovations, which creates cultural homogenisation at the expense of diversity. Moreover, professional trade and association play a vital role in innovation adoption. For example, WHO endorsed a CAD product of the case study; thereby, adding global authority and credibility of the frugal AI innovations. These endorsements usually serve as a catalyst for diffusion, adoption, and impact (see, for instance, He et al. 2022) in a global healthcare supply chain arena, which unlocks trust, funding opportunities, market demand, and competitive edge essential for success. Endorsements also highpoint ethical approvals of the products, which are important for sustainable development goals for well-being and health.

4.6 Conclusions

This chapter used expert-interviews in conjunction with the TOE to analyse the diffusion and impact of frugal AI innovations in paediatric radiology within African healthcare systems. The study results indicated that frugal AI can, among other issues, improve diagnostic capabilities, optimise resource allocation, and bridge healthcare disparities. Moreover, the findings of the study exposed the interconnected and interrelated technological, organisational, and environmental factors that continuously effect the adoption of frugal AI in paediatric radiology supply chain. The study findings inform policymakers, healthcare providers, and technologists about leveraging AI to address systemic challenges in the African healthcare supply chain systems. There's a need to strengthen frugal innovations through government or industry investment to increase local IP generation and limit erosion of expertise to global markets. Policy makers should incentivise frugal innovators with tax breaks and a consented effort in promoting collaborative partnership between local and foreign innovators is necessary for market share and skills transfer. Procurement reform is required in healthcare supply chain, especially in terms of procurement policies and practices. For example, consideration of local products and quality assessment vs. international products. This will guard against trade imbalance, talent migration, job creation losses, and trade deficit for African healthcare supply chain. Even though the study has produced interesting results, it can be extended by interviewing several frugal innovators in the Africa.

References

Aagaard A, Tucci C (2024) AI-driven business model innovation: pioneering new frontiers in value creation. In: Aagaard A (ed) Business model innovation. Palgrave Macmillan, Cham. https://doi.org/10.1007/978-3-031-57511-2_10

Abdel-Wahab M, Giammarile F, Carrara M, Paez D, Hricak H, Ayati N, Li JJ, Mueller M, Aggarwal A, Al-Ibraheem A, Alkhatib S (2024) Radiotherapy and theranostics: a Lancet Oncology Commission. Lancet Oncol 25(11):e545–e580

Acemoglu D, Restrepo P (2018) Artificial intelligence automation and work. Technical report. National Bureau of Economic Research

Ahmed YAH, Althwab AA, Yahya AMF, Qasem AMM, Hussain HTY, Mohammed ASK et al (2024) Pediatric radiology: special considerations and challenges. J Int Crisis Risk Commun Res 7(S9):353–366. Retrieved from https://jicrcr.com/index.php/jicrcr/article/view/342

Albert M (2019) Sustainable frugal innovation—the connection between frugal innovation and sustainability. J Cleaner Prod 237:117747

Anazodo UC, Ng JJ, Ehiogu B et al (2023) A framework for advancing sustainable magnetic resonance imaging access in Africa. NMR Biomed 36(3):e4846. https://doi.org/10.1002/nbm.4846

Babbie E (2015) The practice of social research, 14th edn. Cengage Learning, Boston, MA

Balasubramanian S, Shukla V, Islam N, Upadhyay A, Duong L (2023) Applying artificial intelligence in healthcare: lessons from the COVID-19 pandemic. Int J Prod Res:1–34. https://doi.org/10.1080/00207543.2023.2263102

Bhatti Y, Taylor A, Harris M, Wadge H, Escobar E, Prime M, Patel H, Carter AW, Parston G, Darzi AW, Udayakumar K (2017) Global lessons in frugal innovation to improve health care delivery in the United States. Health Affairs 36(11):1912–1919

Bianchi C, Bianco M, Ardanche M, Schenck M (2017) Healthcare frugal innovation: a solving problem rationale under scarcity conditions. Technol Soc 51:74–80

Bughin J, Hazan E, Ramaswamy S, Chui M, Allas T, Dahlstrom P, Henke N, Trench M (2017) Artificial intelligence: the next digital frontier? https://www.mckinsey.com/mgi.

Choy G, Khalilzadeh O, Michalski M, Do S, Samir AE, Pianykh OS, Geis JR, Pandharipande PV, Brink JA, Dreyer KJ (2018) Current applications and future impact of machine learning in radiology. Radiology 288(2):318–328

Cowls J, Tsamados A, Taddeo M, Floridi L (2023) The AI gambit: leveraging artificial intelligence to combat climate change—opportunities, challenges, and recommendations. AI Soc 38:283–307. https://doi.org/10.1007/s00146-021-01294-x
Dogru AK, Keskin BB (2020) AI in operations management: applications, challenges and opportunities. J Data Inform Manag. https://doi.org/10.1007/s42488-020-00023-1
Dranove D, Garthwaite C (2022) Artificial intelligence, the evolution of the healthcare value chain, and the future of the physician (No. c14761). National Bureau of Economic Research
Frija G, Blažić I, Frush DP, Hierath M, Kawooya M, Donoso-Bach L, Brkljačić B (2021) How to improve access to medical imaging in low- and middle-income countries? EClinicalMedicine 38:101034
Gerring J (2016) Case study research: principles and practices, 2nd edn. Cambridge University Press, Cambridge
Gholizadeh N, Rokni GR, Babaei M (2024) Advantages and disadvantages of using AI in dermatology. Dermatol Rev 5(4):e248
He P, Lovo S, Veronesi M (2022) Social networks and renewable energy technology adoption: empirical evidence from biogas adoption in China. Energy Econ 106:105789
Hsieh HF, Shannon SE (2005) Three approaches to qualitative content analysis. Qual Health Res 15(9):1277–1288
Karera A, Davidson F, Engel-Hills P (2024) Operational challenges and collaborative solutions in radiology image interpretation: perspectives from imaging departments in a low-resource setting. J Med Radiat Sci 71(4):564–572
Kasula BY (2023) Revolutionizing healthcare delivery: innovations and challenges in supply chain management for improved patient care. Trans Latest Trends Health Sector 15(15) Retrieved from https://www.ijsdcs.com/index.php/TLHS/articl
Klein S, Wocke A, Hughes JM (2014) Leaving home: relocation choices of South African multinational enterprise (MNEs). Afr J Bus Manag 8(8):253–269
Kleinheksel AJ, Rockich-Winston N, Tawfik H, Wyatt TR (2020) Demystifying content analysis. Am J Pharm Educ 84(1):7113
Martínez-Arellano G, Ratchev S (2024) Towards frugal industrial AI: a framework for the development of scalable and robust machine learning models in the shop floor. Int J Adv Manuf Technol. https://doi.org/10.1007/s00170-024-14508-5
Molyneux EM (2020) Neglected tropical diseases: public health control programs and mass drug administration. In: Hunter's tropical medicine and emerging infectious diseases. Elsevier, pp 209–213
Morley J, Machado CC, Burr C, Cowls J, Joshi I, Taddeo M, Floridi L (2020) The ethics of AI in health care: a mapping review. Soc Sci Med 260:113172
Panch T, Szolovits P, Atun R (2018) Artificial intelligence, machine learning and health systems. J Global Health 8(2):020303. https://doi.org/10.7189/jogh.08.020303
Qin W (2024) How to unleash frugal innovation through internet of things and artificial intelligence: moderating role of entrepreneurial knowledge and future challenges. Technol Forecast Soc Change 202:123286
Rabinowitz DA, Pretorius ES (2005) Postgraduate radiology training in sub-Saharan Africa: a review of current educational resources1. Acad Radiol 12(2):224–231
Rao D (2023) The urgent need for healthcare workforce upskilling and ethical considerations in the era of AI-assisted medicine. Indian J Otolaryngol Head Neck Surg 75(3):2638–2639
Rosman DA, Bamporiki J, Stein-Wexler R, Harris RD (2019) Developing diagnostic radiology training in low resource countries. Curr Radiol Rep 7:1–7
Rubin GD (2000) Data explosion: the challenge of multidetector-row CT. Eur J Radiol 36(2):74–80
Sarkar S, Mateus S (2022) Doing more with less—how frugal innovations can contribute to improving healthcare systems. Soc Sci Med 306:115127
Siala H, Wang Y (2022) SHIFTing artificial intelligence to be responsible in healthcare: a systematic review. Soc Sci Med 296:114782

Stjepić A-M, Pejić Bach M, Bosilj Vukšić V (2021) Exploring risks in the adoption of business intelligence in SMEs using the TOE framework. J Risk Fin Manag 14(2):58. https://doi.org/10.3390/jrfm14020058

Trauernicht C, Hasford F, Khelassi-Toutaoui N, Bentouhami I, Knoll P, Tsapaki V (2022) Medical physics services in radiology and nuclear medicine in Africa: challenges and opportunities identified through workforce and infrastructure surveys. Health Technol 12(4):729–737

van Leeuwen KG, de Rooij M, Schalekamp S, van Ginneken B, Rutten MJ (2022) How does artificial intelligence in radiology improve efficiency and health outcomes? Pediatr Radiol 52:2087–2093

Verma S (2017) Frugal innovation in medical devices: key to growth in emerging economies. J Med Market 16(2):66–73

Whittaker M, Crawford K, Dobbe R, Fried G, Kaziunas E, Mathur V, West SM, Richardson R, Schultz J, and Schwartz O (2018) AI now report 2018. https://ainowinstitute.org/AINow2018Report.pdf.

Widner J, Woolcock M, Nieto D (2022) Using case studies to enhance the quality of explanation and implementation. In: Widner J, Woolcock M, Nieto D (eds) The case for case studies. Cambridge University Press, pp 1–26

Yeboah-Banin AA, Quaye ES (2021) Pathways to global versus local brand preferences: the roles of cultural identity and brand perceptions in emerging African markets. J Global Market 34(5):372–391. https://doi.org/10.1080/08911762.2021.1886385

Yin RK (2003) Case study research: design and methods. Sage Publications

Yin RK (2017) Case study research and applications: design and methods (6th edition on Kindle). Sage

Prof. Marcia Mkansi is the College Head of Research, Post-graduate Studies, Innovation, and Commercialisation, a Professor of Operations and Supply Chain Management and the former Head of the Department of Operations Management at the College of Economic & Management Sciences, University of South Africa. She serves as a non-executive director for Hellmann Worldwide Logistics, and an advisory board member of the Africa Resource Centre (ARC), a Bill and Melinda Gates Foundation (BMGF)-funded non-governmental organization, set up to be a resource to the public health sector in African governments. Her university-industry alliances include, but are not limited to, Kuehne Foundation, The Innovation Hub, and SAP skills Africa. She is a nominee for the Top Women Standard Bank and UN women projects, and a finalist under the research, innovation, and creative economy category of the National Science and Technology Forum (NSTF)—South32 awards.

Dr. Frank Ranganai Matenda is a Postdoctoral Research Fellow in the Department of Operations Management at the University of South Africa, Pretoria, South Africa. His research interests are related to credit risk, asset pricing, green finance, corporate performance and risk management, investments, corporate finance, financial markets, and small business economics. He is the Coordinator for the International Conference on Business Resilience, Continuity and Regeneration and an Editorial Board Member for the Journal of Inclusive and Innovative Practices.

Godfrey Mugurusi is an Associate Professor of Logistics and Supply Chain Management at the Norwegian University of Science & Technology (NTNU), where he also directs the Bachelor of Logistics Management program. His research focuses on digitalization and sustainability within procurement and supply chain management (PSCM), with publications in leading journals such as the Journal of Purchasing & Supply Management and Operations Management Research. A former practitioner in FMCG and public procurement, he serves on advisory boards for key supply chain research initiatives across Africa.

Aaron L. Nsakanda is an Associate Professor of Management Science and Operations Management at the Sprott School of Business. His expertise lies in applying mathematical modelling and discrete-event simulations to solve complex supply chain and operational challenges. With research focusing on quantitative approaches to real-world problems, Dr. Nsakanda collaborates with businesses to optimize supply chains. A long-standing academic, he is a member of professional societies including INFORMS, CORS, SCS, and DSI, contributing significantly to the field of operations management.

Part III
Governance, Integration, and Trust in Digital Platforms

Chapter 5
Ripple Effect of Using Digital Platforms on Supply Chain Governance, Visibility, and Trust to Improve Medicine Availability

Ramatu Abdulkadir and Andre Kreie

5.1 Introduction

Essential medicine shortages in Public Healthcare Supply Chains (PHSC) in developing countries are of concern to patients and policymakers. The factors contributing to inadequate medicine provision in hospitals include manual supply chain operations (Zuma 2022), inappropriate sourcing strategies, insufficient supply chain capacity, and inadequate infrastructure (Ashiwaju et al. 2024; Gakinahe et al. 2024; Hwang et al. 2019). These issues have prompted calls to adopt digital platforms (DP) to address stock-out problems and improve access to medicine. Enhancing governance structures for health program accountability faces challenges owing to limited technology use and inadequate worker skills to operate advanced digital platforms (Lugada et al. 2022). Digital transformations in healthcare Supply Chains (SCs) necessitate reskilling and upskilling healthcare workers to handle advanced technology in supply chain operations, such as demand planning and forecasting, procurement, warehousing, transportation management, and order fulfilment (Burrell 2017).

R. Abdulkadir (✉) · A. Kreie
LEARN Logistics by Kühne Foundation, Hamburg, Germany
e-mail: ramatu.abdulkadir@kuehne-foundation.org

T. Akenroye et al. (eds.), *Digitalizing Health Care Supply Chains in Africa*, Springer Series in Supply Chain Management 28,
https://doi.org/10.1007/978-3-032-20501-8_5

5.1.1 Adoption of Digital Platforms in African Healthcare Supply Chains

Research has explored the application of technology to address the healthcare supply chain issues in Africa. Overcoming medicine stockouts and enhancing availability depends on structural dynamics, feedback, and behaviours in essential medicine programs (Abdulkadir et al. 2024). The implementation of digital platforms faces challenges due to governance structures and the ability to maintain and upgrade these platforms to meet patient needs (Moucheraud et al. 2017). Nigeria's healthcare sector is slow to adopt digital technologies for supply chain services, requiring more research to assess the impact of digital platforms (DP) on supply chain performance. Some studies have noted improved medicine visibility and accountability with digital platforms (Ottih et al. 2018; Sarley et al. 2017); however, the broader effects on essential medicine programs remain underexplored. Investigating the relationship between DP, governance, visibility, and trust in providing essential medicines for public health remains insufficient. This study addressed two research questions: RQ1: How does the use of digital platforms influence medication availability in PHSC? RQ2: How do the dynamics of digital platforms concerning governance, visibility, and trust within PHSC affect the delivery of medicines to patients? This study examines how adopting digital platforms impacts medicine availability, and explores the effects of this adoption on governance, visibility, and trust.

5.1.2 Context of This Study

This study investigated the impact of digital platform implementation on Supply Chain Governance (SCG), Supply Chain Visibility (SCV), and Stakeholder Trust (ST) within the Essential Medicine Program (EMP) of Kaduna State, Nigeria. The EMP transformation was initiated in 2016 to provide medicine to over 1000 government hospitals using digital technology for demand planning, procurement, warehousing, distribution, and order fulfilment from the central warehouse to hospitals in 23 local government areas.

5.1.3 Theoretical Background

The health care sector is a complex adaptive system in which improvement interventions may cause unintended consequences (Dooley 1997; Sterman 2000). This study uses System Dynamics (SD) theory to explore the relationships between DP adoption and SCG, SCV, and SCT on EMP medicine availability. System dynamics monitors complex system activities over time using stocks, flows, rates, delays, and feedback. This method helps understand policy implementation consequences (Sterman 2000) and is ideal for assessing the impact of digital platform intervention in EMP by tracking behaviour, feedback, and delays over time in nonlinear complex adaptive systems.

5.1.4 Concept of Digital Platform Adoption in EMP

This study argues that healthcare supply chains benefit from digital technology only when integrated with dynamic continuous improvement strategies. Organisations viewing digital technology as a panacea may see initial improvements in medicine availability but will struggle with subsequent challenges and pressures in complex healthcare systems.

The remainder of this paper is organised as follows. Section 2 critically analyses existing literature on the use of digital platforms to address medicine stockouts. Section 3 describes the research methodology. Section 4 presents the results of this study. Section 5 discusses the implications and offers recommendations based on the findings.

5.2 Literature Review

The causes of medicine stockouts in public hospital chains have been explored and DP solutions have been proposed to minimise their impact on medicine delivery (Table 5.1). Ibeneme et al. (2022) enumerated the challenges with DP integration in the African healthcare sector which include the cost, capacity, governance, infrastructure, resistance to change, and systems fragmentation. The imperative for SCG to advocate sustainable digital investments in healthcare supply chains becomes evident when considering the prevalence of fragmented digital transformation efforts (Gebremeskel et al. 2021; Karamagi et al. 2022; Tambo et al. 2016). The necessity of digital interconnectivity has been further highlighted during the COVID pandemic, as emphasised by Rinke et al. (2022s). In Nigeria, the use of (DP) for supply chain operations is minimal in government-owned hospitals (Onoja et al. 2021). Interactions between various stakeholders in the healthcare sector necessitate a holistic digital transformation which provides visibility and access to information for all stakeholders to engage in and make decisions in real time.

Research conducted in Africa has explored the use of smartphones for monitoring and tracing health products (Egharevba et al. 2019; Lamanna and Byrne 2019), big data, artificial intelligence platforms (Bag et al. 2023), and drone logistics (Wang 2021). The adoption of DP in healthcare networks offers benefits, such as cost reduction, increased efficiency, enhanced visibility, and improved customer service delivery (Table 5.2).

Table 5.1 Summary of the causes behind medicine stock outs and proposed digital solutions for mitigation across Africa

Authors (Year)	Causes of medicine stockouts	Digital solutions proposed	Location	Type of supply chain	Methodology
Zuma (2022)	Manual processes for medicine supply	Use of electronic stock management system	South Africa	Essential medicines	Qualitative exploratory Semi-structured interviews Thematic analysis
Wagenaar et al. (2014)	Distance from central warehouse	Innovative methods for forecasting, medicine ordering, and communication among partners	Mozambique	Essential medicines	Survey Questionnaire Statistical analysis
Mikkelsen-Lopez et al. (2014)	Inadequate supplies	System strengthening and use of mobile health solutions	Tanzania	Malaria supply chain	Short message service Mobile phone Statistical analysis
Gakinahe et al. (2024)	Travel distance and unsuitable storage facilities	Improve transport and storage infrastructure	Rwanda	Malaria supply chain	Survey Statistical analysis
Hwang et al. (2019)	Sourcing from a single company and lack of visibility	Supply chain monitoring	South Africa	Antiretroviral and TB medicines programs	Survey Telephone
Leung et al. (2016)	Inadequate inventory management policies	Strengthen forecasting capabilities	Zambia	Essential medicines	Survey Modelling and simulation
Abdulkadir et al. (2024)	Inefficient procurement and inventory management practices. Inadequate supply chain capacity	Shared digital platforms, pooled procurement, and knowledge sharing	Nigeria	Essential medicines	Mixed method

Table 5.2 Digital platforms used in African public healthcare supply chains

Authors (Year)	Digital product	Digital product objective	Study objective	Location	Supply chain focus	Methods
Egharevba et al. (2019)	Logistic management information system	Track and trace medicines	Evaluate the capability of the information system	Nigeria	All health products	Pilot study, field work
Bag et al. (2023)	Use of big data and artificial intelligence platform for decision-making	Capacity and resource management	Examine the effects of collaborative platform on absorptive capacity of omni-channel processes	South Africa	Omni-channel supply chain	Questionnaire
Lamanna and Byrne (2019)	Mobile health solution	Report vaccine stock in real-time	Vaccine supply chain optimisation	Zambia	Vaccine supply chain	Track vaccine stock data
Wang (2021)	Drone services	Delivery of medical products	Ethical consideration and impact of drone usage in healthcare SCs	Malawi	Laboratory products	Field study
Sato (2023)	eHealth solution	Direct delivery of vaccine to manage stock outs	Cost analysis of vaccine program	Nigeria	Vaccine supply chain	Review of expense reports
Shieshia et al. (2014)	Mobile health solution	Community stock reporting tool	Supply chain performance	Malawi	Community health	Mixed methods

5.2.1 *Supply Chain Governance*

Provan and Kenis (2008) categorised network governance models by their autonomy level. Autonomous networks operate without external controls, semi-autonomous networks are managed by a leading organisation within the network, and dependent networks are governed by an external entity. In the context of this research, SCG is defined as a collaborative network of organisations striving to achieve a common objective of customer satisfaction, while simultaneously promoting inclusivity, adaptability, and efficiency through the utilisation of digital technology. In this context, the role of DP in supply networks is to mitigate the risks inherent in each governance model by promoting the active participation of internal and external stakeholders in decision-making processes. The employment of digital communication platforms enhances the efficiency of the SCG by fostering greater transparency and accountability, thereby bolstering the SCT between government and hospital managers for EMP.

The perception of mistrust and mismanagement of funds for EMP has hindered government investment, resulting in the exacerbation of bottlenecks to access funds and ultimately leading to medicine stockouts (Abdulkadir, 2024). Healthcare supply networks can benefit from using both formal and informal governance instruments to enhance service delivery performance, as demonstrated by Martins et al. (2020). The use of governance instruments, such as supply chain trust, negotiations, and contracts, can help guide supply chain relationships and create value for the network (Ghosh & Fedorowicz, 2008). Research has shown that the adoption of DP is more effective when hospital chains implement a centralised governance framework, which enables better monitoring and tracing of medications and ultimately improves performance (Zhu et al. 2022). Thus, the governance structure of hospitals' supply networks must be supported by the DP to facilitate information sharing and improve decision-making for demand and supply planning to foster trust in the system.

5.2.2 Supply Chain Visibility

Barratt and Oke (2007) defined SCV as the degree of quality information sharing in a supply network for improved performance. SCV in healthcare organisations encompasses the gathering and examination of data for supply chain operations such as the tracking and tracing of pharmaceuticals (Bvuchete et al. 2018). The use of digital technology to capture information, such as radio frequency identification, barcodes, and quick response codes, improves the visibility of medicine products and decision-making (Bvuchete et al. 2018; Musa et al. 2014). The provision of real-time visibility of health products facilitates the identification of waste within healthcare systems, thereby placing pressure on managers and policymakers to enhance transparency and accountability in the management of financial resources (Finkenstadt and Handfield 2021). The necessity to incorporate DP into public healthcare systems arises because of the intricate nature of these systems, which involve numerous stakeholders, and the requirement to stay and respond to evolving healthcare needs (Tiwari et al. 2024). Hence, DP supports the collection, analysis, and sharing of critical supply chain information between network partners to make informed decisions that determine the availability of medicines.

5.2.3 Supply Chain Trust

Trust in the supply chain denotes confidence in the reliability of business partners, expecting their actions to be advantageous rather than harmful (Mayer et al. 1995). Supply chains are vulnerable to attacks from competitors or malicious third parties as any partner within the network can be targeted. Enhancing trust requires the cooperation of all stakeholders, including customers. Therefore, data within the supply network must be safeguarded against misuse and breach. To build trust in supply chains, governments should invest in improving the information and technology infrastructure and advocate the adoption of blockchain technology (Kshetri and Voas 2019; Musamih et al. 2021; Panda and Satapathy 2021).

Ineffective communication and information sharing among stakeholders has led to counterfeit medicines in developing countries, significantly threatening patient health and safety (Kritchanchai 2014). Information flow with products builds trust and improves communication and product distribution (Ghosh and Fedorowicz 2008), whereas digital platforms strengthen interbusiness connections and enhance performance (Kim and Lee 2021). Consequently, research indicates that trust aids the adoption of digital technologies, whereas digitalisation enhances relational assets, thereby improving business performance.

5.2.4 Research Gaps

The literature indicates that DP adoption has a positive impact on information sharing and visibility (Egharevba et al. 2019; Lamanna and Byrne 2019). However, no study has investigated the dynamic effects of technology adoption on public health supply chains. While Ibeneme et al. (2022) highlighted capacity, governance, and systems resistance as factors affecting DP adoption, they did not explore the ripple effects of these elements on medicine availability. This study aims to address these gaps by applying system dynamics methods to analyse the various factors that influence digital platform adoption and medicine availability in a multi-stakeholder medicine supply chain.

5.3 Methodology

Document reviews and in-depth interviews were conducted with EMP teams across five healthcare organisations in Kaduna (Table 5.3). All organisations fulfilled the selection criteria of being publicly funded and operating an essential medicine program with digital implementation maturity levels (Duncan et al. 2022). See Appendix A.1 for DP maturity assessment.

Twenty-two experts with more than 5 years of experience in EMP were selected from the five supply chains (Table 5.4). Transcripts from the interviews were documented and transcribed using Otter software. The transcripts were refined and analysed using quotation analysis to identify cause-and-effect statements (Abdulkadir 2024; Abdulkadir et al. 2024; Tomoaia-Cotisel et al. 2022). Vensim PLE plus 2024 was used for modelling and simulation using the Sterman (2000) distribution model.

Table 5.3 Case descriptions with digital tools and maturity levels

Case descriptions	Type of EMP	Local government area	Digital tools	DP maturity level (%)
SC1: Kaduna state health supplies management agency	General and specialist care medicines	Kaduna south	Microsoft azure, Msupply, SMS platform, cash collection platform	86
SC2: National ear care Centre	Specialist ear, nose, and throat medicines	Kaduna north	Microsoft excel	14
SC3: Ahmadu Bello University	General and specialist care medicines	Zaria	Hospipharm software	14
SC4: Federal Neuropsychiatric Hospital	Specialist eye care medicines	Kaduna south	Manual system with occasional use of Microsoft excel	14
SC5: National eye Centre	Specialist psychiatric care medicines	Kaduna south	Hospipharm software	14

Table 5.4 EMP experts interviewed on digital technology adoption

EMP interview experts	SC1	SC2	SC3	SC4	SC5	Total
EMP managers	1	1	1	1	1	5
Logistics officers	2	1	1	1	1	6
Sourcing managers	1	1	1	1	1	5
Medicine suppliers	2	1	1	1	1	6
Total	6	4	4	4	4	22

5.4 Findings

Findings from this study showed that SC1 had the highest level of digital platform adoption, with 95% of the participants explicitly identifying collaboration, information sharing, visibility, trust, and data-driven operations as crucial for an improved 75% medicine availability (Table 5.5). The medicine availability in SC2 was 65%, 75% in SC3, 65% in SC4, and 45% in SC5. Although there was a 100% consensus on the need for digital information sharing across all organisations, partner collaboration was the least developed variable across SCs, except SC1, which has advanced collaboration with partners due to the implementation of digital transformation, integration of platforms, and capacity-building of cross-functional teams. Information sharing is recognised across all SCs as integral to improving performance and reducing medicine stock outs. The adoption of digital platforms has increased the collaboration between EMP network partners. The 100% score on data-driven decisions by SC3 shows that information sharing takes place only internally, as the organisation has 0% partner collaboration. The relationship with

Table 5.5 Percentage of participants identifying variables for digital platform adoption in public health supply chains

Variables	EMP model variables	SC1 participants (%)	SC2 participants (%)	SC3 participants (%)	SC4 participants (%)	SC5 participants (%)	Total (%)
Partner collaboration	Stakeholder trust Medicine sales Government allocation Medicine expiries	100	25	0	25	0	30
Information sharing	Customer orders Medicine order rate	100	100	100	100	100	100
Visibility	Time to correct inventory Time to average orders	100	25	75	75	25	60
Trust	Time to hold medicines Adequate medicines	100	100	100	100	50	90
Data-driven decisions	Fill rate Order fulfilment	75	75	100	25	50	65
Average score		**95**	65	75	65	45	

partners was mainly transactional which could be responsible for its lowest medicine availability score of 45%. SC5 had a 0% score for partner collaboration, with a marginal improvement in medicine availability of 50%. See Appendix A.2 for the sample quotation analysis for the model simulation and model formulas.

5.4.1 Effects of DP on Supply Chain Governance

The operational processes of demand planning, forecasting, and supply planning were conducted using a cloud-based system in SC1. SC2 uses Excel software for data collection and demand planning, whereas SC3 uses hospital pharmacy software for inventory management which is not connected to the Internet. SC4 operates a manual system, whereas SC5 uses electronic medical record software for inventory management at the point-of-care (Fig. 5.1). Only SC1 operates a

Quotations (Q) for DP adoption strategies in EMPs	**Interview expert**
Q1: "We use the warehouse management software to manage inventory and the short message service platform to collect data from facilities like consumption data. I have been privileged to use the analytic platform, which gives you general visibility from the warehouse to the point of consumption. The other systems plug into the analytic platform to give a one-time view of product availability the state." Q2: "It's boils down to visibility, being customer-focused having the entire team knowing that their purpose is to serve the citizen of Kaduna state and having visibility across the agency.	SC1 EMP manager
Q1: "We use Microsoft Excel to visually carry out inventory count exercise."	SC2 EMP manager
Q1: "... there is a software we use for our inpatient where we are able to monitor their treatment right from their admission to when they are discharged to see what they have consumed during their stay and the cost implication." Q1: "...management have tried to introduce a hospital software. I think we have attained 50% coverage. But all other places, including our stations have not keyed in and the program unfortunately is on hold for now."	SC3 EMP manager SC3 Logistic manager
Q1: "digital technology is a welcome development if we can have such facilities."	SC4 Sourcing manager
Q1: "...we do stocktaking on paper, you have to write, it takes us just a week, that's the annual stock taking. The monthly stock taking is done in a day, may be two, three. Now that we have intranet, we are hoping to get a system in the store ... for [medicine] requisition so that you don't have to come to the store."	SC5 Logistic manager

Fig. 5.1 Quotations on digital adoption strategies in EMP supply chains

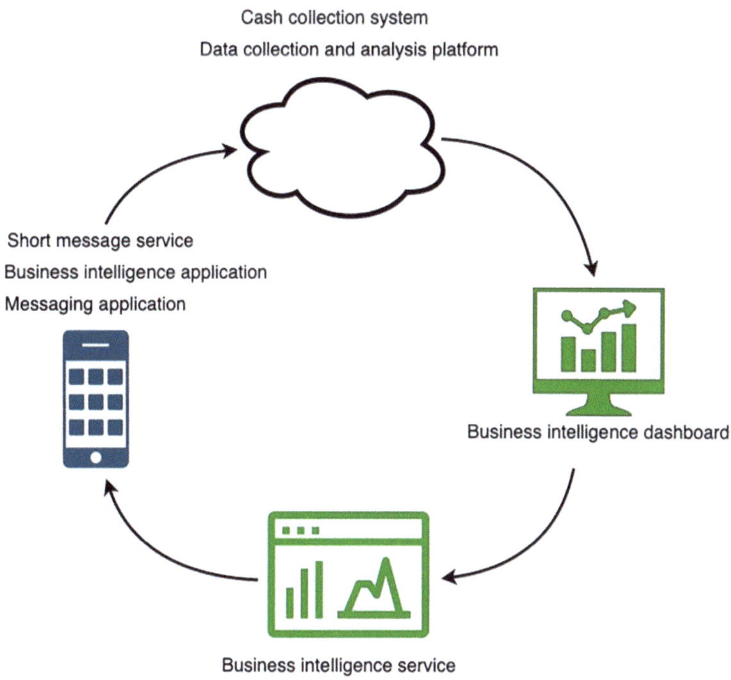

Fig. 5.2 SC1 integrated digital platform

cloud-based interoperable supply chain system which supports superior performance compared to the other four supply chains. There are some marginal benefits with the use of siloed software as compared to manual operations in the prevention of medicine stockouts, but the lack of an integrated platform leads to information asymmetry and deepens mistrust between partners.

Procurement, inventory management, warehousing, order management, and order fulfilment are all operated manually in SC2, SC3, SC4, and SC5, except in SC1 where Electronic Procurement (e-procurement) and warehouse management software are used for inventory management. SC1 uses mobile short message service codes to collect, analyse, and visualise a business-intelligence platform (Fig. 5.2). The platform connects all EMP managers and operation staff and allows communication and information sharing with customers, suppliers, service providers, stakeholders, and policymakers.

5.4.2 *Effects of DP on Supply Chain Visibility*

SC1 higher technology adoption rate led to increased demand for digital capacity, information sharing, and integration of DP with partners, as shown in Fig. 5.3. The reinforcing loops of digital performance, information sharing, and digital integration are balanced by the need for capacity-building. Visibility derived from the use of technology platforms empowers healthcare workers to participate in the

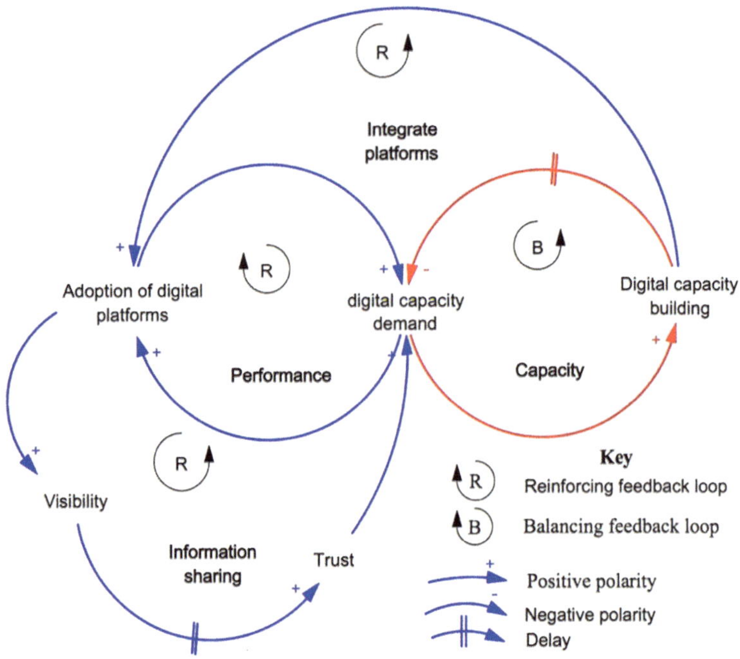

Fig. 5.3 Digital performance dynamics and increased demand for digital capacity

order-fulfilment process. Shaping the state government's policies toward a more digitally inclusive approach. Staff have been trained in digital data collection and analytics for demand-driven supply chains. The use of data analytics for the replenishment of medicines has reduced waste and medicine expiries. Data-driven demand and supply planning ensures prudent allocation of scarce resources. Cloud-based platforms require a digital supply chain governance framework.

Over 400 staff in 23 local government areas communicate and share information in real-time to ensure timely medical deliveries to hospitals. The findings of this study indicate that adopting technology platforms significantly affects supply chains. SC1, which had the highest technology adoption rate, experienced fewer medicine stockouts and higher customer service levels than did the other four cases with lower technology adoption rates.

5.4.3 Effects of DP on Supply Chain Trust

The adoption of DP in SC1 increases the need for digital supply chain auditing and tracking of funds. SC1 tracks medicines and funds from warehouses to all hospitals, leading to increased transparency and accountability in resource management. Information sharing with partners and stakeholders increased trust, leading to higher investment from the government in digital infrastructure. The government acquired and maintained a business-intelligence platform for SC1. Investments were made in digital capacity-building for all SC1 staff members. The SCI also engaged in the training of over 400 hospital staff in digital technology use for data collection and order management. The diffusion of knowledge within the SC1 system was very high compared to SC2, SC3, SC4, and SC5, which are fragmented systems that hinder the seamless flow of information and products. Price transparency in SC1 is demonstrated by the monthly online publication of medication prices for over 1000 government hospital. These publications increase trust, transparency, and visibility, allowing patients to plan and manage their own health. The capacity to monitor and track medicines and transactions across the supply chain enhances public trust in government.

5.4.4 *The Effect of Digitally Enabled Governance, Visibility, and Trust in Medicine Availability*

Integrating digitalisation into a continuous improvement plan enhances governance, visibility, and trust and increases medicine availability in SC1 by 24,000 units, achieving 100% of the desired medicines at week 100. Conversely, SC2, SC3, and SC4 had 11,379 units, covering 47% of the desired medicines owing to fragmented systems. SC5, however, is currently stocked out (see Fig. 5.4).

The adoption of DP improves trust through enhanced information sharing and data-driven decision-making, thereby increasing the availability of medicine. Stakeholder trust at 100 weeks was 96% in SC1, 30% in SC2, SC3, and SC4, and 10% in SC5. Trust reduces uncertainty and the bullwhip effect (see Fig. 5.5).

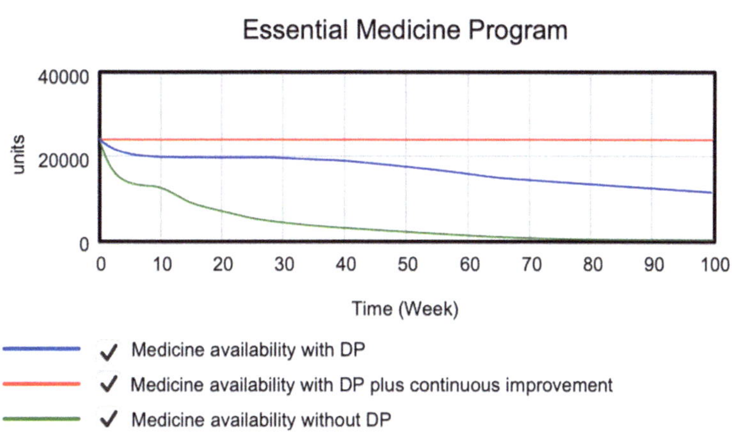

Fig. 5.4 Improved medicine availability with the adoption of digital platform

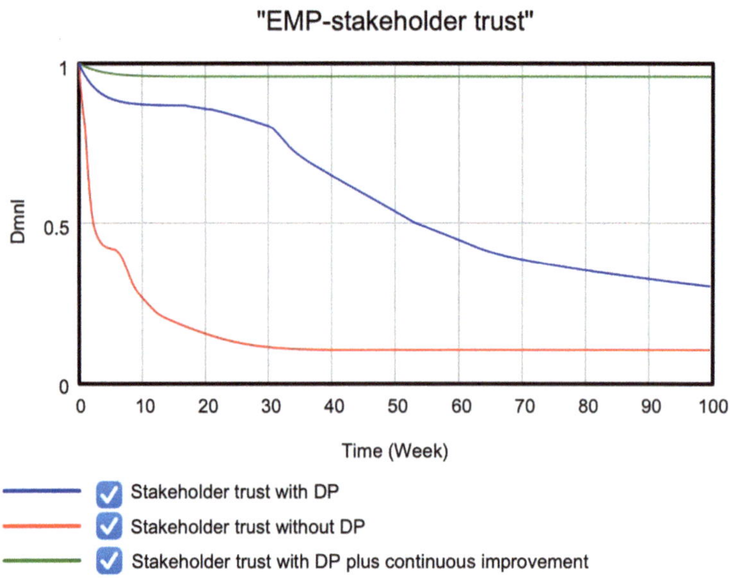

Fig. 5.5 Digital platform adoption increases stakeholder trust

5.4.5 Ripple Effects from DP Adoption

The findings from this study show that the SC1 use of DP leads to various ripple effects within the healthcare system and across industries. Table 5.6 outlines the cross-industry effects of SC1 DP interventions.

- The adoption of DP for SC1 increased the use of advanced technologies, such as drone delivery of medicines, cloud computing, electronic procurement, control towers, demand for digital skills, demand for digital technology policies, and incentives.
- There is an increased demand to build the capacity of healthcare workers and network partners in digital supply chain governance, network master coordination, cloud-based solutions, customer relationship management, and drone logistics.
- Pressure to promote transparency and accountability by adopting electronic procurement, supplier relationship management, supplier integration, and digital supply chain governance.
- Increase demand for on-time medicine delivery to hospitals and end-user visibility.
- Increased demand for capacity-building and DP adoption by SC2, SC3, SC4, and SC5.

Table 5.6 Effects of DP implementation across ministries and industries in SC1

Ministries and industries	Effect of DP implementation
Justice	Establish partnership agreements with donors and third-party service providers, such as those involved in drone logistics and pharmaceutical manufacturing, digital platform enterprise
Legislation	Establishing new regulatory frameworks to facilitate the integration of digital platforms in healthcare supply chain management
Education	Undertake new collaborations to educate specialists in DP competencies and proficiencies, commence instruction in logistics and supply chain management
Telecommunication	Enhance the digital infrastructure to extend coverage to remote areas and villages
Security services	Undertake the engagement of security agencies to guarantee the secure delivery of pharmaceuticals to areas that are challenging to access and remote locations

SC1 Drone Delivery of Medicines

Enhanced technological capabilities accelerate the adoption of advanced drone services in SC1. The integration of third-party drone services signals supply chain maturity. The implementation of a digital governance framework aids in drafting and adopting laws that support autonomous product delivery. Additional impacts include technology knowledge transfer, economic growth, research and development, highly skilled drone professionals, increased collaboration with supply chain stakeholders, and improved supply chain resilience. Reducing greenhouse gas emissions and promoting eco-friendly instant logistics can lead to cross-industry adoption.

SC1 Electronic Procurement

E-procurement in SC1 shortens procurement cycles and diversifies suppliers to include both local and national participants. Manual medicine procurement in public health supply chains is cumbersome and resource intensive. Transitioning to DP for electronic procurement broadens the supplier reach.

SC1 Network Master Coordination

As a network master, SC1 oversees planning, procurement, logistics, and inventory management to enhance the system resilience. This role supports hospitals in sensing, collaborating, optimising, and resolving network issues, such as facilitating accountable stock transfers between hospitals.

SC1 Digital Supply Chain Capacity Improvement

SC1 partners with digital solution providers to improve network capabilities and extend services to hospitals statewide. Healthcare workers, typically not digital experts, need basic technical skills to use systems effectively. Integrating digital skills into healthcare education ensures a consistent supply of skilled personnel and reduces staff turnover by enhancing job satisfaction. These challenges have prompted SC1-university collaborations to facilitate learning dissemination.

SC1 Digital Supply Chain Governance

Implementing digital platforms (DP) in healthcare supply chains necessitates a new governance framework because of their novelty and the need for healthcare worker reskilling and upskilling. Utilising mobile technology and short message services for data collection and demand-driven planning to minimise expiries reduced medicine stockouts, but caused system tensions, ripple effects, and heightened demand for visibility and partner collaboration.

5.5 Implications and Recommendations for Supply Chain Management Practices in Africa

Adopting DP and enhancing supply chain processes improves medicine availability. Healthcare organisations should implement innovative digital strategies to ensure the provision of medication and achieve Universal Health Coverage. DP adoption boosts supply chain resilience and allows for advanced technology integration including drone logistics, e-procurement, network coordination, digital capacity-building, and digital governance. Furthermore, five key players from industries beyond healthcare were identified along with their roles in fostering the digital transformation of public healthcare. Supply chains adopting technology benefit from digital platforms and recognise the necessity for further digitalisation of operations and processes. This aligns with Ibeneme et al. (2022), who assert the need for additional resources to enhance optimisation and capacity development. Addressing the complexities and uncertainties of digital healthcare transformation requires a flexible and evolving approach. University-industry collaborations are advantageous because they provide access to knowledge, skilled professionals, and sustain digital projects through human resource capacity.

The development of efficient and secure transportation methods led SC1 to collaborate with a third-party drone service to reduce hospital delivery times, underscoring the study's main finding that organisations must continually improve to effectively manage the impact of digital platforms. The acquisition of DP does not guarantee the improved availability of essential medicines, as demonstrated by the disjointed digital chains in SC2, SC3, SC4, and SC5. This fragmentation arises from insufficient partner collaboration and inadequate financial support from the government as highlighted by Gebremeskel et al. (2021), Karamagi et al. (2022), and Tambo et al. (2016). The answer to the first research question revealed that digital platforms (DPs) reduce stockouts and enhance medicine availability through better partner collaboration. The answer to the second research question highlights that DP implementation requires a digital governance framework, capacity-building, collaboration, innovative coordination, and continuous improvement to sustain third-party relationships and improve transparency, accountability, and medicine availability.

Essential medicine programs that are unable to implement digital governance or meet capacity development demands in digital transformation will likely face ongoing medical shortages and eroding public trust. This study suggests that SC2, SC3, SC4, and SC5 should utilise SC1's digital resources to reduce digitalisation costs. Dooley (1997) posits that organisations improve existing practices (first-order change), alter their operations (second-order change), or either adapt or perish (third-order change). For successful digital transformation in PHSCs, continuous adaptation to evolving system requirements is essential to meet customer expectations. This study aids managers, policymakers, donors, and investors in understanding the impacts of digital transformations, supporting medicine programs in addressing emerging needs and managing unintended consequences. It also helps healthcare stakeholders comprehend the broader effects of interventions on sectors such as education, policy, telecommunications, and transportation.

Appendices

Appendix 1

Digital maturity framework assessment for SC1, SC2, SC3, SC4, and SC5

EMP Digital capability	SC1	SC2	SC3	SC4	SC5	Total count
Availability of digital adoption strategy plan: Standard operating procedure for DP adoption	1	0	0	0	0	1
Availabile DP infrastructure and capacity	1	0	0	0	0	1
DP interoperability	1	0	0	0	0	1
Data-driven decision-making	1	0	0	0	0	1
Customer relationship management	0	0	0	0	0	0
Staff IT capacity	1	1	1	1	1	5
DP Governance	1	0	0	0	0	1
Total (%)	86	14	14	14	14	

Key: Yes-1 No-0

Appendix 2

SC1 EMP manager interview quotation analysis on DP adoption

Quote number) "... Simulation variables in phrase(s)"	Phrase(s) from quote denoting model variables	Model variables	Causal link between variables(→=causal link, --‖→=causal link with delay, +/-=positive or negative polarity)
01) "We can bring in any data analytics to improve that. The analytic platform provides visibility for everyone. It makes it easy to explain and transparency in procurement when we are stocked out. In relation to patient, we supply medicines to facilities. We expect them to feed us back with consumption data. We use it to make informed decision on what to procure. If there's no downstream consumption, then no need to call suppliers to resupply medicines. For the supplier's, we have prequalified suppliers whom we onboard and explain our processes. We also build the supplier's capacity in some instances, so that we can benefit from each other. we've been able to build that bond of relationship so that we can make medicines available to the patients."	-visibility - transparency - stocked out - procure - resupply - benefit from each other -available to the patients	Visibility Transparency Stockout Order procurement Order fulfilment EMP-Stakeholder relationship (trust) Fill rate	Visibility→+Transparency→-Stockout→-Order procurement→+Order fulfilment→+EMP-Stakeholder relationship (trust)→+Fill rate
02) "It boils down to visibility, they need to understand what the the upstream does. ... Understanding the importance of sending the consumption data will help us procure and better service terms. when they understand the entire process and having visibility of why we do what we do will help in building that relationship. Whenever suppliers come to supplier medicines, there're some criteria we look at in terms of their performance, lead time of delivery, quality of products. We give the suppliers feedback on how to improve their services because we believe that it's a working relationship and both parties need to benefit as a win-win situation. that has helped to improve their capacity. For the organisation, it has improved the quality of service and product. The suppliers have been able to deliver products."	- visibility - service terms - relationship - lead time - feedback - win-win - product	Visibility Fill rate EMP-Stakeholder relationship (trust) Supply delay Information sharing Collaboration Medicine inventory	Visibility→+Fill rate→+EMP-Stakeholder relationship (trust)→-Supply delay→-Information sharing→+Collaboration→+Medicine inventory
03) "With critical stakeholders, there's need for continuous stakeholder engagement, having review meetings, keeping them abreast with recent development in the agency through social media platforms, face to face visit, government media and report disseminations. We give visibility of our product prices, we put the price list on the government website. ... overtime we've had engagements and quarterly review meetings."	-engagement -abreast with recent development - prices - overtime	Communication Information sharing Sell price Time delay	Communication--//→+Information sharing→-Sell price
04) "With patients, we review prices of products using a unified selling pricelist and disseminate on telegram social media platforms. The CSOs are usually involved in program medicines and the medicine procured by the government. CSOs in the past have followed up on the procurement of program medicines like family planning and last mile distribution of the medicines. The pricelist on the government website has helped and I hope it will further broaden and strengthen our relationship with them. For government agencies, we have our supervising ministry ..., at any point when they need information, our doors are open. we send quarterly reports to them and [...] reports to them to give them necessary feedback."	- review prices - procured - last mile distribution - relationship - information	Sell price Order procurement Order fulfilment EMP-Stakeholder relationship (trust) Information sharing	Sell price→-Order procurement→+Order fulfilment→-EMP-Stakeholder relationship (trust)→+Information sharing
05) "For our government agency, with the analytic platform, ..., they have access to that's they can see how medicines are distributed across the state. For CSOs, we share some data and details to them on to see the medicines available in facilities at specific times. For health facilities, shipment data, consumption data. In line with the development at the agency, looking at the entire supply chain. The whole situation can be messy but with the introduction of digital technology, it has gone a long way to help us track and trace our health commodities at any point in time. That visibility from the warehouse to the health facility is a good development. It's the only way to go considering ...the past when we had parallel supply chain and you can't track medicines."	- analytic platform - data - medicines - messy - track and trace - in time	Visibility Information sharing Medicine inventory Stockout Shrinking and expiring inventory Time delay	Visibility→+Information sharing→+Medicine inventory→-Stockout→-Shrinking and expiring inventory Visibility--//→-Shrinking and expiring inventory
06)"We use the warehouse management software to manage inventory and the short message service platform to collect	-Software	Time period for averaging orders	Time period for averaging orders→-Customer orders→+Fill rate

data from facilities like consumption data. I have been privileged to use the analytic platform, which gives you general visibility from the warehouse to the point of consumption. The other systems plug into the analytic platform to give a one-time view of product availability the state."	- consumption - availability	Customer orders Fill rate	
07) "...measure the order fill rate which is a measure of the number of products ordered vs what has been supplied. The request from facility e.g 50 items, the number of products supplied to them is product availability. We categorise health products, what no of critical items have been supplied to the facilities? If orders fill rate is around 90-95%, that is good compared to measuring the money used for procurement because the items procured may be in the warehouse leading to expiries. The best way of measuring performance is the order fill rate."	- fill rate - expiries	Fill rate Shrinking and expiring inventory	Fill rate→-Shrinking and expiring inventory
08) "It's boils down to visibility, being customer-focused having the entire team knowing that their purpose is to serve the citizen of Kaduna state and having visibility across the agency."	- visibility - customer-focused - team	Visibility Fill rate Teamwork	Visibility→+ Teamwork→+Fill rate
09) "For the suppliers, whenever they bring in the products, they need to follow up in facilities to see the consumption. Depending on the supplier maturity and the level of visibility we are ready to share, going forward we can plug the suppliers to the digital platform to allow have visibility to see how their products are performing. It will be like a vendor-managed inventory where the supplier is plugged into the same system. Before we call for resupply, the supplier can plan ahead to provide the products due to longstanding relationship with the organisation. That will reduce the supplier lead time and any emergencies that might arise."	- products - maturity - visibility -products are performing - plugged into the same system - resupply - relationship	Order fulfilment Supplier performance Visibility Fill rate Digital technology Order procurement	Order fulfilment→+ Digital technology→+ Visibility→+ Order procurement→+ Fill rate--//→+ EMP-Stakeholder relationship (trust)→+ Supplier performance
	- lead time	EMP-Stakeholder relationship (trust) Time delay	

Appendix 3

EMP model simulation variables and formulas for DP adoption

Variables and formulars for EMP Model Simulation
1. EMP fill rate=effect of EMP medicine adequacy on fill rate, Units: Dmnl 2. "EMP-stakeholder trust"= effect of EMP medicine adequacy of product mix on trust, Units: Dmnl 3. Essential Medicine On Order= INTEG (EM procurement-EM fulfillment, 3000), Units: units 4. Essential Medicine Inventory= INTEG (EM order fulfillment-EM selling-shrinking and expiring inventory, 24000), Units: units 5. government funding="EMP-stakeholder trust"*allocated funding per week, Units: naira/Week 6. EMP average order rate=SMOOTH(EMP customer orders,time period to average orders), Units: units/Week 7. EMP customer orders=normal customer orders, Units: units/Week 8. EMP desired medicine inventory=EMP average order rate*EMP time period for medicine inventory holding, Units: units 9. EMP medicine inventory correction=(EMP desired medicine inventory-Essential Medicine Inventory)/time period for reconciling medicine inventory, Units: units/Week 10. EMP selling=min(EMP customer orders,Essential Medicine Inventory/"1 week")*EMP fill rate, Units: units/Week 11. EMP time period for medicine inventory holdings=8, Units: Week 12. INITIAL TIME = 0, Units: Week 13. FINAL TIME = 100, Units: Week

References

Abdulkadir R (2024) The dynamics of supply chain integration: empirical evidence from public health supply chains in Kaduna state, Nigeria. Doctoral Thesis, Liverpool John Moores University. https://doi.org/10.24377/LJMU.t.00022145

Abdulkadir R, Matellini DB, Jenkinson ID, Pyne R, Nguyen TT (2024) Assessing performance using maturity model: a multiple case study of public health supply chains in Nigeria. J Hum Logist Supply Chain Manag 14(1):17–70. https://doi.org/10.1108/JHLSCM-05-2022-0053

Ashiwaju BI, Agho MO, Okogwu C, Orikpete OF, Daraojimba C (2024) Digital transformation in pharmaceutical supply chain: an African case. Matrix Sci Pharm 7(3):95–102. https://doi.org/10.4103/mtsp.mtsp_16_23

Bag S, Dhamija P, Singh RK, Rahman MS, Sreedharan VR (2023) Big data analytics and artificial intelligence technologies based collaborative platform empowering absorptive capacity in health care supply chain: an empirical study. J Bus Res 154:113315. https://doi.org/10.1016/j.jbusres.2022.113315

Barratt M, Oke A (2007) Antecedents of supply chain visibility in retail supply chains: a resource-based theory perspective. J Oper Manag 25(6):1217–1233. https://doi.org/10.1016/j.jom.2007.01.003

Burrell DN (2017) Creating inclusive, diverse, and psychologically safe workplaces for African-American women working in public health response supply chain and logistics. Land Forces Acad Rev 27(2):134–140. https://doi.org/10.2478/raft-2022-0018

Bvuchete M, Grobbelaar SS, Van Eeden J (2018) A case of healthcare supply chain visibility in South Africa. In: 3rd biennial south African biomedical engineering conference, pp 1–5. https://doi.org/10.1109/SAIBMEC.2018.8363179

Dooley KJ (1997) A complex adaptive systems model of organization change. Nonlinear Dynamics Psychol Life Sci 1:69–97. https://doi.org/10.1023/A:1022375910940

Duncan R, Eden R, Woods L, Wong I, Sullivan C (2022) Synthesizing dimensions of digital maturity in hospitals: systematic review. J Med Internet Res 24(3):e32994. https://doi.org/10.2196/32994

Egharevba HO, Fatokun O, Aboh M, Kunle OO, Nwaka S, Gamaniel KS (2019) Piloting a smartphone-based application for tracking and supply chain management of medicines in Africa. PLoS ONE 14(7):e0217976. https://doi.org/10.1371/journal.pone.0217976

Finkenstadt DJ, Handfield R (2021) Blurry vision: supply chain visibility for personal protective equipment during COVID-19. J Purch Supply Manag 27(3):100689. https://doi.org/10.1016/j.pursup.2021.100689

Gakinahe GU, Rutungwa E, Mbonyinshuti F, Kayitare E (2024) Availability of antimalarial medicines and inventory management at the community level: a case study of Bugesera district in Rwanda. BMC Health Serv Res 24:136. https://doi.org/10.1186/s12913-024-10605-z

Gebremeskel AT, Otu A, Abimbola S, Yaya S (2021) Building resilient health systems in Africa beyond the COVID-19 pandemic response. BMJ Glob Health 6(6):e006108. https://doi.org/10.1136/bmjgh-2021-006108

Ghosh A, Fedorowicz J (2008) The role of trust in supply chain governance. Bus Process Manag J 14(4):453–470. https://doi.org/10.1108/14637150810888019

Hwang B, Shroufi A, Gils T, Steele SJ, Grimsrud A, Boulle A et al (2019) Stock-outs of antiretroviral and tuberculosis medicines in South Africa: a national cross-sectional survey. PLoS ONE 14(3):e0212405. https://doi.org/10.1371/journal.pone.0212405

Ibeneme S, Karamagi H, Muneene D, Goswami K, Chisaka N, Okeibunor J (2022) Strengthening health systems using innovative digital health technologies in Africa. Front Digital Health 4:854339. https://doi.org/10.3389/fdgth.2022.854339

Karamagi HC, Muneene D, Droti B, Jepchumba V, Okeibunor JC, Nabyonga J, Asamani JA, Traore M, Kipruto H (2022) eHealth or e-chaos: the use of digital health interventions for health systems strengthening in sub-Saharan Africa over the last 10 years: a scoping review. J Glob Health 12:1–9. https://doi.org/10.7189/jogh.12.04090

Kim HK, Lee CW (2021) Relationships among healthcare digitalization, social capital, and supply chain performance in the healthcare manufacturing industry. Int J Environ Res Public Health 18(4):1–13. https://doi.org/10.3390/ijerph18041417

Kritchanchai D (2014) A framework for healthcare supply chain improvement in Thailand. Oper Supply Chain Manag 5(2):103–113. https://doi.org/10.31387/oscm0120080

Kshetri N, Voas J (2019) Supply chain trust. IT Professional 21(2):6–10. https://doi.org/10.1109/MITP.2019.2895423

Lamanna C, Byrne L (2019) A pilot study of a novel, incentivised mHealth technology to monitor the vaccine supply chain in rural Zambia. Pan Afr Med J 33(1). https://doi.org/10.11604/pamj.2019.33.50.16318

Leung NHZ, Chen A, Yadav P, Gallien J (2016) The impact of inventory management on stock-outs of essential drugs in sub-Saharan Africa: secondary analysis of a field experiment in Zambia. PLos ONE 11(5):0156026. https://doi.org/10.1371/journal.pone.0156026

Lugada E, Komakech H, Ochola I, Mwebaze S, Olowo Oteba M, Okidi Ladwar D (2022) Health supply chain system in Uganda: current issues, structure, performance, and implications for systems strengthening. J Pharm Policy Pract 15(1):14. https://doi.org/10.1186/s40545-022-00412-4

Martins SADS, Machado MC, Queiroz MM, Telles R (2020) The relationship between quality and governance mechanisms: a qualitative investigation in healthcare supply-chain networks. BIJ 27(3):1085–1104. https://doi.org/10.1108/BIJ-03-2019-0114

Mayer RC, Davis JH, Schoorman FD (1995) An integrative model of organizational trust. Acad Manag Rev 20(3):709–734. https://doi.org/10.5465/amr.1995.9508080335

Mikkelsen-Lopez I, Shango W, Barrington J, Ziegler R, Smith T, DeSavigny D (2014) The challenge to avoid anti-malarial medicine stock-outs in an era of funding partners: the case of Tanzania. Malar J 13:1–9. https://doi.org/10.1186/1475-2875-13-181

Moucheraud C, Schwitters A, Boudreaux C, Giles D, Kilmarx PH, Ntolo N, Bangani Z, St. Louis ME, Bossert TJ (2017) Sustainability of health information systems: a three-country qualitative study in southern Africa. BMC Health Serv Res 17:1–11. https://doi.org/10.1186/s12913-016-1971-8

Musa A, Gunasekaran A, Yusuf Y (2014) Supply chain product visibility: methods, systems and impacts. Expert Syst Appl 41(1):176–194. https://doi.org/10.1016/j.eswa.2013.07.020

Musamih A, Salah K, Jayaraman R, Arshad J, Debe M, Al-Hammadi Y, Ellahham S (2021) A blockchain-based approach for drug traceability in healthcare supply chain. Inst Electr Electron Eng Access 9:9728–9743. https://doi.org/10.1109/ACCESS.2021.3049920

Onoja AJ, Sanni OF, Awelewa O, Peterside S, Onoja SI (2021) Poor availability of information communication and technology in sub-saharan africa health sector: a case study of nigerian health facilities: availability of information communication and technology in nigerian health facilities. J Health Inf Dev Countries 15(1):1–9. https://mail.jhidc.org/index.php/jhidc/article/view/313. Accessed 15 July 2024

Ottih C, Cussen K, Mustafa M (2018) Building strong health supply chain systems: the visibility and analytics network approach to improving the Nigeria immunisation supply chain. BMJ Health Care Inform 25(4). https://doi.org/10.14236/jhi.v25i4.944

Panda SK, Satapathy SC (2021) Drug traceability and transparency in medical supply chain using blockchain for easing the process and creating trust between stakeholders and consumers. Pers Ubiquit Comput 28:75–91. https://doi.org/10.1007/s00779-021-01588-3

Provan KG, Kenis P (2008) Modes of network governance: structure, management, and effectiveness. J Public Adm Res Theory 18(2):229–252. https://doi.org/10.1093/jopart/mum015

Rinke de Wit TF, Janssens W, Antwi M, Milimo E, Mutegi N, Marwa H, Ndili N, Owino W, Waiyaiya E, Garcia Rojas DC, Dolfing M (2022) Digital health systems strengthening in Africa for rapid response to COVID-19. Front Health Serv 2:987828. https://doi.org/10.3389/frhs.2022.987828

Sarley D, Mahmud M, Idris J, Osunkiyesi M, Dibosa-Osadolor O, Okebukola P, Wiwa O (2017) Transforming vaccines supply chains in Nigeria. Vaccine 35(17):2167–2174. https://doi.org/10.1016/j.vaccine.2016.11.068

Sato R, Metiboba L, Galadanchi JA, Adeniran MF, Hassan SH, Akpan D, Odogwu J, Fashoto B (2023) Cost analysis of an innovative eHealth program in Nigeria: a case study of the vaccine direct delivery system. BMC Public Health 23(1):1691. https://doi.org/10.1186/s12889-023-16575-x

Shieshia M, Noel M, Andersson S, Felling B, Alva S, Agarwal S, Lefevre A, Misomali A, Chimphanga B, Nsona H, Chandani Y (2014) Strengthening community health supply chain performance through an integrated approach: using mHealth technology and multilevel teams in Malawi. J Glob Health 4(2):1. https://doi.org/10.7189/jogh.04.020406

Sterman J (2000) Business dynamics. McGraw-Hill, New York

Tambo E, Madjou G, Mbous Y, Olalubi OA, Yah C, Adedeji AA, Ngogang JY (2016) Digital health implications in health systems in Africa. Eur J Pharm Med Res 3(1):84–90. https://storage.googleapis.com/journal-uploads/ejpmr/article_issue/1451541580.pdf. Accessed 12 July 2024

Tiwari M, Bryde DJ, Stavropolou F, Dubey R, Kumari S, Foropon C (2024) Modelling supply chain visibility, digital technologies, environmental dynamism and healthcare supply chain resilience: an organisation information processing theory perspective. Transp Res Part E Logist Transp Rev 188:103613. https://doi.org/10.1016/j.tre.2024.103613

Tomoaia-Cotisel A, Allen SD, Kim H, Andersen D, Chalabi Z (2022) Rigorously interpreted quotation analysis for evaluating causal loop diagrams in late-stage conceptualization. Syst Dyn Rev 38(1):41–80. https://doi.org/10.1002/sdr.1701

Wagenaar BH, Gimbel S, Hoek R, Pfeiffer J, Michel C, Manuel JL, Cuembelo F, Quembo T, Afonso P, Gloyd S, Sherr K (2014) Stock-outs of essential health products in Mozambique–longitudinal analyses from 2011 to 2013. Trop Med Int Health 19(7):91–801. https://doi.org/10.1111/tmi.12314

Wang N (2021) "As it is Africa, it is ok"? Ethical considerations of development use of drones for delivery in Malawi. Inst Electr Electron Eng Trans Technol Soc 2(1):20–30. https://doi.org/10.1109/TTS.2021.3058669

Zhu X, Tao Y, Zhu R, Wu D, Ming WK (2022) Impact of hospital characteristics and governance structure on the adoption of tracking technologies for clinical and supply chain use: longitudinal study of US hospitals. J Med Internet Res 24(5):33742. https://doi.org/10.2196/33742

Zuma SM (2022) Assessment of medicine stock-outs challenges in public health services. Africa's Public Serv Deliv Perform Rev 10(1):578. https://doi.org/10.4102/apsdpr.v10i1.578

Ramatu Abdulkadir is a Senior Program Manager at LEARN Logistics by Kühne Foundation, Germany. She holds a PhD in Transport Logistics from Liverpool John Moores University, United Kingdom. Her research interests cover health supply chains, sustainable and circular supply chains. She is a Certified Supply Chain Professional and a Fellow of the West African Postgraduate College of Pharmacists. Dr. Abdulkadir is dedicated to leveraging research to address intricate supply chain challenges and advance sustainable economic development in Africa.

Andre Kreie is Managing Director at LEARN Logistics by Kühne-Foundation, based in Hamburg, Germany. He is a Business Economist and holds a PhD and a Masters in Logistics and Supply Chain Management (LSCM) from Heriot-Watt University, Edinburgh, UK. Dr. Kreie leads the education unit LEARN that addresses capacity building in middle- and low-income countries related to LSCM, leadership, and strategy. He is a regular member of the International Advisory Boards of Edinburgh Business School (EBS), UK, and Arizona State University (ASU), US, on the CARISCA Project in collaboration with Kwame Nkrumah University of Science and Technology (KNUST) in Ghana. Since October 2023, Dr. Kreie also chairs the International Advisory Board of the Logistics Institute of Central Asia (LICA).

Chapter 6
Healthguider: A Master Healthcare Supply Chain File and Database System

Frank Ranganai Matenda, Marcia Mkansi, and Phumeza Saliwe

6.1 Introduction

Access to healthcare is a vital human right (Hashemi et al. 2020; Peprah et al. 2020) and it is one of the objectives of the global health development agenda. However, attaining this goal is a substantial problem in many African economies as a result of restricted resources, systemic inefficiencies and infrastructural limitations. In the same vein, Yenet et al. (2023) propounded that financial restrictions, scarce human resources, high cost of existing medications on the market, manual consumption prediction, poor inventory management, inadequacies in drug registration and trade--associated issues of intellectual property rights agreement regulations are some of the challenges African countries face when it comes to the obtainability of vital medicines. Interestingly, one of the most serious matters within the African healthcare sector is the inadequacy of traditional booking and appointment systems, which are usually paper-based (Mavuso et al. 2023; Ramutumbu et al. 2023; Yenet et al. 2023). These systems are prone to delays, errors and mismanagement, hampering timely patient care and accounting for poor health results (see, for instance, Mavuso et al. 2023; Jimma and Enyew 2022). Further, paper-premised systems find it difficult to deal with the swelling patient load related to urbanisation, population growth and increasing appearance of chronic diseases in Africa.

F. R. Matenda (✉) · M. Mkansi
College of Economic and Management Sciences, The University of South Africa, Pretoria, South Africa

P. Saliwe
Operations Management, University of South Africa, Pretoria, Republic of South Africa
e-mail: saliwp@unisa.ac.za

T. Akenroye et al. (eds.), *Digitalizing Health Care Supply Chains in Africa*, Springer Series in Supply Chain Management 28,
https://doi.org/10.1007/978-3-032-20501-8_6

Generally, for daily processes, institutions are contingent on appointments and scheduling (Pariyar et al. 2023). Interestingly, methods of scheduling appointments are cautiously changing. Institutions are now moving from paper-based systems to all-in-one paperless booking and appointment systems. The move to paperless systems agrees with global attempts to digitalise healthcare and achieve the United Nations Sustainable Development Goal 3, which aspires to promote healthy lives and enhance well-being for all people (Peprah et al. 2020). The dawn of all-in-one paperless booking and appointment systems provides a transformative solution to the challenges posed by paper-based systems (see Jimma and Enyew 2022 and references therein). Such systems take advantage of digital technologies to streamline appointment scheduling, lessen administrative loads and enhance patient data management; thereby promoting effectiveness and augmenting the patient experience. Moreover, these electronic systems offer vital data analytics abilities, allowing healthcare providers and policymakers to make informed verdicts and optimise resource allocation.

Africa has distinct healthcare settings which are characterised by a combination of urban and rural settings (see Norris et al. 2022). This further highlights the dire need for innovative digital solutions. Non-existence of physical infrastructure and long travel distances to clinics in rural areas (Peprah et al. 2020; Lu et al. 2010) can discourage patients from looking for medical care timeously. For instance, digital systems that allow remote appointment scheduling can address these challenges, thereby enhancing accessibility by underserved populace. In urban areas, where healthcare amenities are usually congested, paperless systems can alleviate bottlenecks by eliminating waiting times and promoting effective and efficient management of patient flows.

Nevertheless, the implementation of the paperless systems in different parts of the world faces distinct challenges such as restricted internet penetration, high costs of technology adoption and resistance to change among healthcare staff (Jimma and Enyew 2022; Tsai et al. 2020). Africa is not an exception. In South Africa, Healthguider, an innovation that provides an all-in-one paperless booking and appointment system and mobile application to streamline clinic operations, saving resources and time, was introduced. Its integrated features include ticketing system, patient diagnosis, billing and switching, tele-medicine, stock management system, medication reminders, patient referrals/medical check-ups, and access to doctors. Basically, it provides efficient appointment scheduling, patient diagnosis and management, automated prescription management, and centralised medical data and insights. However, access to the healthcare value chain remains the primary obstacle for Healthguider in South Africa. This chapter explores the necessity of all-in--one paperless booking and appointment systems in Africa's healthcare sector, analysing the benefits, technical structure, impact, and opportunities and challenges of Healthguider.

This chapter is structured as follows. Section 2 outlines the review of literature, and Sect. 3 outlines the methodology adopted in the study. In Sect. 4, study results are presented. Section 5 concludes the study and presents the implications and opportunities for further research.

6.2 Literature Review

Healthcare remains a pressing global issue (Peprah et al. 2020). How to deliver healthcare and make it accessible is an issue of concern. Equitable access to health-care for all people is a vital tenet of each healthcare system (Peprah et al. 2020). Generally, there have been rigorous attempts to reinforce healthcare systems glob-ally. To promote equitable access to quality healthcare for all people, countries have been adopting technologies that are transforming the healthcare sector. Interestingly, countries have been witnessing a huge shift from paper-premised health records to electronic records since the 1990s. Among other issues, paper-premised systems utilise greater space and, specifically, delay access to appropriate medical care (Jimma and Enyew 2022). Further, paper-based systems are subject to physical damage, misplacement, human error and theft (Alsanad et al. 2023). Of late, hospi-tals and clinics have been implementing paperless systems such as master file and database systems commonly referred as Enterprise Resource Planning (ERP) sys-tems to streamline their operations.

With growing recognition of the significance of seamless data integration across various departments, ERP systems have become vital for promoting operational efficiency (Kulkarni et al. 2023). ERP systems promote reliable access to informa-tion throughout the whole institution by allowing integration of data from diverse departments (Al-Assaf et al. 2024). Usually, an ERP system has numerous function-alities such as finance, purchasing, accounting, human resources, manufacturing and sales (Mladenova 2020). Al-Assaf et al. (2024) postulated that the integration of different departments promotes better strategic planning and decision-making. Interestingly, since their first introduction in the 1960s, ERP systems are continuing to advance and with the advent of technologies such as artificial intelligence they won't stop developing (Mladenova 2020). Chiarini et al. (2018) examined ERP implementation in public healthcare and discovered that its benefits can be catego-rised into four: stakeholders' satisfaction, patients' satisfaction, operations effi-ciency, and strategic and performance management. However, the authors (Chiarini et al. 2018) further opined that the complication of the project, process reengineer-ing and staff's participation can obstruct ERP implementation in public healthcare. Almajali et al. (2016) proffered that implementing ERP system fruitfully is complex and expensive, and regularly results in high disappointment rates and abandonments as a result of the need to fit with the social or business culture.

Generally, paperless systems enhance health care improvement in quality patient safety, patient care and cost reduction by offering easy access to medical data (Jimma and Enyew 2022). They offer instant access to the patient records to all service providers in the healthcare chain, thereby allowing them to offer precise and unswerving care (Alsanad et al. 2023; Adler-Milstein and Bates 2010). Alsanad et al. (2023) also indicated that specialists, general practitioners and other healthcare providers within a facility can monitor a patient's records in real time, minimising the risk of errors in analysis and decision-making. Further, Alsanad et al. (2023) showed that paperless systems promote continuous information transfer, allowing patient health data to be easily shared between hospitals or clinicians. Basically, paperless systems provide enormous and simple methods of storing, retrieving, and distributing data in healthcare management.

Despite great advances in technology in the healthcare sector, implementation and adoption challenges continue. Tsai et al. (2020) propounded that resource restrictions, inadequate/poor training and educational/technical support for users, and poor literacy and skills in technology are some of the obstacles to the adoption and use of the paperless systems. Jimma and Enyew (2022) identified technical, financial, time, legal, organisational, psychological, and social barricades to the acceptance of electronic medical records from the perceptions of nurses and physicians. Moreover, these paperless systems are exposed to cyber-attacks, accidental modifications, accidental and/ or unauthorised access (see, for example, Alsanad et al. 2023; Javaid et al. 2023). The existing literature also indicated that the performance of these systems can be reduced as databases grow, hence scalability issues. All these heightened interest on the technical structures that underpin these systems.

6.3 Methodology

This study used semi-structured interviews to examine the benefits, technical structure, impact, and opportunities and challenges of Healthguider. Healthguider is a South African innovation that encapsulates an all-in-one healthcare supply chain file and database system. The benefits, technical structure, impact, and opportunities and challenges of Healthguider influences its effective diffusion among downstream and upstream healthcare supply chain stakeholders.

6.3.1 Healthguider Context

The Healthguider innovation is particularly crucial as it is one of the master file and database systems or ERP systems. Healthguider revolutionises healthcare by integrating electronic medical records abilities with a patient-focused mobile application, dealing key problems such as inefficient patient flow, fragmented records and high operational costs. Healthguider improves provider efficiency, patient satisfaction and data security by centralising patient information, automating processes and providing real-time access. This user-friendly and compliant platform allows patients to take an active role in managing their health, promoting a more connected and streamlined healthcare experience. Healthguider target market includes independent doctors, clinics, specialists seeking digital tools for patient care, nurses, laboratories, and pharmacies. ERPs have been introduced to a myriad of sectors like education, retail, finance, healthcare, insurance, and hotel chains (Shehab et al. 2004). Interestingly, the success rates of ERP systems are low (Garg and Agarwal 2014; Dezhar 2012; Huang et al. 2004), especially in public healthcare supply chain. However, the implementation of ERP systems in downstream and upstream healthcare supply chain stakeholders can offer benefits and intelligence necessary for fostering partnerships and stakeholders' intention to implement.

6.3.2 Data Collection

We used semi-structured interviews with the founder and co-founder of Healthguider a South African start-up servicing healthcare supply chains. Semi-structured interviews were adopted due to the exploratory nature of the study (Patton 2002). Semi--structured interviews allow reciprocity between the participant and interviewer (Galletta 2012). This allowed the participant to provide varied responses and the interviewer to make follow-ups on certain issues and to observe the verbal expressions of the participant. The founder has 5 years in business development, as an UI/UX software analyst, 7 years plus in software development environment, and has a diploma in computer system engineering and master's in computer science. Supporting the founder are four employees, i.e., chief financial officer (CFO), data analyst, business administrator, and scrum master. The CFO has 7 years' experience in accounting, auditing, business development, and has a Bachelor of Technology in Internal Auditing. The data analyst led sales and has a degree in Economics and Statistics.

The business administrator is a bookkeeper and the scrum master, who is a software developer, has a master's in computer science. The founder and co-founder were purposively selected as they are the key architects of the innovation's technical structure. They are at the forefront of its implementation in South Africa and Democratic Republic of Congo (DRC). The two separate interviews lasted an hour and half, with a complimentary pitch deck presentation and technology demonstration. Purposive sampling was implemented to select the participants. Purposive sampling better matches the sample to the objectives and aims of the study, thereby enhancing the robustness of the study and reliability of the data and results (Campbell et al. 2020). Thematic content analysis was used to interpret patterns, gain nuanced understanding of how they emerge and identify implications thereof. The latter approach is endorsed by advocates of content analysis (see Maier 2017).

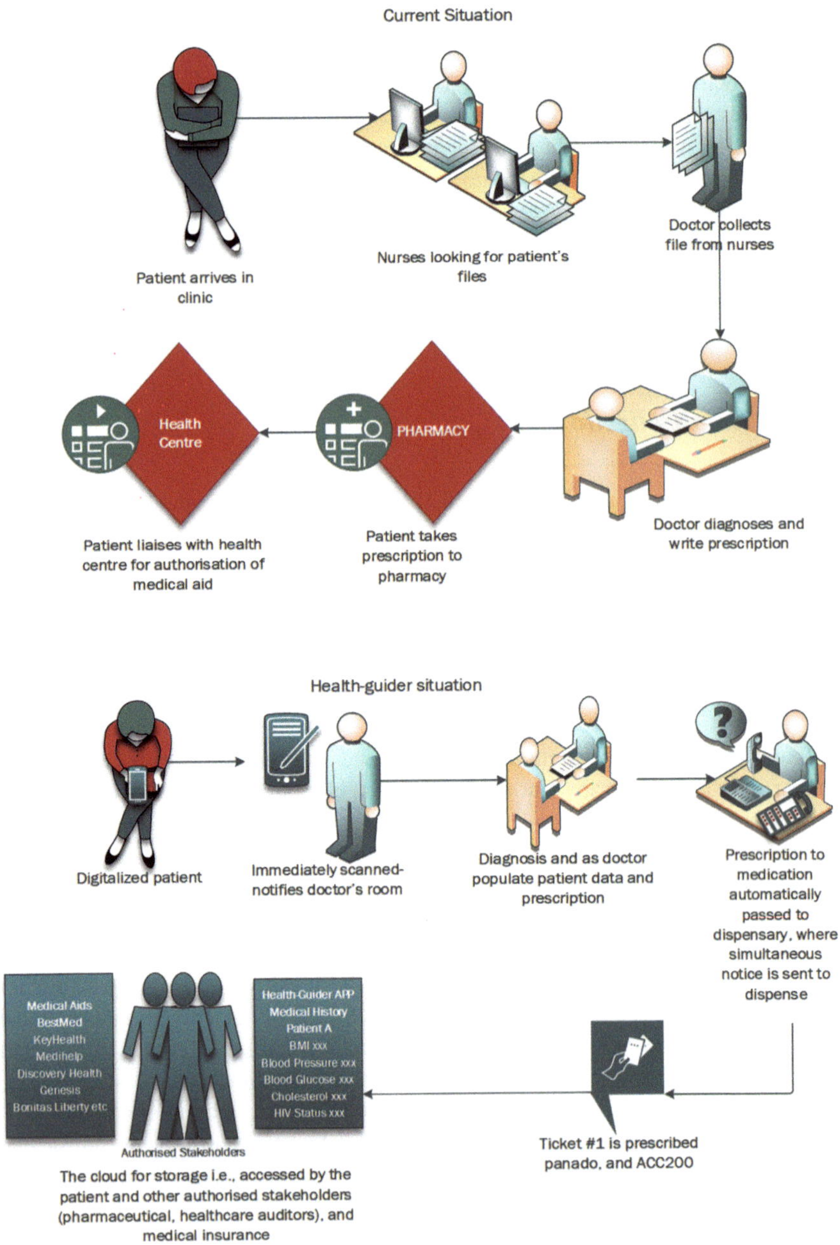
Current Situation
Patient arrives in clinic
Nurses looking for patient's files
Doctor collects file from nurses
Doctor diagnoses and write prescription
PHARMACY
Patient takes prescription to pharmacy
Health Centre
Patient liaises with health centre for authorisation of medical aid
Health-guider situation
Digitalized patient
Immediately scanned-notifies doctor's room
Diagnosis and as doctor populate patient data and prescription
Prescription to medication automatically passed to dispensary, where simultaneous notice is sent to dispense
Ticket #1 is prescribed panado, and ACC200
Health-Guider APP
Medical History
Patient A
BMI xxx
Blood Pressure xxx
Blood Glucose xxx
Cholesterol xxx
HIV Status xxx
Medical Aids
BestMed
KeyHealth
Medihelp
Discovery Health
Genesis
Bonitas Liberty etc
Authorised Stakeholders
The cloud for storage i.e., accessed by the patient and other authorised stakeholders (pharmaceutical, healthcare auditors), and medical insurance

6.4 Findings

The study findings are presented in this section.

6.4.1 *Challenges Addressed by the Healthguider Innovation and Its Benefits*

Participants in the study propounded that the Healthguider innovation addresses the challenge of uncoordinated, and in most cases, manual processes of the public healthcare supply chain, which remains one of the greatest challenges in South Africa. The insight from the founder reveals a huge healthcare market for the innovation in both public and private systems, with the latter using fragmented systems. In public healthcare systems, most processes are manual, consequently creating bottlenecks in service delivery from poor patient experience, delayed patient scheduling, data silos, increased costs, poor medical audits, to redundant efforts whereby different healthcare centres perform similar tasks leading to resource inefficiency, i.e., redundant and duplication of efforts. Further, the participants highlight challenges relating to patients' adherence to medical prescriptions. This argument is supported by the following quote:

> $218.7 million mhealthcare market, but we still have a problem of patient scheduling and manual processing and in clinics, there's a prolonged delay that has compromised medical audits. This increases patient risk and furthermore, we try to solve a problem of medication adherence. In South Africa, between 50% and 60% of patients with chronic conditions fail to adhere to prescribed medication as reported by of the South African Journals and there is a huge pool of electronic medical records (EMR) systems, but organisations store them locally and isolated systems are one of the biggest problems. Founder

The Healthguider innovation, mobile and web applications, adopt an integrated approach that can provide healthcare centres a harmonised process to minimise redundancy, whilst improving communication and data sharing. The application has the possibility to establish central authority in healthcare supply chain processes necessary to foster the culture of stakeholder collaboration, improve efficiency, reduce costs, and enhance patient experience and high-quality service. The emphasis on patient health management is notable, creating shared responsibilities between patient and healthcare facilities. This argument is supported by the following quote:

> Healthguider revolutionises healthcare by integrating EMRs capabilities with patient focused mobile application, it deals with key challenges like fragmented medical records, inefficient patient flow and high operational cost by centralising patient data, automating tasks and enabling real-time access. Healthguider enhances provider efficiency, patient satisfaction and data security. The seamless compliant platform empowers patients to manage their health, proactively, create a more connected and efficient healthcare experience. Founder

6.4.2 Technical Structure of the Healthguider Innovation

Through an integrated, streamlined, and multi-functional digital platform, the innovation provides significant supply chain implications across various healthcare domains. From the downstream chain, it offers opportunities for operational efficiency that can reduce costs associated with multiple platforms, whilst improving speed and accuracy of service delivery. The automation of prescription management can elevate patient experience through its seamless interface whilst offering personalised experience across multiple touchpoints and responsiveness. The upstream chain can optimise the innovation for analytics and intelligence necessary for creating agile and quick decision-making in transfers of patients, referrals, service flows, and patient processing times, invoicing etc. Furthermore, the public healthcare supply chain can enhance interoperability of its technological infrastructure to ensure proper alignment of application programming interfaces and standardise protocols for compatibility and cross functional collaboration, efficient appointment scheduling, patient diagnosis and management, automated prescription management, and centralised medical database. The quotes that support this are as follows:

> The innovation offers efficient appointment scheduling, patient diagnosis and management, automated prescription management, centralised medical data and insights. We have two platforms, a mobile application and cloud practice management system (PMS) …. Regardless of whether the patient moves from Gauteng to Cape Town, that patient should have their information. Even if the patient flies to the United States, doctors should know that this is the way you treat me. This is my medical history, with that consent, this is my medical history. This is what I'm taking through my application. Founder, Co-Founder and Presentations

Furthermore, the innovation proposes a core master file that serves multi-healthcare stakeholders from medical insurance, pharmaceuticals, auditors, patients, and other healthcare centres. The database can be the central data warehouse for health supply chain that holds consolidated and authoritative data necessary to revolutionise public healthcare. This will ensure uniformity and eliminate conflicting data. Thus, there is a need to enforce data and cyber security and control, whereby every entry automatically reflects across linked systems for data consistency. The responses of the participants are shown as follows:

> A patient is digitalised, given a ticket number that is immediately shown on doctor's screen, as soon as diagnosis is complete, the prescription side has the information, and form sent to the medical aid while on the outside the very same prescription and diagnosis are sent to cloud so much that the patient has a medical history there. If the patient has an application, it means that the patient can access the medical history and get an application for referral and medical history audit. Founder

6.4.3 Impact of the Healthguider Innovation

The impact of Healthguider innovation can be traced from its accessibility on android and iPhone operation system to its 3-pilot test report and engagements with 4 healthcare providers, insurance company, and other 12 stakeholders. Early engagements reveal partnership opportunities with an industry player, DRC and selected doctors' centres in South Africa. This highlights critical innovation ecosystem and healthcare supply chain stakeholders necessary to drive cultural shifts for experimentation and continuous improvement. It further highpoints innovation risk management strategy which minimises negative shocks in the healthcare supply chain as the technical feasibility and glitches are validated in real operational environment. Technology validation serves as evidence for industry and government regulation adherence which is crucial for system compliance. The participants reveal faster adoption rate of five thousand doctors in the DRC as compared to 17 stakeholders in South Africa. The combined adoption rate from the pilot phase cemented Healthguider innovation as a validated technology ready for commercialisation. Most importantly, the pilot report reveals health benefit that yielded about 35% savings per insured person and enhanced stock management and better utilisation of time. The following quote supports this argument:

> We engaged our product with four healthcare providers and an insurance company and insights from over 12 stakeholders. Now, we have a product that is on Play Store and App Store. And then we have a web application which is the PMS. ... We have done a three-pilot test and a three-year contract with a company called On Point Healthcare that offers us AB slices free of about 1800 + 115 per user. We have been utilised by two companies. There is the third one which is very big. It's from the DRC...There is appetite because immediately when I moved to the DRC I had instantly 5000 doctors.... Our ticketing system promotes saving health which is about 0.35% per person's policy. Founder and Co-Founder

Following a successful pilot phase in South Africa and the DRC, Healthguider attracted the attention of Technology Innovation Agency (TIA). Far from financial support, the founder highlights the need for experience and technology validation. Put differently, experience supersedes financial investment in new innovation as it affords innovators practical knowledge of implementation, including a platform to address obstacles and leverage opportunities, without which, the innovation may be underutilised. It allows for efficient and effective resource utilisation, which minimises misallocation of resources and reduce failures in diffusion efforts. The latter is a crucial ingredient for trust and credibility necessary to facilitate faster adoption and partnerships. Participants in this study shared similar sentiments on this as reported in the following response:

> TIA is coming on board and the Department of Trade, Industry and Competition was impressed too, they are coming on board. We are funding you further to commercialise your product. The biggest thing about our government is sometimes we don't need you to give us money, but we need you to give us experience. We need you to say here is one or two clinics, pilot on them. We don't necessarily need to get paid because we did this out of love. We did it to improve service delivery. You can throw millions, but what we want is to see our innovation change lives in the public space because the absorption in the private space is there. There's nothing that is worse than building a great product and not get it into the hands of the customer. It can be great sitting on a shelf. But there is no greater thing putting this in the hands of people that really need it. Founder

6.4.4 Opportunities and Challenges Associated with the Healthguider Innovation

There are learning curves which highlight opportunities and challenges in the participants' narrative. In townships, general practitioners prefer a walk-in system over booking system. However, suburban areas are accustomed to scheduling systems. The insight reveals peculiar dynamics of township and rural downstream healthcare supply chain context. There is an element of practicality of patients' access and convenience, which might be induced by the digital divide, data issues and limited alternative health alternatives. In this case, a first come first serve scheduling system supersedes digital scheduling system. Consequently, the downstream of a township healthcare supply chain deals with unpredictable patient volumes. Whilst the latter reduces idle periods, increases revenue and accommodates uninsured patient segments, it highlights a challenge for Healthguider ambition and efforts for digitising healthcare scheduling system. In practice, it reveals challenges related to unpredictable workloads, and limited capacity to maintain continuous care for chronic patients. For Healthguider, these learning curves helped shape the direction of innovation offerings from patient to organisational features. This was evidenced by the participants' responses in the following quotes:

> What I have learned was that people who will use the application are specialists. GPS don't do bookings. They don't do bookings because anyone can walk anytime. And I'm talking about locations (townships). The suburbs have Vitality, Bonitas, etc. I'm talking about the locations where the masses don't have access to healthcare. The biggest challenges are clients change every time. Now, we need to learn that we cannot do 100% system for everyone. But, if we have 80% to 90% of the functionalities that an organisation would need, that is the best we could do. Founder

Also, within the downstream healthcare supply chain practitioners, there are heterogenous system requirements that need to be factored. The findings present two distinct perspectives of township supply chain stakeholders' requirements. On one hand, a walk-in preference is hard to digitise due to high revenue, and patient access limitations. On the other hand, heterogenous digital requirements with an unpredictable patient volume can benefit from a master file and database system. The two-healthcare perspective signals the approach and the environment for digital technical structure necessary for the transformation of township healthcare supply chain. An example of workload minimisation is the system's ability to produce patient's leave notice if required, which saves practitioners time. The quote to support this is as follows:

> "And one of the challenges is, you know, when we went out to the market, we learnt that a GP, a dentist, a gynaecologist uses different templates. We had to go back to development and say, ok, well, you know what? Let's understand how these people work". "And it automatically calculates to say from the 22nd to the 23rd cannot work due to injuries".

A further challenge is legal costs for contracting supply chain stakeholders and the needs for license agreement. This challenge highlights how regulatory compliance and contractual legal costs can make or break the implementation of innovation in the healthcare supply chain. Technically, it highlights the need to embed industry regulations in new technology. Strategically, it reveals litigation and risk measures required for the implementation of master file and database systems in healthcare supply chain. Furthermore, legal variation across boarders necessitates cross licencing agreements to avoid high legal costs and battles; whilst fostering a collaborative environment. The quote to support this is as follows:

> I remember a lawyer billing me R50 000 for contract with On Point Healthcare.So, DRC is going to be even worse? Because DRC wants something called a license agreement. Healthguider will be white labelled, and DRC will be offering it to doctors as DRC application. Founder

6.4.5 *System Demonstration by the Founder*

In demonstration of Healthguider digital product, the founder highlights some of the conflicting priorities between organisational requirements and development requirements. For example, restricted access to some data and patients' system features due to Protection of Personal Information Act (POPI Act). This was evidenced by their responses in the following quotes:

> This is the dashboard waiting time, in progress. Completed patients, total patients and revenues generated. Now, I cannot go to patients because of POPI Act, but I can go into appointments. System demonstration by the Founder

6.5 Discussions

The study discovered that most processes are manual in South African public healthcare systems. Alsanad et al. (2023) propounded that healthcare record management has historically depended on manual, paper-based systems, providing a tangible and easily identifiable method for storing patient information. However, manual systems create challenges in the delivery of service from poor patient experience, data silos, delayed patient scheduling, amplified costs, compromised medical audits and redundant efforts whereby diverse healthcare institutions execute related duties resulting in resource inefficiency, Also, manual systems result in problems related to patients' adherence to medical prescriptions. Under the same line of reasoning, Alsanad et al. (2023) opined that in paper-premised systems, papers may be misplaced, lost, or torn and may be destroyed by floods, fire outbreaks and other natural disasters. For more information on the drawbacks of paper-based systems, the reader is referred to, among other authors, Alsanad et al. (2023).

The study found that Healthguider innovation addresses the challenge of uncoordinated, and in most cases, manual processes of the public healthcare supply chain, which remains one of the greatest challenges in South Africa. Health-guider innovation is designed to streamline upstream and downstream healthcare supply chain from medical order processing, referrals logistics, distribution of prescriptions, to data storage through a master file and database system. Put differently, it proposes a core database that can serve multi-supply chain stakeholders' interests in both the upstream (government officials, doctors, pharmaceuticals, medical insurance/aid) and downstream chain (healthcare facilities, patients). That is to say, it provides an integrated approach that can provide healthcare stakeholders a harmonised process to minimise redundancy, whilst improving communication and data sharing. An indirect implication of the innovation is digital and healthcare equity which creates inclusion and accessibility to the vulnerable public healthcare supply chain.

Further, the innovation serves as a transformational tool that can ensure efficient utilisation of human capital and technology by eliminating repetitive tasks and improving digital proficiency, resulting in simplification through consolidation of task management and resource savings, i.e., time and money. Interestingly, it helps bridge the gap between public and private healthcare systems, thus leading to democratisation of healthcare by digital innovators in partnership with governors of public healthcare. Alsanad et al. (2023), Jimma and Enyew (2022) and Adler-Milstein and Bates (2010) submitted that paperless systems have a plethora of benefits such as the provision of immediate access to patient records to all service providers in the healthcare chain, thus permitting them to offer accurate and unswerving care. Nonetheless, it should be noted that paperless systems are exposed to accidental modifications, cyber-attacks, accidental and/or unauthorised access (Alsanad et al. 2023; Javaid et al. 2023), which may negatively impact efficient and effective service delivery.

When it comes to its technical structure, the Healthguider innovation is an integrated, streamlined, and multi-functional digital platform that offers significant supply chain implications across several healthcare domains. The Healthguider innovation is a paperless booking/appointment Software as a Service (SaaS) system and mobile application that modernises clinic operations, thereby saving resources and time. It is compatible with iPhone Operating System (iOS), Android and personal computer (PC), thereby guaranteeing accessibility and reliability. The innovation provides appointment scheduling, medication and appointment reminders, referrals, and beneficiary bookings in an attempt to support the patients in their healthcare journey. The innovation has a central master file that serves multi-healthcare stakeholders such as medical insurance companies, pharmaceuticals, auditors, patients, and other healthcare centres. This promotes uniformity and eradicates conflicting data. The innovation's structure is valuable in the healthcare supply chain. From the downstream chain, it decreases costs associated with numerous platforms and enhances speed and precision of service delivery. In the upstream chain, the innovation can be optimised for analytics and intelligence essential for flexible and swift decision-making in various areas such as patient transfers and referrals. In support of this, Mladenova (2020) opined that ERP systems have functionalities and Al-Assaf et al. (2024) proffered that the integration of diverse departments enhances better strategic planning and decision-making.

To further validate this argument, Chiarini et al. (2018) indicated that stakeholders' satisfaction, patients' satisfaction, operations efficiency, and strategic and performance management are some of the benefits of the ERP systems in the healthcare. Moreover, the technical structure of the innovation can be aligned to the existing technological infrastructure to enhance efficient service delivery. Validating this point, Velcu (2010) propounded that ERP systems merge business processes and information technology of the adopting institution to ease the movement of information via business functions. This indicates that amalgamating an ERP system with current business processes is vital for a continuous flow of information and operational continuousness.

The Healthguider innovation is accessible on iOS, Android and PC and has been pilot tested and adopted by several stakeholders such as insurance companies in DRC and South Africa. For instance, Healthguider has attracted the interest of the TIA. This indicates that the innovation's benefits, technical feasibility and glitches have been validated in real operational environment (see, for instance, Murphy et al. 2024; Tanaka et al. 2024; Feldacker et al. 2023). Technology validation provides evidence that the innovation adheres to industry and government regulations, making it easy to commercialise the innovation. This is validated by Shema-Shiratzky et al. (2022) and Schauffel et al. (2021), among other authors. Further, the adoption rates of the innovation are different in diverse countries due to several reasons (see Garcia and Crenner 2022; Afzal et al. 2021; and reference therein).

It has also been revealed that experience supersedes financial investment in novel innovations. Experience provides innovators with empirical knowledge of implementation, allowing them to deal with problems and leverage opportunities. Experience permits efficient and effective resource utilisation, thereby minimising misallocation of resources and enhancing diffusion. Validating this point, Wieder et al. (2006) confirmed that the longer the experience of institutions with ERP systems, the greater their overall performance. Even though ERP systems can have significant impact in institutions, some studies (Garg and Agarwal 2014; Dezhar 2012; Huang et al. 2004) have indicated that the success rates of ERP systems are low.

General practitioners, in townships, prefer walk-in systems over booking systems, while those in suburban or urban areas are used to scheduling systems. This indicates that the dynamics of township and rural downstream healthcare supply chain are different from those of suburban or urban areas. The driving force can be the issue of patients' access and convenience, which is fuelled by digital divide, data issues and restricted substitute health alternatives. Since the downstream of a township or rural healthcare, supply chain deals with erratic patient volumes, a first come first serve scheduling system can be a better option than a digital scheduling system. This might be a challenge for Healthguider's determination and attempts to digitise the healthcare scheduling system. These learning curves assist in shaping the direction of the Healthguider innovation offerings from patient to organisational features.

Under the same line of reasoning, Atherton et al. (2024) propounded that patients in rural areas are less probable to be aware of or use online appointment booking and patients in deprived areas are bunched in practices with low consciousness and implementation of online appointment booking. Hawe et al. (2023) indicated that restricted access to the technology and low literacy skills in utilising the technology are some of the problems for some rural patients when using technology-enabled healthcare. In support of this, in one huge tertiary public hospital outpatient service centre in China, Zhang et al. (2014) discovered that only 17% of patients used an online appointment booking system, while 90% of the doctors thought there was a need to offer alternative forms of appointment booking systems for outpatients.

Further, it has been indicated that within the downstream healthcare supply chain practitioners, there are heterogenous system requirements. The findings present two unique viewpoints of township supply chain stakeholders' requirements. On one hand, a walk-in preference is hard to digitise due to high revenue and patient access limitations. On the other hand, heterogenous digital requirements with an unpredictable patient volume can benefit from a master file and database system. The two-healthcare perspective signals the approach and the environment for digital technical structure necessary for the transformation of township healthcare supply chain.

Legal costs for contracting supply chain stakeholders and the need for licence agreements is a challenge. Regulatory compliance and contractual legal costs can make or break the application of innovation in the healthcare supply chain (see, for instance, Phares, Dobrzykowski and Prohofsky, 2021; Lee Mendoza, 2019; Hu and Schwarz, 2011). Also, legal variation across boarders necessitates cross licencing agreements to evade high legal costs and battles; whilst promoting a collaborative environment. Moreover, there are conflicting priorities between organisational requirements and development requirements, i.e., conflicting priorities by potential adopters. For instance, the need for balancing operational excellence with compliance to national laws such as POPI Act and a tug of war between change management vis-à-vis overcomplexity as users finds new features overwhelming.

From the discussion above, the following strategic measures for the implementation of innovation are proposed: (i). Practical knowledge supersedes financial investment: Finance can assist in developing new tools and strategies, but without experience, there could be misallocation of resources and underutilisation; (ii) Agile and enhanced problem solving: Access to chain partners assist in building robust supply chain partners for troubleshooting and adaptation of innovation to local context. It enhances trust and credibility amongst supply chain stakeholders; (iii) Access to healthcare supply chain partners requires a great deal of understanding cultural and social dynamics rife in Africa. The latter is crucial for adjusting and adapting innovation to healthcare segment nuances; (iv) Overtime, the chain testers should build a learning hub and data necessary for enhancing healthcare knowledge for new products and similar innovations. Thus, reducing trial and error phase, costs and efforts for future innovations. The learning curve creates the depth of knowledge and sustainability of intellectual capital; (v) Regulatory and legal compliance are strategic measures that require both technical and contractual integration.

6.6 Conclusions

Implementing semi-structured interviews, the study examined the benefits, technical structure, impact, and opportunities and challenges of Healthguider. The findings of the study highlight that the Healthguider innovation provides several benefits and its technical structure is good, has a significant impact in the healthcare and is exposed to numerous opportunities and challenges. The study findings inform policymakers, healthcare providers and technologists that Africa does not lack innovation but rather faces challenges in overcoming market access barriers. Even though the study has produced interesting results, it can be extended by interviewing the adopters of the Healthguider innovation.

References

Adler-Milstein J, Bates DW (2010) Paperless healthcare: Progress and challenges of an IT-enabled healthcare system. Bus Horiz 53(2):119–130

Afzal F, Ahmad AA, Ali QA, Joshi S, Mehra S (2021) Fulfilling the need of hour: systematic review of challenges associated with electronic medical record (EMR) implementation-SBEA model. Vidyabharati Int Interdiscipl Res J 13(8):649–662

Al-Assaf K, Alzahmi W, Alshaikh R, Bahroun Z, Ahmed V (2024) The relative importance of key factors for integrating Enterprise resource planning (ERP) systems and performance management practices in the UAE healthcare sector. Big Data Cogn Comput 8(9):122. https://doi.org/10.3390/bdcc8090122

Almajali DA, Masa'deh R, Tarhini A (2016) Antecedents of ERP systems implementation success: a study on Jordanian healthcare sector. J Enterp Inf Manag 29(4):549–565. https://doi.org/10.1108/JEIM-03-2015-0024

Alsanad IS, Aldarbi SA, Aljohani MA, Alhejaili MAM, Aldhahri AM, Alarfi MDM (2023) Data security challenges in medical records: a comparative analysis of digital and paper systems. Int J Health Sci 7(S1):3813–3828. https://doi.org/10.53730/ijhs.v7nS1.15402

Atherton H, Eccles A, Poltawski L, Dale J, Campbell J, Abel G (2024) Investigating patient use and experience of online appointment booking in primary care: mixed methods study. J Med Internet Res 26:e51931

Campbell S, Greenwood M, Prior S, Shearer T, Walkem K, Young S, Bywaters D, Walker K (2020) Purposive sampling: complex or simple? Research case examples. J Res Nurs 25(8):652–661. https://doi.org/10.1177/1744987120927206

Chiarini A, Vagnoni E, Chiarini L (2018) ERP implementation in public healthcare, achievable benefits and encountered criticalities-an investigation from Italy. Int J Serv Oper Manag 29(1):1–17

Dezhar S (2012) Strategic and tactical factors for successful ERP projects: insights from an Asian country. Manag Res Rev 35(11):1070–1087

Feldacker C, Mugwanya R, Irongo D, Kathumba D, Chiwoko J, Kitsao E, Sippell K, Wasunna B, Jonas K, Samala B, Mwakanema D (2023) A community-based, Mobile electronic medical record system app for high-quality, integrated antiretroviral therapy in Lilongwe, Malawi: design process and pilot implementation. JMIR Form Res 7(1):e48671

Galletta A (2012) Mastering the semi-structured interview and beyond: from research design to analysis and publication. New York University Press, New York

Garcia G, Crenner C (2022) Comparing international experiences with electronic health records among emergency medicine physicians in the United States and Norway: semistructured interview study. JMIR Hum Factors 9(1):e28762

Garg P, Agarwal D (2014) Critical success factors for ERP implementation in a Fortis hospital: an empirical investigation. J Enterp Inf Manag 27(4):402–423

Hashemi G, Wickenden M, Bright T, Kuper H (2020) Barriers to accessing primary healthcare services for people with disabilities in low and middle-income countries, a meta-synthesis of qualitative studies. Disabil Rehabil 44(8):1207–1220. https://doi.org/10.1080/09638288.2020.1817984

Hawe N, Seaton CL, Corman K, Burton L, Rush KL (2023) 'There'sa lot less time on small talk': rural patient perspectives on shifting to technology-enabled healthcare in Canada during COVID-19. SSM Health Syst 1:100002

Hu Q, Schwarz LB (2011) Controversial role of GPOs in healthcare-product supply chains. Prod Oper Manag 20(1):1–15

Huang S, Chang I, Li S, Lin M (2004) Assessing risk in ERP projects: identify and prioritize the factors. Ind Manag Data Syst 104(8):681–688. https://doi.org/10.1108/02635570410561672

Javaid, M., Haleem, A., Singh, R. P., & Suman, R. (2023). Towards insighting cybersecurity for healthcare domains: A comprehensive review of recent practices and trends. Cyber Secur Appl 1:100016

Jimma BL, Enyew DB (2022) Barriers to the acceptance of electronic medical records from the perspective of physicians and nurses: a scoping review. Inf Med Unlock 31:100991

Kulkarni ND, Director EAS, Bansal S (2023) Manager, EAS defining data migration strategies for seamless ERP transformation case study. J Econ Manag Res 4(3):1–7

Lee Mendoza R (2019) Incentives and disincentives to drug innovation: evidence from recent literature. J Med Econ 22(8):713–721

Lu N, Samuels ME, Kletke PR, Whitler ET (2010) Rural-urban differences in health insurance coverage and patterns among working-age adults in Kentucky. J Rural Health 26(2):129–138

Maier M (2017) Content analysis: advantages and disadvantages. In: The SAGE encyclopedia of communication research methods, vol 4. SAGE, pp 240–242. https://doi.org/10.4135/9781483381411

Mavuso N, Jere N, Lwanga A, Makalima C (2023) An integrated web based patient records application for sustainable healthcare services. In: 2023 2nd Zimbabwe conference of information and communication technologies (ZCICT). IEEE, pp 1–8

Mladenova T (2020, October) Open-source ERP systems: an overview. In: 2020 international conference automatics and informatics (ICAI). IEEE, pp 1–6

Murphy CJ, Narala V, Katiki A, Martinez MS, Cerasale MT, Nguyen KT (2024) Bundled de-implementation of recurring hospital orders with a novel electronic medical record order set. BMJ Open Qual 13(4):e002889. https://doi.org/10.1136/bmjoq-2024-002889

Norris M, Klabbers G, Pembe AB, Hanson C, Baker U, Aung K, Mmweteni M, Mfaume RS, Beňová L (2022) A growing disadvantage of being born in an urban area? Analysing urban–rural disparities in neonatal mortality in 21 African countries with a focus on Tanzania. BMJ Glob Health 7(1):e007544

Pariyar A, Swapna HR, Kaur N (2023) Enhancing the healthcare system through Mobile-based doctor's appointment booking application. Ann For Res 66(1):3143–3150

Patton MQ (2002) Qualitative research & evaluation methods, 3rd edn. Sage, Thousand Oaks, CA

Peprah P, Budu HI, Agyemang-Duah W, Abalo EM, Gyimah AA (2020) Why does inaccessibility widely exist in healthcare in Ghana? Understanding the reasons from past to present. J Public Health 28:1–10

Phares J, Dobrzykowski DD, Prohofsky J (2021) How policy is shaping the macro healthcare delivery supply chain: the emergence of a new tier of retail medical clinics. Bus Horiz 64(3):333–345

Ramutumbu NJ, Ramathuba DU, Maputle MS (2023) Barriers to accessing oncology services for effective cancer care in the public health institutions in Limpopo Province, South Africa: a qualitative study. Nurs Rep 13(3):956–968

Schauffel N, Schmidt I, Peiffer H, Ellwart T (2021) Self-concept related to information and communication technology: scale development and validation. Comput Hum Behav Rep 4:100149

Shehab EM, Sharp MW, Supramaniam L, Spedding TA (2004) Enterprise resource planning: an integrative review. Bus Process Manag J 10(4):359–386

Shema-Shiratzky S, Beer Y, Mor A, Elbaz A (2022) Smartphone-based inertial sensors technology–validation of a new application to measure spatiotemporal gait metrics. Gait Posture 93:102–106

Tanaka Y, Masukawa K, Sakuramoto H, Kato A, Ishigami Y, Tatsuno J, Ito K, Kizawa Y, Miyashita M (2024) Development of quality indicators for palliative care in intensive care units and pilot testing them via electronic medical record review. J Intensive Care 12(1). https://doi.org/10.1186/s40560-023-00713-z

Tsai CH, Eghdam A, Davoody N, Wright G, Flowerday S, Koch S (2020) Effects of electronic health record implementation and barriers to adoption and use: a scoping review and qualitative analysis of the content. Life 10(12):327

Velcu O (2010) Strategic alignment of ERP implementation stages: an empirical investigation. Inf Manag 47(3):158–166

Wieder B, Booth P, Matolcsy ZP, Ossimitz M (2006) The impact of ERP systems on firm and business process performance. J Enterp Inf Manag 19(1):13–29. https://doi.org/10.1108/17410390610636850

Yenet A, Nibret G, Tegegne BA (2023) Challenges to the availability and affordability of essential medicines in African countries: a scoping review. ClinicoEcon Outcomes Res 15:443–458. https://doi.org/10.2147/CEOR.S413546

Zhang M, Zhang C, Sun Q, Cai Q, Yang H, Zhang Y (2014) Questionnaire survey about use of an online appointment booking system in one large tertiary public hospital outpatient service center in China. BMC Med Inform Decis Mak 14:1–11

Frank Ranganai Matenda is a Postdoctoral Research Fellow in the Department of Operations Management at the University of South Africa, Pretoria, South Africa. His research interests are related to credit risk, asset pricing, green finance, corporate performance and risk management, investments, corporate finance, financial markets, and small business economics. He is the Coordinator for the International Conference on Business Resilience, Continuity and Regeneration and an Editorial Board Member for the Journal of Inclusive and Innovative Practices.

Marcia Mkansi is the College Head of Research, Post-graduate Studies, Innovation, and Commercialisation, a Professor of Operations and Supply Chain Management and the former Head of the Department of Operations Management at the College of Economic & Management Sciences, University of South Africa. She serves as a non-executive director for Hellmann Worldwide Logistics, and an advisory board member of the Africa Resource Centre (ARC), a Bill and Melinda Gates Foundation (BMGF)-funded non-governmental organization, set up to be a resource to the public health sector in African governments. Her university-industry alliances include, but are not limited to, Kuehne Foundation, The Innovation Hub, and SAP skills Africa. She is a nominee for the Top Women Standard Bank and UN women projects, and a finalist under the research, innovation, and creative economy category of the National Science and Technology Forum (NSTF)—South32 awards.

Phumeza Saliwe is a Lecturer in Operations Management at the University of South Africa (UNISA). She is also a PhD candidate in Human Resources Management at the University of South Africa and holds an MCom degree in Business Management. Her research interests cover organisational commitment, ethical leadership, conflict management styles, and career guidance. She is also registered as an HR Associate with the South African Board for People Practices (SABPP).

Part IV
Impact of Digital Supply Chain Transformation on Healthcare Delivery

Chapter 7
Leveraging Mobile Health Interventions to Improve Health Literacy and Combat Non-Communicable Diseases in Sub-Saharan Africa

Stephen Ogweno, Harrison Roger, George William Kajjumba, and Dorcus Bateefu Nakiganda

7.1 Introduction

Non-communicable diseases (NCDs), such as cardiovascular diseases, diabetes, and obesity present a challenge—in an estimated 40·five million (71%) of the 56·nine million worldwide deaths were from NCDs (Anyanwu et al. 2024; Bennett et al. 2018). The burden is disproportionately felt in low- and middle-income countries, including Sub-Saharan Africa (SSA) (Gouda et al. 2019). In this region, NCDs are responsible for 37% of deaths, a figure projected to rise as populations age and urbanize (Anyanwu et al. 2024). SSA faces unique challenges in addressing NCDs due to a combination of insufficient healthcare infrastructure, limited healthcare literacy, and a fragmented healthcare supply chain (Heine et al. 2021; Moner-Girona et al. 2021). These factors exacerbate the challenges in managing NCDs, leaving millions without timely diagnosis, treatment, or preventive care.

S. Ogweno (✉)
Faculty of Biology Medicine and Health, the University of Manchester, Manchester, UK

Stowelink Foundation - Research Division, Nairobi, Kenya
e-mail: founder@stowelink.com

H. Roger
Faculty of Biology Medicine and Health, the University of Manchester, Manchester, UK
e-mail: Roger.Harrison@manchester.ac.uk

G. W. Kajjumba
Department of Civil and Environmental Engineering, University of Nevada, Las Vegas, NV, USA

D. B. Nakiganda
Department of Accounting & Finance, Makerere University, Kampala, Uganda

T. Akenroye et al. (eds.), *Digitalizing Health Care Supply Chains in Africa*, Springer Series in Supply Chain Management 28,
https://doi.org/10.1007/978-3-032-20501-8_7

The healthcare supply chain in SSA plays a critical role in the availability and accessibility of essential resources for NCD prevention and management (Nagitta et al. 2021a; Nagitta and Mkansi 2019). Weaknesses in supply chain infrastructure, including poor road networks, inconsistent medication supplies, and inadequate cold chain systems, have significantly hindered efforts to tackle NCDs. For example, 40% of health facilities in SSA report regular stockouts of essential medications for conditions like diabetes and hypertension, leading to preventable complications and deaths (Nagitta et al. 2021b). Beyond physical supply chain challenges, there is a significant gap in intellectual health capital—specifically, the population's ability to understand and use health information effectively, which is essential for managing chronic diseases.

Health literacy is a cornerstone of health promotion and a critical determinant of health outcomes. It enables individuals to understand disease risks, adhere to treatment regimens, and make informed health decisions. However, in SSA, where literacy levels vary widely, the lack of targeted health education campaigns further deepens health inequities. Less than 50% of adults in the region are estimated to have sufficient health literacy to manage their health effectively (Odusina et al. 2021). Cultural barriers, language diversity, and low general literacy further compound the challenge (Zickafoose et al. 2024). Improving health literacy is particularly urgent for managing NCDs, as these diseases often require long-term lifestyle changes and self-management skills, which are difficult to implement without adequate knowledge.

Mobile health (mHealth) has emerged as a transformative tool for addressing healthcare challenges, including supply chain inefficiencies and low health literacy (Ng et al. 2021). mHealth encompasses a wide range of interventions, from SMS reminders for medication adherence to mobile apps providing education about NCDs. The integration of mHealth into the healthcare supply chain offers additional benefits by improving communication, reducing logistical bottlenecks, and increasing the reach of health promotion campaigns. Digital platforms can track medication stock levels in real-time, ensure timely delivery of critical supplies, and disseminate health education materials across diverse populations.

Despite its potential, mHealth adoption in SSA faces several challenges, including limited internet connectivity, varying digital literacy levels, and inconsistent policy support across countries. Furthermore, the majority of existing mHealth interventions have been limited to pilot studies or single-country initiatives, leaving significant research gaps in understanding the scalability and sustainability of cross-country interventions. Research also predominantly focuses on SMS-based communication, neglecting other platforms that could potentially offer greater engagement and effectiveness.

This study aims to fill these gaps by evaluating the feasibility and effectiveness of cross-country mHealth interventions for improving health literacy and strengthening the healthcare supply chain in SSA. By analyzing data from the NCD365 project, it seeks to provide actionable insights into platform-specific strategies, regional differences, and the interplay between health literacy and supply chain efficiency. The findings aim to inform policy and practice, ensuring that mHealth is effectively integrated into efforts to combat NCDs and improve health outcomes in the region.

7.2 Literature and Hypotheses

Hypothesis 1: Exposure to mHealth interventions aimed at health promotion can lead to an increase in individuals' health literacy levels in Sub-Saharan Africa

Exposure to information through targeted interventions has consistently been shown to lead to significant increases in knowledge, awareness, and behavioral changes across various domains (Al-Dmour et al. 2022; Witzling et al. 2015). For instance, studies on public health campaigns have demonstrated how repeated exposure to anti-smoking messages significantly increased awareness about smoking-related risks, leading to a decline in smoking prevalence (Finney Rutten et al. 2009; Upadhyay et al. 2019). Similarly, educational campaigns on HIV prevention, delivered through community-based programs and digital platforms, have successfully increased condom use and reduced risky behaviors (Muessig et al. 2015; Purdy 2011).

Applying these principles to Sub-Saharan Africa, where health literacy levels are generally low, mHealth interventions hold significant promise. By delivering consistent, accessible, and culturally relevant content, these interventions can bridge knowledge gaps and empower individuals to make informed health decisions. The NCD365 project's year-long engagement is expected to lead users to measurable improvements in literacy about NCD prevention and management, particularly among populations with prior limited exposure to health information.

Hypothesis 2: There is a significant difference in the effectiveness of different online communication channels, such as social media platforms and websites, for mHealth interventions in promoting health in Sub-Saharan Africa

Effective communication channels are pivotal to the success of any project, particularly those focused on information dissemination and behavior change. Different communication strategies can yield varying outcomes depending on the target audience, content, and platform used. For instance, health promotion campaigns conducted through television broadcasts have been shown to reach broader but less interactive audiences compared to community-based workshops, which tend to foster deeper engagement and understanding (Beck 2003; Burzyńska et al. 2015; Chew and Palmer 2005). Similarly, during vaccination campaigns, the use of SMS reminders significantly improved appointment adherence (Chew and Palmer 2005; Domek et al. 2016; Eze et al. 2021). While face-to-face education sessions led to better comprehension of vaccine safety (Johri et al. 2020).

In the digital realm, the choice of online communication channels can greatly influence the reach and effectiveness of health promotion efforts. Social media platforms, in particular, have demonstrated diverse impacts based on their unique functionalities and user demographics (Ghahramani et al. 2022; Korda and Itani 2011). For example, Instagram's visual appeal has been successful in engaging younger audiences with health promotion messages (Huang and Su 2018), while LinkedIn's professional focus makes it more suitable for reaching healthcare workers and policymakers (Smith and Watkins 2020). WhatsApp, on the other hand, has proven effective for personalized communication and group interactions.

This study will leverage a range of online platforms, including WhatsApp, Twitter (now X), Facebook, Instagram, LinkedIn, and dedicated websites, to explore their effectiveness in promoting health literacy and awareness in Sub-Saharan Africa. These platforms are expected to yield significant outreach by catering to diverse audience needs and preferences. For instance, WhatsApp's group messaging features will facilitate community discussions, while Twitter's (X) real-time updates can provide rapid information dissemination. Facebook and Instagram will target general audiences through multimedia storytelling, and LinkedIn will focus on engaging professionals and stakeholders in the healthcare sector. Websites will serve as repositories of detailed health information, offering users comprehensive resources at their convenience.

By analyzing the outcomes across these platforms, this study aims to identify the most effective strategies for maximizing engagement and information retention, ultimately contributing to the success of mHealth interventions in Sub-Saharan Africa. For example, Facebook's visual storytelling capabilities may be leveraged for awareness campaigns, while websites can serve as repositories for detailed health information. Thus, it is hypothesized that the effectiveness of mHealth interventions will vary depending on the social media platform used, as each platform caters to different audience needs and engagement styles.

7.3 Methodology

The study was conducted in five Sub-Saharan African countries: Nigeria, Kenya, Uganda, Cameroon, and Zimbabwe. These countries were selected to represent the broad cultural diversity of the region. Each participating country was represented by an organization involved in the NCD365 program. The partner organizations from each country are listed in Table 7.1.

From each country, 80 participants were recruited at the start of the project, bringing the total to 400 participants. The selection was carried out using a purposive sampling technique to ensure the inclusion of individuals with varying degrees of prior exposure to NCD information. This approach was chosen to target individuals most likely to benefit from the intervention and provide a comprehensive assessment of its impact.

The project spanned 1 year, during which participants received NCD-related information tailored to their local contexts. Each month, as detailed in Table 7.1, participants were exposed to a specific focus area, including topics such as cancer prevention, drug use, obesity, and general health promotion strategies. The information was disseminated via various social media platforms, including WhatsApp, Facebook, Twitter (X), Instagram, LinkedIn, and dedicated websites.

Table 7.1 Participating countries, organizations, and NCDs monthly thematic focus

Participating countries and organizations	Country	Participating organizations
	Nigeria	Food and Genes Initiative
	Kenya	Stowelink Foundation
	Uganda	Berna Acargo Foundation
	Cameroon	Reconciliation and Development National[π]
	Zimbabwe	Health Access Initiative[∞]
NCD information	Month	Thematic focus
	January	Introduction to NCDS—Basics
	February	Cancer
	March	Drugs and substance abuse and NCDS
	April	NCDS and COVID 19 link
	May	Cardiovascular diseases
	June	Diabetes
	July	Mental health (depression and anxiety)
	August	Chronic kidney diseases
	September	Sickle cell disease
	October	Childhood obesity
	November	Less talked about NCDs
	December	NCDs prevention tips

[∞]Community-based organization
[π]Civil society organization

After 1 year, an assessment was conducted to evaluate the participants' health literacy levels and the effectiveness of information dissemination across the different platforms. The evaluation utilized both quantitative surveys and qualitative feedback mechanisms. Quantitative methods measured changes in knowledge related to NCDs, while qualitative data provided insights into participant experiences and preferences for specific communication channels.

The results of the assessment were analyzed to determine the relationship between mHealth interventions and improvements in health literacy, as well as to identify the most effective platforms for information dissemination in promoting health literacy in Sub-Saharan Africa.

7.4 Findings

7.4.1 Demographic Characteristics

Out of the 400 respondents who started the program, 349 completed it and responded to the questionnaires after 1 year. Of these, 336 provided complete responses, while 13 respondents did not complete the questionnaires, resulting in their data being excluded from the analysis. This represents a response rate of 84%, which provides

Table 7.2 Demographic characteristics of the study population (n = 336)

Variable	Category	n	Percentage (%)	Variable	Category	n	Percentage (%)
Age	18–24	159	46.1	Country	Cameroon	63	18.8
	25–34	127	37.8		Kenya	71	21.1
	35–44	25	7.4		Nigeria	69	20.5
	45–54	25	7.4		Uganda	70	20.8
Sex at birth	Female	179	53.3		Zimbabwe	63	18.8
	Male	156	46.4	Platform	WhatsApp	197	58.6
	Others	1	0.3		Twitter	70	20.8
Settlement	Rural	21	6.3		Facebook	23	6.8
	Semi-urban	114	33.9		Instagram	20	5.9
	Urban	201	59.8		Websites	18	5.4
Education	Postgraduate	77	22.9		LinkedIn	8	2.4
	Undergraduate	207	61.6				
	Secondary	51	15.2				
	Primary	1	0.3				

a sufficiently large and representative dataset to conduct meaningful analyses and draw valid conclusions. Table 7.2 summarizes key demographic characteristics of the participants. Among the respondents, 52% were female and 48% male, reflecting a near-gender balance. Age groups were distributed as follows: 18–24 years (46%), 25–34 years (38%), and above 35 years (14%). Educational levels showed that 99% of participants had secondary-level education or higher. Participants engaged with different social media platforms throughout the intervention. WhatsApp was the most used platform (59%), followed by Twitter/X (21%), Facebook (7%), and Instagram and LinkedIn (8% combined). These usage patterns highlight the importance of tailoring mHealth interventions to leverage platforms with higher engagement rates. These demographics and platform engagement patterns suggest a diverse and representative sample, providing valuable insights into how mHealth interventions can address health literacy needs across varied populations.

7.4.2 mHealth Exposure and Literacy Levels

NCDs General Knowledge Changes

After exposing the participants to mHealth material for 1 year, they were asked questions related to their understanding of NCDs. Table 7.3 summarizes the percentage of participants who answered the questions correctly across different topic areas. The survey results revealed varying levels of knowledge and understanding among participants regarding NCDs and their risk factors. Questions assessing general knowledge about NCDs, such as G1 ("What statement best describes a

Table 7.3 Health literacy assessment scores after 1 year of exposure to mHealth materials

	Question	Score (%)*
G1	What statement best describes a non-communicable disease	93.8
G2	Which of the following is not a non-communicable disease	69.0
G3	Non-communicable diseases are the leading killer diseases globally	83.6
G4	Click all the right ones. Non-communicable diseases risk factors include:	52.9
G5	Select the correct statement: People with non-communicable diseases	90.5
G6	Can smoking tobacco affect your health?	97.6
G6A	If yes, can you select all the diseases that could be caused by the habit?	48.2
G6B	If smoking causes cancer, which cancers are caused by smoking?	40.2
G7	Can tobacco chewing affect your health?	87.8
G7A	If yes, can you name the diseases that could be caused by tobacco chewing?	31.1
G7B	If tobacco chewing causes cancer, check all cancers are caused by the habit?	37.9
G8	Can drinking alcohol affect your health?	97.0
G8A	If yes, can you name the diseases that could be caused by drinking alcohol?	36.0
P1	How much do you know about high blood pressure?	98.5
P1A	If you know something about high blood pressure, is it important to have blood pressure checked?	97.9
P1B	If yes, how often blood pressure should be checked?	86.6
P2	How much do you know about heart attack?	97.3
P2A	If you know something about heart attack, do you agree that it can be prevented?	83.0
P3	How much do you know about stroke?	95.8
P3A	If you know something about stroke, do you agree that people with high blood pressure are more likely to have a stroke?	86.3
P4	How much do you know about diabetes?	99.4
P4A	If you know something about diabetes, what can an individual do to reduce the chance of getting the disease?	58.5
P5	How much do you know about long-term lung diseases?	87.5
P5A	Tick all appropriate. How many lung diseases do you know of?	38.0
P5B	If you know something about long-term lung diseases, what can an individual do to reduce the chance of getting the disease?	96.4
P6	How much do you know about mental health?	96.4
P6A	Tick all appropriate, how many mental health conditions do you know of?	57.2
P6B	If you know something about mental health, what can an individual do to reduce the chance of getting the disease?	39.9

*Participants who answered the questions correctly

non-communicable disease?") and G3 ("Non-communicable diseases are the leading killer diseases globally"), received relatively high percentages of correct responses (93.8% and 83.6%, respectively). This indicates a strong awareness among participants about the nature and global impact of NCDs.

However, when it came to identifying specific diseases caused by risk factors, such as smoking, tobacco chewing, and alcohol consumption, the percentages of correct responses were comparatively lower. For instance, G6A ("If yes, can you select all the diseases that could be caused by smoking?") and G6B ("If smoking causes cancer, which cancers are caused by smoking?") had response rates of 48.2% and 40.2%, respectively, indicating a knowledge gap in understanding the precise health risks associated with smoking. Similarly, G7A ("If yes, can you name the diseases that could be caused by tobacco chewing?") and G7B ("If tobacco chewing causes cancer, check all cancers that are caused by the habit") had response rates of 31.1% and 37.9%, respectively.

Questions related to preventive measures and understanding the link between NCDs and other health conditions also received varying levels of correct responses. For example, P4 ("How much do you know about diabetes?") showed a high percentage of correct responses (99.4%), indicating a relatively strong understanding of this particular NCD. Conversely, P5A ("Tick all appropriate. How many lung diseases do you know of?") had a lower response rate of 38%, suggesting a need for more comprehensive knowledge about different types of long-term lung diseases.

These findings highlight both the strengths and areas for improvement in the mHealth intervention's educational impact. High awareness of general NCD concepts and diabetes prevention suggests effective content delivery in those areas, whereas lower knowledge on the risks of smoking, tobacco chewing, and lung diseases indicates the need for more targeted information in future interventions.

Literacy Level Improvements and Education Status

The results of the adjusted literacy rates based on the highest education level are presented in Table 7.4. The table shows the percentage of individuals within each education level category and their corresponding adjusted literacy rates. Among individuals with a primary school education, the adjusted literacy rate was 0.23%. For individuals with secondary school education, the adjusted literacy rate increased to 11.80%. The highest adjusted literacy rate was observed among individuals with an undergraduate education, reaching 47.68%. Those with postgraduate education also demonstrated a relatively high adjusted literacy rate of 17.86%. Overall, when considering all education levels together, the adjusted literacy rate was 77.57%.

The significant differences in adjusted literacy rates by education level can be attributed to varying access to health information and cognitive abilities associated with formal education. Higher education levels likely provided participants with better skills for understanding and applying health-related knowledge, enabling

Table 7.4 Adjusted rate for literacy based on education level

Education level	Adjusted literacy rate
Primary school	0.23%
Secondary school	11.80%
Undergraduate	47.68%
Postgraduate	17.86%
Total	77.57%

Table 7.5 Relationship between health literacy and exposure duration

	Type III sum of squares	df	Mean square	F	Sig.
Corrected model	2452.378[a]	3	817.459	8.033	0.000
Intercept	1887428.93	1	1,887,429	18,546	0.000
Duration	2452.38	3	817.459	8.033	0.000
Error	33787.05	332	101.768		
Total	2061218.79	336			
Corrected total	36239.42	335			

df, Degrees of freedom; *F*, Represents the ratio of the variance between groups to the variance within groups
[a]$R^2 = 0.068$

them to make informed decisions about NCD prevention and management (Bay et al. 2017; Yenit et al. 2023). Additionally, individuals with undergraduate and postgraduate education may have had prior exposure to relevant information, which contributed to their higher literacy rates.

Hypothesis 1: Exposure to mHealth Interventions Increase Health Literacy Levels

Based on the ANOVA results (Table 7.5), the analysis indicates a significant relationship between exposure to mHealth interventions aimed at health promotion (represented by the variable "Duration") and individuals' health literacy levels in Sub-Saharan Africa. The effect size, as indicated by the R^2 value of 0.068, suggests that the exposure to mHealth interventions explains approximately 6.8% of the variance in literacy levels. While this effect size is relatively small, it is still statistically significant, underscoring the importance of mHealth interventions as a factor in improving health literacy. However, this also highlights the need to explore additional contributing factors that could enhance literacy levels further. Factors such as socio-economic status, internet accessibility, baseline literacy levels, and cultural influences may play crucial roles in determining the effectiveness of health interventions.

Previous studies have similarly demonstrated that while mHealth interventions can significantly improve health literacy, their impact is often mediated by external factors. For instance, research by Atun et al. (2015) found that individuals with better socio-economic resources were more likely to benefit from digital health initiatives, emphasizing the need for interventions tailored to diverse population needs. Similarly, Noar (2006) highlighted that the frequency and quality of content exposure are critical in determining the success of health campaigns. In addition, a study by Gonzalez et al. (2021) showed that culturally sensitive content delivery significantly enhanced engagement and understanding among diverse communities, reinforcing the importance of localized strategies in digital health interventions. Furthermore, Wei et al. (2020) noted that the integration of interactive features, such as quizzes and feedback mechanisms in mobile applications, increased retention of health information and motivated behavioral changes in underserved populations. These examples underscore the multifaceted nature of health literacy improvement and the importance of leveraging a combination of content quality, delivery mechanisms, and user-centered design to maximize the effectiveness of mHealth interventions.

In summary, the findings provide robust evidence supporting the hypothesis that mHealth interventions positively influence health literacy levels in Sub-Saharan Africa. To maximize their impact, future studies should aim to identify and integrate complementary strategies addressing other potential determinants of health literacy.

7.4.3 Media Platform Usage

Literacy Levels Per Platform

The majority of participants (197 out of 336, approximately 59%) used WhatsApp, followed by Twitter with 70 participants (approximately 21%). The remaining platforms had much lower representation, with Facebook, Instagram, websites, and LinkedIn accounting for 7%, 6%, 5%, and 2% participants, respectively (Table 7.6). These usage patterns align with existing literature, which highlights WhatsApp as a widely used communication platform in Sub-Saharan Africa due to its accessibility, low data consumption, and group messaging features (Kituyi 2017). Twitter's (X) significant presence can be attributed to its ability to provide real-time updates and facilitate discussions, which makes it appealing for health communication efforts. Platforms like Facebook, while globally popular, showed a smaller footprint in Sub-Saharan Africa, likely due to banning of Facebook in some African countries. Websites and LinkedIn had the lowest number of participants, reflecting their limited reach in communities where internet access and professional networking are less prevalent.

Table 7.6 Platform usage and adjusted literacy levels after 1 year

Platform	n	Mean literacy level	Adjusted literacy levels (%)
WhatsApp	197	78%	45.12
Twitter	70	77%	16.01
Facebook	23	75%	5.13
Instagram	20	80%	4.76
Websites	18	81%	3.86
LinkedIn	8	80%	1.90

Adjusted Literacy Levels per Platform

The adjusted literacy levels provide a nuanced view of the effectiveness of each platform in promoting health literacy. Table 7.6 summarizes the adjusted literacy levels per platform. Despite being the most widely used platform, WhatsApp's adjusted literacy level was the highest among all platforms. This can be attributed to its ability to deliver personalized and interactive content, such as videos, infographics, and group discussions, which enhance understanding and retention of health information (Fernández-robin et al. 2019; Puspita and Dhimas Herdhianta 2021). Twitter's moderate adjusted literacy level suggests that while it is effective for disseminating quick updates and engaging in conversations, it may not provide the depth of information needed for significant literacy improvements. The platform's character limit and fast-paced nature could limit comprehensive educational efforts. Websites had the highest mean literacy level (81%), suggesting they are a valuable resource for those who access them. However, their adjusted literacy level was lower, likely due to limited accessibility and navigation challenges for participants with low digital literacy (Soleimani et al. 2024). The lowest adjusted literacy level was observed on LinkedIn, which is not surprising given its focus on professional networking rather than health education. Its small user base among the participants further limits its impact.

Hypothesis 2: Platform Effectiveness and Literacy Levels

The Kruskal-Wallis test was conducted to investigate whether there were significant differences in information exposure among different platforms (Table 7.7). This non-parametric test was chosen because it does not assume normality and is well-suited for comparing more than two independent groups with ordinal or non-normal data, which aligns with the characteristics of literacy level distributions across platforms (McKight and Najab 2010). The test results indicate no statistically significant differences in information exposure across the platforms ($p = 0.765$). This suggests that while platforms varied in terms of adjusted literacy levels (as shown in the previous table), the usage of a given platform did not significantly impact overall information intake. For instance, WhatsApp had the highest adjusted literacy level (45.12%), while LinkedIn had the lowest (1.90%), yet these differences were not sufficient to yield statistically significant variation in the Kruskal-Wallis test.

This finding aligns with previous literature emphasizing that content quality, frequency, and user engagement are critical determinants of health literacy outcomes,

Table 7.7 Kruskal-Wallis test for literacy level among different platforms

Statistic	Value
Chi-Square	41.582
Degrees of freedom	49
Asymptotic significance	0.765

regardless of the platform used (Kituyi 2017). Platforms like WhatsApp may excel in user accessibility and content delivery, but their comparative advantage may diminish when broader metrics of exposure are considered. Additionally, the lack of significant differences suggests that the choice of platform might not inherently determine the effectiveness of mHealth interventions, but rather how the platform is utilized. For example, culturally tailored content and interactive features have been shown to enhance engagement and comprehension (Gonzalez et al. 2021; Wei et al. 2020). These insights highlight the importance of optimizing content delivery across all platforms to achieve consistent health literacy improvements.

7.5 Implications and Recommendations

7.5.1 Implications

Impact of mHealth on Health Literacy

The study provides strong evidence supporting the hypothesis that exposure to mHealth interventions can significantly improve health literacy levels in Sub-Saharan Africa. Although the effect size ($R^2 = 0.068$) indicates that mHealth interventions explain only a small portion of the variance in health literacy levels, this underscores their relevance in addressing the region's health literacy challenges. However, the findings suggest that mHealth alone cannot fully address the gaps, emphasizing the need to integrate complementary strategies to maximize its impact. This demonstrates that targeted, accessible, and culturally tailored mHealth content is vital in empowering individuals with the knowledge and skills needed for NCD prevention and management. The intervention's success in improving understanding of NCD basics and diabetes prevention suggests that mHealth can effectively disseminate key health messages, particularly when addressing widely understood or relatable conditions.

Platform Effectiveness

The Kruskal-Wallis test showed no statistically significant differences in the effectiveness of various platforms for disseminating mHealth content, suggesting that the choice of platform does not inherently determine the success of health literacy campaigns. This finding highlights that the quality and delivery of content, rather than the platform itself, are the primary drivers of mHealth intervention success. Platforms like WhatsApp and Twitter (X), while popular, must be leveraged with targeted, engaging, and user-friendly content to maximize their potential.

Role of Education in Health Literacy

The analysis showed a significant correlation between higher education levels and improved health literacy. Participants with undergraduate or postgraduate education had markedly higher adjusted literacy rates, emphasizing the importance of formal education in enhancing individuals' ability to process and utilize health information. This suggests that mHealth interventions need to incorporate simplified and inclusive content that caters to populations with lower levels of formal education.

Integration with Supply Chain Systems

mHealth can play a pivotal role in integrating supply chain systems by providing real-time updates on NCDs and ensuring timely delivery of essential medicines and resources. This integration could also improve trust in healthcare systems, as individuals are more likely to engage with mHealth platforms that offer practical solutions to immediate healthcare needs.

7.5.2 Recommendations

While the choice of platform did not significantly affect health literacy outcomes, tailoring content to the strengths of each platform is essential. For instance: Use WhatsApp for group discussions, direct messaging, and video-based health education. Leverage Twitter (X) for real-time updates and quick health tips. Engage professionals through LinkedIn for knowledge sharing and training.

Integrating mHealth platforms with healthcare supply chains can improve access to critical resources for NCD prevention and management. For instance: mHealth platforms can track stock levels of essential medications and notify users about availability at nearby healthcare centers.

The study revealed knowledge gaps in lesser-discussed NCDs such as the risks of tobacco chewing and long-term lung diseases. Future mHealth interventions should prioritize these areas by creating campaigns that address these conditions in greater depth.

References

Al-Dmour H, Masa'deh R, Salman A, Al-Dmour R, Abuhashesh M (2022) The role of mass media interventions on promoting public health knowledge and behavioral social change against COVID-19 pandemic in Jordan. SAGE Open 12(1). https://doi.org/10.1177/21582440221082125

Anyanwu C, Bikomeye JC, Beyer KMM (2024) The impact of environmental conditions on non-communicable diseases in sub-Saharan Africa: a scoping review of epidemiologic evidence. J Glob Health 14:04003. https://doi.org/10.7189/JOGH.14.04003

Atun R, Odorico L, De Andrade M, Almeida G, Cotlear D, Dmytraczenko T, Frenz P, Garcia P (2015) Universal health coverage in Latin America 1 health-system reform and universal health coverage. Lancet 385:1230–1247. https://doi.org/10.1016/S0140-6736(14)61646-9

Bay JL, Hipkins R, Siddiqi K, Huque R, Dixon R, Shirley D, Tairea K, Yaqona D, Mason-Jones A, Vickers MH (2017) School-based primary NCD risk reduction: education and public health perspectives. Health Promot Int 32(2):369–379. https://doi.org/10.1093/heapro/daw096

Beck V (2003) Working with daytime and prime-time television shows in the United States to promote health. In: Entertainment-education and social change, 1st edn. Routledge, London, pp 229–246. https://doi.org/10.4324/9781410609595-18

Bennett JE, Stevens GA, Mathers CD, Bonita R, Rehm J, Kruk ME, Riley LM, Dain K, Kengne AP, Chalkidou K, Beagley J, Kishore SP, Chen W, Saxena S, Bettcher DW, Grove JT, Beaglehole R, Ezzati M (2018) NCD countdown 2030: worldwide trends in non-communicable disease mortality and progress towards sustainable development goal target 3.4. Lancet 392(10152):1072–1088. https://doi.org/10.1016/S0140-6736(18)31992-5/ATTACHMENT/23D1B457-1120-4064-B3EF-AAB6481D5F9D/MMC3.PDF

Burzyńska J, Binkowska-Bury M, Januszewicz P (2015) Television as a source of information on health and illness—review of benefits and problems. Progr Health Sci 5(2):174–184

Chew F, Palmer S (2005) Television health promotion in four countries. Nutrition 21(5):634–638. https://doi.org/10.1016/J.NUT.2004.09.022

Domek GJ, Contreras-Roldan IL, O'Leary ST, Bull S, Furniss A, Kempe A, Asturias EJ (2016) SMS text message reminders to improve infant vaccination coverage in Guatemala: a pilot randomized controlled trial. Vaccine 34(21):2437–2443. https://doi.org/10.1016/J.VACCINE.2016.03.065

Eze P, Lawani LO, Acharya Y (2021) Short message service (SMS) reminders for childhood immunisation in low-income and middle-income countries: a systematic review and meta-analysis. BMJ Glob Health 6(7):5035. https://doi.org/10.1136/BMJGH-2021-005035

Fernández-robin C, Yáñez D, Mccoy S (2019) Intention to use WhatsApp. In: Harkut DG (ed) Artificial intelligence—scope and limitations. Intech Open. https://doi.org/10.5772/intechopen.81999

Finney Rutten LJ, Augustson EM, Doran KA, Moser RP, Hesse BW (2009) Health information seeking and media exposure among smokers: a comparison of light and intermittent tobacco users with heavy users. Nicotine Tob Res 11(2):190–196. https://doi.org/10.1093/NTR/NTN019

Ghahramani A, de Courten M, Prokofieva M (2022) The potential of social media in health promotion beyond creating awareness: an integrative review. BMC Public Health 22(1):1–13. https://doi.org/10.1186/S12889-022-14885-0/FIGURES/5

Gonzalez C, Early J, Gordon V, Teresa D, Carolina M (2021) Promoting culturally tailored mHealth: a scoping review of Mobile health interventions in Latinx communities. J Immigr Minor Health 23(5):1065–1077. https://doi.org/10.1007/s10903-021-01209-4

Gouda HN, Charlson F, Sorsdahl K, Ahmadzada S, Ferrari AJ, Erskine H, Leung J, Santamauro D, Lund C, Aminde LN, Mayosi BM, Kengne AP, Harris M, Achoki T, Wiysonge CS, Stein DJ, Whiteford H (2019) Burden of non-communicable diseases in sub-Saharan Africa, 1990–2017: results from the global burden of disease study 2017. Lancet Glob Health 7(10):e1375–e1387. https://doi.org/10.1016/S2214-109X(19)30374-2

Heine M, Lategan F, Erasmus M, Lombaard CM, Mc Carthy N, Olivier J, van Niekerk M, Hanekom S (2021) Health education interventions to promote health literacy in adults with selected non-communicable diseases living in low-to-middle income countries: a systematic review and meta-analysis. J Eval Clin Pract 27(6):1417–1428. https://doi.org/10.1111/JEP.13554

Huang YT, Su SF (2018) Motives for Instagram use and topics of interest among young adults. Future Internet 10(8):77. https://doi.org/10.3390/FI10080077

Johri M, Chandra D, Kone KG, Sylvestre MP, Mathur AK, Harper S, Nandi A (2020) Social and behavior change communication interventions delivered face-to-face and by a mobile phone to strengthen vaccination uptake and improve child health in rural India: randomized pilot study. JMIR Mhealth Uhealth 8(9):e20356. https://doi.org/10.2196/20356

Kituyi GM (2017) Social media and health behaviour in sub Saharan Africa [ICT University]. https://www.ritsumei.ac.jp/ir/isaru/assets/file/raris/raris-14-03_Iwata.pdf

Korda H, Itani Z (2011) Harnessing social media for health promotion and behavior change. Health Promot Pract 14(1):15–23. https://doi.org/10.1177/1524839911405850

McKight PE, Najab J (2010) Kruskal-Wallis Test. The Corsini Encyclopedia of Psychology, 1–1. https://doi.org/10.1002/9780470479216.CORPSY0491

Moner-Girona M, Kakoulaki G, Falchetta G, Weiss DJ, Taylor N (2021) Achieving universal electrification of rural healthcare facilities in sub-Saharan Africa with decentralized renewable energy technologies. Joule 5(10):2687–2714. https://doi.org/10.1016/J.JOULE.2021.09.010/ASSET/F01939FC-8DC9-485B-888C-34CB593C1D11/MAIN.ASSETS/GR16.JPG

Muessig KE, Nekkanti M, Bauermeister J, Bull S, Hightow-Weidman LB (2015) A systematic review of recent smartphone, internet and web 2.0 interventions to address the HIV continuum of care. Curr HIV AIDS Rep 12(1):173–190. https://doi.org/10.1007/S11904-014-0239-3/METRICS

Nagitta OP, Mkansi M (2019) Exploring the supply chain coordination dimensions for artemisinin-based combination therapies in Uganda. Int J Supply Chain Manag 8(4):134–151

Nagitta OP, Mkansi M, Kajjumba GW (2021a) The relationship between market environment dimensions and availability of malaria pills in Uganda. Glob Adv Health Med 10:1–10. https://doi.org/10.1177/21649561211002126

Nagitta OP, Mkansi M, Nyesiga SD, Kajjumba GW (2021b) A structural equation modeling of supply chain strategies for artemisinin-based combination therapies in Uganda. Med Access 5:239920262110647. https://doi.org/10.1177/23992026211064711

Ng WY, Tan TE, Movva PVH, Fang AHS, Yeo KK, Ho D, Foo FSS, Xiao Z, Sun K, Wong TY, Sia ATH, Ting DSW (2021) Blockchain applications in health care for COVID-19 and beyond: a systematic review. Lancet Digit Health 3(12):e819–e829. https://doi.org/10.1016/S2589-7500(21)00210-7/ATTACHMENT/B4F3DE7E-7D2C-40AB-A2C8-4E0760F68FF4/MMC1.PDF

Noar SM (2006) A 10-year retrospective of research in health mass media campaigns: where do we go from here ? J Health Commun 11:21–42. https://doi.org/10.1080/10810730500461059

Odusina EK, Ahinkorah BO, Ameyaw EK, Seidu AA, Budu E, Zegeye B, Yaya S (2021) Noncompliance with the WHO'S recommended eight antenatal care visits among pregnant women in sub-Saharan Africa: a multilevel analysis. Biomed Res Int 2021(1):6696829. https://doi.org/10.1155/2021/6696829

Purdy CH (2011) Using the internet and social media to promote condom use in Turkey. Reprod Health Matters 19(37):157–165. https://doi.org/10.1016/S0968-8080(11)37549-0

Puspita N, Dhimas Herdhianta A (2021) The effect of health promotion with WhatsApp media and booklets on knowledge level and attitude about HIV/Aids. Int J Multicult Multireligious Understand 8(7):500–508. https://doi.org/10.18415/IJMMU.V8I7.2849

Smith SA, Watkins B (2020) Millennials' uses and gratifications on LinkedIn: implications for recruitment and retention. Int J Bus Commun 60(2):560–586. https://doi.org/10.1177/2329488420973714

Soleimani H, Elango B, Hassanzadeh M (2024) A systematic review of a web-based system for selective dissemination of information in developing nations: benefits, challenges, and key features. InfoScience Trends 1:43–55. https://doi.org/10.61186/ist.202401.01.16

Upadhyay S, Lord J, Gakh M (2019) Health-information seeking and intention to quit smoking: do health beliefs have a mediating role? Tobacco Use Insights 12:1179173X1987131. https://doi.org/10.1177/1179173X19871310

Wei Y, Zheng P, Deng H, Wang X, Li X, Fu H (2020) Design features for improving mobile health intervention user engagement: systematic review and thematic analysis. J Med Internet Res 22(12):1–14. https://doi.org/10.2196/21687

Witzling L, Shaw B, Amato MS (2015) Incorporating information exposure into a theory of planned behavior model to enrich understanding of proenvironmental behavior. Sci Commun 37(5):551–574. https://doi.org/10.1177/1075547015593085

Yenit MK, Kolbe-Alexander TL, Gelaye KA, Gezie LD, Tesema GA, Abebe SM, Azale T, Shitu K, Gyawali P (2023) An evaluation of community health workers' knowledge, attitude and personal lifestyle behaviour in non-communicable disease health promotion and their association with self-efficacy and NCD-risk perception. Int J Environ Res Public Health 20(9):1–17. https://doi.org/10.3390/ijerph20095642

Zickafoose A, Ilesanmi O, Diaz-Manrique M, Adeyemi AE, Walumbe B, Strong R, Wingenbach G, Rodriguez MT, Dooley K (2024) Barriers and challenges affecting quality education (sustainable development goal #4) in sub-Saharan Africa by 2030. Sustainability 16(7):2657. https://doi.org/10.3390/SU16072657

Stephen Ogweno is a multi-award-winning global public health researcher and innovator, renowned for his pioneering work in non-communicable diseases and digital health interventions. He earned his Master's in Public Health (Global Health) from the University of Manchester, following his undergraduate studies in Population Health at Kenyatta University. His research focuses on the intersection of non-communicable diseases with health technology, health literacy, and climate change effects in low-resource settings. Ogweno serves in several key roles, including as a Steering Member at WHO NCD Labs and NCD Alliance, and as a director at the World Obesity Federation, amplifying his work in global health. With over 20 peer-reviewed publications and recognitions such as winning the WHO Hideyo Noguchi Prize for Young African Researchers in 2022, Ogweno continues to advance evidence-based public health research, developing sustainable, innovative solutions to reduce health inequities and transform healthcare outcomes globally.

Harrison Roger I am a Senior Lecturer in Public Health at the Centre for Epidemiology, University of Manchester, with a research focus on public health interventions, lifestyle-related health outcomes, and chronic disease prevention. My work primarily involves assessing the effectiveness and impact of public health interventions, particularly in relation to health behaviors and disease prevention strategies. I also have a strong research interest in public health education, with a focus on transnational students and distance learning. My current research explores the experiences of students studying public health remotely across different countries, contributing to the broader understanding of global education accessibility. Additionally, I have extensive expertise in developing and evaluating online distance learning programs in public health and serve as the Programme Director for the Population Health MOOCs projects at the University. My research continues to inform best practices in both public health education and intervention evaluation.

George William Kajjumba is a researcher in the Department of Civil and Environmental Engineering at the University of Nevada, Las Vegas (UNLV), USA. His work focuses on pioneering water treatment technologies aimed at ensuring sustainable, high-quality drinking water. He has led and designed innovative treatment strategies to remove lithium, disinfection by-products, and emerging contaminants from water sources. Additionally, his research has been instrumental in identifying and mitigating small organic molecules post-reverse osmosis systems, significantly contributing to advancements in water quality management.

Dorcus Bateefu Nakiganda is a Finance and Accounting Specialist with expertise in financial management, procurement, and supply chain logistics. She holds a Bachelor of Commerce and an MBA from Makerere University and has over 11 years of experience spanning finance, grants management, and taxation. Her work integrates financial systems with operational efficiency, particularly in healthcare logistics and resource allocation. Dorcus is passionate about optimizing supply chain processes to enhance accessibility and delivery of essential healthcare services, including non-communicable disease (NCD) management. Her ability to bridge finance, logistics, and human behavior has been instrumental in improving resource distribution in both Africa and North America.

Chapter 8
Lifesten Health: Quick Diagnostic Mobile Application for Non-Communicable Disease

Marcia Mkansi, Stephen Ogweno, Frank Ranganai Matenda, and Peace Iraguha

8.1 Introduction

Against a background of the COVID-19 pandemic, special focus has been directed toward non-communicable diseases (NCDs) (Zhao et al. 2024). NCDs, such as cardiovascular diseases, diabetes, cancer, musculoskeletal and mental diseases and chronic respiratory diseases, refer to a cluster of conditions associated with modern lifestyle that can be elucidated by assessing epidemiological transitions and demographic (Wolf et al. 2021). Allen et al. (2018) postulated that the four most common ones are cardiovascular disease, diabetes, cancers and chronic respiratory disease. Zhao et al. (2024) articulated that the World Health Organisation (WHO) indicated that more than 42 million people die due to NCDs on a yearly basis. Interestingly, NCDs excessively impact people in low- and middle-income economies, where more than three quarters of worldwide NCD deaths per year—32 million—transpire (World Health Organization 2021). Atewologun et al. (2024) opined that NCDs are becoming a global and public health issue, particularly in Africa. Elkomy and Jackson (2024) indicated that NCDs are the major contributors to the disease burden

M. Mkansi (✉) · F. R. Matenda
College of Economic and Management Sciences, The University of South Africa, Pretoria, South Africa
e-mail: mkansm@unisa.ac.za

S. Ogweno
Faculty of Biology Medicine and Health, the University of Manchester, Manchester, UK

Stowelink Foundation - Research Division, Nairobi, Kenya
e-mail: founder@stowelink.com

P. Iraguha
Department of Gender, Sexual and Reproductive Health, University of Global Health Equity, Kigali, Rwanda

T. Akenroye et al. (eds.), *Digitalizing Health Care Supply Chains in Africa*, Springer Series in Supply Chain Management 28,
https://doi.org/10.1007/978-3-032-20501-8_8

in Sub-Saharan African countries. Extant literature has revealed that the Sub-Saharan region has restricted ability to prevent, diagnose and treat NCDs. Therefore, NCDs are the major cause of deaths in our communities (Murray et al. 2012) and they threaten the attainment of several sustainable development goals.

Since NCDs usually are associated with prolonged durations and excessive treatment costs, they put a substantial burden on communities and families; thereby forcing them into poverty (Zhao et al. 2024). WHO has predicted that management and surveillance of NCDs might cost the world economy up to US$47 trillion by 2030 (World Health Organization 2018). This indicates that there is an urgent need to deal with NCDs using any means possible. Zhao et al. (2024) postulated that there is convincing evidence that shows that effective interventions can decrease premature deaths as a result of NCDs. Existing literature has indicated that these interventions include bolstering health and medical interventions (by early detection, prevention, treatment and continuous management) and mitigating modifiable risk factors (such as adopting a healthy diet, quitting smoking, increasing physical activity and restricting alcohol consumption) (Banatvala et al. 2023; Shah et al. 2022). Basically, the prevention and management of NCDs is one of the priorities of global policy priorities.

There are several challenges that should be addressed to reduce the burden of NCDs. These embrace the need for healthcare innovations, especially for under-resourced countries. Of late, AI has been effectively implemented in the prevention and control of NCDs (see, for example, Zhao et al. 2024). It has been used to fortify medical and health interventions. AI tools are progressively being implemented in the healthcare sector for several purposes. Deniz-Garcia et al. (2023) postulated the integration of AI into mobile health (mHealth) apps, which has the ability to substantially support people and healthcare experts in preventing and managing NCDs in a personalised manner. The authors further stated that mHealth apps are extensively available, low in cost and can assist enhance healthy behaviours. Milne-Ives et al. (2020) opined that mHealth apps could encourage healthy food selections, upsurge in physical activity and decrease of sedentary time. El-Rashidy et al. (2021) proffered that AI-powered mHealth apps can be utilised for the remote monitoring of people with chronic diseases, assisting to lower diagnostic costs and time while enhancing healthcare delivery.

In Africa, the growing adoption of mobile devices has not only led to a surge in Internet users, but has also established alternative supply chain channels across various industries, including healthcare. However, the number of AI-based mobile applications for diagnostics for NCDs is restricted. The situation is even worse when we refer to AI-based mobile applications that integrate quick diagnostics with patient wellness and loyalty programs. Further, in Africa, substantial progress has been attained in developing technologies to fight diseases, even though the majority of research is executed outside the continent (Atewologun et al. 2024). This poses challenges to the long-term sustainability of addressing NCDs within Africa (Atewologun et al. 2024).

Implementing semi-structured interviews with Lifesten, a Rwanda-based startup, this case study examines the use of AI and mobile applications to enhance the diagnostics of NCDs and promote wellness. Lifesten expands the digital healthcare supply chain beyond conventional healthcare facilities, incorporating pharmaceutical companies, health insurers, retailers, patients and community forums. This chapter is organised as follows. Section 8.2 presents the review of literature and Sect. 8.3 summarises the methodology implemented in this study. In Sect. 8.4, study results are outlined. Section 8.5 concludes the study and exhibits the implications and avenues for future research.

8.2 Literature Review

Digital health incorporates all healthcare technologies such as mHealth and cuts across numerous areas (Mescher et al. 2024). U.S. Food and Drug Administration (2020) indicated that digital health is associated with "the vast potential to improve our ability to accurately diagnose and treat disease and to enhance health care delivery to all people". mHealth implements smartphone and mobile device apps to achieve these goals (Chan 2021). In practice, mHealth has become a crucial component of the health care information technology industry, experiencing substantial growth of late (Chib and Lin 2018). Extant literature has indicated that this expansion has been partly powered by the proliferation of devices such as wearable technologies, mobile sensors and Internet of Things devices which are widely used for monitoring in medical institutions and hospitals. Interestingly, some of these devises are even used outside hospital sites for remote in-home care. Further, the adoption of mHealth has increased exponentially over the past two decades, coinciding with the improved functionality and widespread adoption of smartphones, tablets and other personal electronic devices (Mescher et al. 2024). Therefore, the quantity of direct-to-consumer mHealth apps has increased to hundreds of thousands (Mescher et al. 2024).

Figure 8.1 illustrates the functioning of mHealth apps, which integrate data from various sources into a smartphone-premised platform to deliver guidance and advice for health care patients, professionals and healthy individuals (Deniz-Garcia et al. 2023).

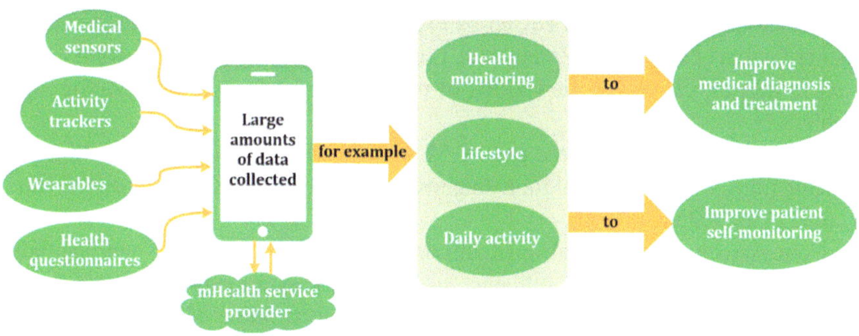

Fig. 8.1 Conceptual block illustration of mHealth app function. Source: Deniz-Garcia et al. (2023)

Of late, AI has transformed health care delivery (Bhatt et al. 2022). The authors (Bhatt et al. 2022) further stated that AI techniques have been implemented to design forecasting models for the early detection of diseases and these forecasting models leverage mHealth data to determine new ways for managing and detecting mental health conditions and chronic diseases. The use of AI-powered mHealth applications has become a fast-growing research area. Among other reasons, the aim of implementing AI to design mHealth apps is to enhance treatment, thwart diseases, monitor people with chronic diseases remotely, reduce costs and time to diagnosis, offer improved health care delivery (El-Rashidy et al. 2021), and offer more personalised health care (Johnson et al. 2021; Mesko 2017).

Even though AI-based mHealth applications have potential to improve healthcare delivery, there are numerous challenges that limit their use in medical practices. Mescher et al. (2024) opined that mHealth apps are usually unregulated by global regulatory organisations and are seldom assessed for quality, effectiveness, safety and data security. In the same vein, Deniz-Garcia et al. (2023) postulated that, in spite of an expanding mHealth apps body of literature, their efficacy is still an issue of debate. Existing literature has indicated that clinical efficacy of mHealth apps is debateable and these apps are not able to maintain user engagement. The authors (Mescher et al. 2024) indicated that, in practice, several evaluation frameworks and scales are in place, but the responsibility of appraising mHealth apps is with the end users. Consequently, it is difficult to identify mHealth apps that must be endorsed by healthcare givers and implemented by patients since there is a multiplicity of these apps, and there is lack of evaluation and oversight (Mescher et al. 2024). Bhatt et al. (2022) proffered that, presently, not much is acknowledged concerning the implementation of AI-powered mHealth settings. Deniz-Garcia et al. (2023) (and references therein) indicated that the evidence buttressing the implementation of mHealth apps is not convincing.

Internet connections and smartphones are not accessible all over and the costs related to their implementation can be an obstacle even if they are accessible (Deniz-Garcia et al. 2023). This study further suggested that physical restrictions like blindness; language, digital and health literacy; and the lack of awareness of safe and efficient mHealth apps are some of the challenges. Brault and Saxena (2021) showed that AI is unable to critically think, thereby it cannot execute an intellectual and epistemic examination of the results found. This indicates that the validity of the results should be critically assessed by experts to evade problems. As indicated by Deniz-Garcia et al. (2023), Zhang et al. (2018) revealed the challenges for AI adoption in mHealth from the viewpoints of medical research and AI technology (see Table 8.1).

Other challenges facing the use of AI in mHealth apps include algorithm processing time, which is critical for a diagnostic tool that requires rapid results (Deniz-Garcia et al. 2023).

Concussively, even though mHealth apps are projected to grow exponentially, their efficacy and long-term influence usually differ as a result of technical challenges, user obstacles or inadequately designed interventions (Holtz and Mitchell 2024). Many existing apps lack efficacy or fail to sustain user engagement. These authors further opined that these obstacles highpoint the requirement for enhanced

Table 8.1 Challenges for AI adoption in mobile health from the viewpoints of medical research and AI technology

AI technology-associated matters	Medical research-associated matters
• Structure and data origin - presence of varied and sophisticated databases: diverse data sources do not offer standardised data that can be simply merged - laboratory results uncertainty as a result systematic and random errors: the acquirement of high-quality data is occasionally operator-dependent - requirement for huge data amounts for AI algorithms training • Algorithms architecture - lack reproducibility of results: diverse training processes can offer diverse forecasting results in diverse clinical settings - Problems of overfitting: AI models may not be capable to generalise for huge and diverse populations - high computational power and time needs: as a result algorithm sophistication and data volume - intra- and interindividual data variability	• Interdisciplinary nature of research - data security and privacy: data from many people is required to train the algorithm • Learning process of deep learning - need to circumvent black-box technology: necessary to know why a classification process functions or not - medical specialist assessment: need for clinical approval and validation of the data patterns recognised

Source: Deniz-Garcia et al. (2023)

deliberations when building these apps and the creation of best practices for designing mHealth apps that are efficient. In summary, more research is required on the implementation of AI in mHealth apps.

8.3 Methodology

The study conducted a semi-structured interview with the chief executive officer (CEO) of Lifesten to analyse the implementation of AI and mobile applications to augment the diagnostics of NCDs and promote wellness. The CEO has a master's degree in digital global health from the University of Manchester and has also studied at Cambridge University. Further, the CEO has worked with a few local and global organisations, including the WHO, the Global Non-communicable Disease Alliance and the World Obesity Federation. These organisations have been working primarily at the intersection of digital health advocacy and NCDs. The interview lasted for an hour. We use semi-structured interviews since they are suitable for dealing with more sophisticated social-behavioural research questions (Adeoye-Olatunde and Olenik 2021). *The interviewer can ask more questions to comprehend the perspectives of the participant.* In the same vein, Belina (2023) propounded that semi-structured interviews are efficient in gathering perceptions into concealed facets of social life, challenges that are not closely noticeable. The author also indicated that semi-structured interviews allow for the exploration of under-researched areas. Sampling is a vital facet of qualitative research design since it affects the study findings' trustworthiness (Adeoye-Olatunde and Olenik 2021). Purpose sampling was used in this study. We adopted it because it studies only the population that is of particular interest (Andrade 2021). Literature also indicated that purposive sampling is usually viewed as more effective in apprehending the insights of senior elites (López 2023 and references therein). The study adopted content analysis. Maier (2017) propounded that content analysis is valuable in describing communicative messages, the research process is comparatively unobtrusive, and content analysis offers a comparatively safe process for examining communicative messages.

8.4 Findings

This study analyses the implementation of AI and mobile applications to enhance the diagnostics of NCDs and promote wellness. The study findings are presented in this section.

Lifesten is one of the two companies in the Sub-Saharan Africa that have applied the use of transdermal optical imaging technology via smartphones at a population level and optimised the intersection of mobile applications, AI algorithm and wellness programs to achieve United Nations Sustainable Development Goal 3 of good health and wellness. From the diagnostic perspective, it offers a versatile transdermal optical imaging innovation that uses near infrared light for quick capturing of blood flow in the face and using the data for diagnostic and analysis of NCDs. The strength of transdermal optical imaging is its AI unique properties that leverage light to provide non-invasive, detailed real time diagnosis. Loyalty programs are integrated as a strategic tool to foster patient engagement, promote repeat utilisation, enhance profitability, harness health related data, retain and attract users, encourage proactive good health and well-being, and promote diffusion of the innovation. The smartphone or mobile application serves as a remote and digital healthcare supply chain pipeline that connects different stakeholders from patients, doctors, healthcare facilities to responsible government officials. Through the digital platform, several stakeholders produce and deliver healthcare services from diagnostics, referral logistics, prescriptions and analyse healthcare products or inventory. The following quote supports this argument:

> Lifesten Health is for profit enterprise that has a digital innovation. We are the second company in sub-Saharan Africa, to introduce Transdermal optical imaging to the public. Transdermal optical imaging is technology where with your smartphone you can be able to scan your face and we look at the flow of blood under. Through an algorithm and in 30 seconds we're able to give your blood pressure, your body mass index, your stress index, your cardiovascular disease risk, and 13 other critical health diagnostics and we're able to give you all of that data in in 30 seconds. It is literally a 30 second facial scan or a 30 second selfie as we communicate it to our people and then off getting the results, individuals get personalized health plans. **CEO**

The intersection of technology, supply chain and loyalty create a triple helix and complex supply chain approach to healthcare service. The structure is a multi-tier chain with three strands of partners with varied needs and businesses. The first stand constitutes digital entrepreneurs and their investors such as Lifesten Health, PricewaterhouseCoopers (PwC) and Norvatis Foundation. The second strands are public or government ministers of health, Information and Communication Technology (ICT), and research health centres. The third strand constitutes production and retail supply chain stakeholders. This was showed by the response in the succeeding quote:

> From the stakeholder standpoint, we have a lot of stakeholders who saw the vision, saw the innovation and really worked with us to ensure that we're able to bring this to life. So, we have the Novartis Foundation as an example, who was a financier. We are also very lucky to have the government such as the Ministry of Health and the Ministry of ICT in Rwanda. Another key stakeholder is PwC. **CEO**

Of particular interest was the understanding of the unique business needs of the chain stakeholders. Government partners such as the minister of health and ICT appears to bridge infrastructural challenge, whilst delivering healthcare with limited resources and stress to healthcare budgets. Academics and research partners harness high impact research data, with evidence-based impact. Loyalty partners such as pharmaceuticals, health stores, gyms, nutritionists and physiotherapists encourage repeat purchases and retention crucial for profit and sustainability. Technology owners and investors increase adoption, impact and return on investment. The healthcare data and database serve as critical intelligence for new businesses opportunities and healthcare products. Furthermore, it's a repository of insight necessary for predictive and preventive healthcare for global and national stakeholders. The quote to support this is as follows:

> A big opportunity that Lifesten Health is working on is to transform the data into predictive and behavioural use cases for the user. For predictive analysis, we will offer this for governments, for institutions, for organisations that are interested in predictive health of users to better prepare them to react to and also prevent, the rise of new diseases. So, that is a pioneering field where we are continuously gathering these data points and hoping that in a very near future within the next 18 months that we are able to begin capitalising on these data points that we are currently collecting or working on. **CEO**

The digital affordance of mobile applications makes it possible for multiple digital products to be delivered simultaneously for a transformative e-supply chain. Lifesten AI-based application leverage its high penetration in Africa and the in-built capabilities to diagnose and visualise cardiovascular NCDs at a cellular level. As an e-supply chain channel, it's able to capture, in real time, fine details at a cellular or molecular level necessary for instantaneous quick diagnostics. Rewards and loyalty programs are by design strategic tools to manipulate human behaviour towards a positive outcome, in this case, health goals, whilst simultaneously fostering customer retention for participating gyms, health stores, nutritionist, etc. The participant observed the following:

> We all know from health economics that doing things that are healthy is hard. Going to the gym, working out, eating the right food is hard. So, individuals need ways to be incentivised to engage in this healthy behaviour. Engaging in healthy behaviour in the short term does not give you visible results. Rather, the results usually come in the long term and individuals are wired to primarily want to get or do activities that give them short term rewards. That's why junk foods, alcohol and betting and these kinds of things are usually more attractive to individuals because they give short term rewards. How can I create innovations that essentially help in incentivising individuals to adopt healthy behaviour so that we are able to prevent NCDs or lifestyle diseases? That is how I came to develop Lifesten. **CEO**

The impact of Lifesten's supply chain and business model can be measured by the company's supply chain partners, investors, government partnership, media attention, projected income and the number of healthcare users enrolled in less than a year. The company's business model captures profit at both ends of its chain. The business to business to customer model (B2B2C) offers corporates a wellness package or program at $119 per person per year. Hence the business to customer (B2C) model offers health insurance plans of $36–96 per person per year. For a population of 1.6 million, the corporate program of $199 plus customers' health insurance at $96, the projected and estimated revenue is $344,000,000 per year. The quote to support this is as follows:

> We reached 1.6 million people in a span of 10 months with our government partners. This also attracted international attention from organizations like CNN and DW, who also featured Lifesten innovation on the global system. So, those are the initial reactions in terms of the innovation and it being on the market. Being in the market for a while, we've seen a rising interest from other countries. Lifesten Health, by the way, is accessible globally and we have 64 countries all over the world or users from 64 countries all over the world. **CEO**

> PERSONAL PLANS B2C (Health Insurance Plans) $36–96 PER PERSON PER YEAR. WORKPLACE PLANS B2B2C (Cooperate Wellness Programs), $119 PER PERSON YEAR. **Pitch Deck**

8.5 Discussion

The study findings highlight a pathway for achieving unified vision amongst supply chain stakeholders. The partnership between several stakeholders like investors and government, and wellness is geared towards achieving a unified vision of United Nations Sustainable Development Goal 3 of good health and wellness, whilst fostering economic growth through consumption of products. Sustainable Development Goal 3 vows to "ensure healthy lives and promote well-being for all at all ages" (United Nations 2015). For example, retail partners such as health stores, pharmaceuticals and gyms foster consumption of goods and services necessary for economic growth. Government partners deliver healthcare service to the public. Investors pave way for new markets and comprehensive digital products, enabling the implementation of advanced technology such as cloud platforms, AI and IoT to optimise operations for predictive health and preventative analytics that deliver automated and instantaneous diagnosis and decision-making.

In support of this, Aminizadeh et al. (2024) propounded that the dawn of AI has steered a wave of transformative applications developed to augment healthcare services, with Machine Learning as a remarkable subclass of AI. Tiwari and Waoo (2024) and Haleem et al. (2022) are some of the authors that indicated that the implementation of technology in healthcare is restructuring the industry, providing unparalleled prospects to improve diagnostic accuracy, enhance patient care and elevate operational efficiency. The study also highlights the possibilities of enhanced communication and collaboration through the Lifesten platform, necessary for establishing trust and sustaining relationships. In the same vein, Nielsen and Sahay (2022) postulated that digital platforms and ecosystems transform how users cooperate, interact and collaborate in the health sector.

Interestingly, the case study offers empirical insight of remote digital production and e-service delivery of healthcare through diagnostic, delivery and sale of insurance products, tech products (AI-application), gym service, nutritional products and pharmaceutical and health products, among other things. The quick diagnostic mobile application innovation has the ability to configure e-supply chain that delivers the triple objective of right product at right place at the right time. Put differently, the case study reveals a transformed integrated logistics solution that produces and delivers digital products and services remotely. The quick diagnostic and referral system creates a dynamic e-routing system that optimise mobile phones as delivery channels using real time data for cost and time effective solutions across regions and countries.

Lifesten Health is a reformed digital conglomerate company. That is to say, it is a diversified organisation that functions across numerous industries or sectors, with its main foundation focus erected on digital technologies. This company leverages digital platforms, online services and advanced technologies like AI to create, deliver and monetise its products and services. It is an epitome of a disruption company, which transcends industries to optimise economies of scale through the power of mobile application as a shared resource for centralised management, revenue generation, collaboration platform with a unique purchasing power between B2C and B2B markets. In the same vein, Walton (2014) proffered that Internet-premised companies have a huge influence upon traditional value creation actions via the disintermediation of supply chains. The authors further stated that these companies leverage core competencies and attain profits ascending from better resources, and this novel configuration of competitive advantage is premised on possessing a better ecosystem that implements data as the key resource as an alternative to capital.

Obviously, the diverse portfolio is critical for diversification of risks where poor performance in one area can be offset by better performance in another area. Thus, creating a sustainable and profitable model necessary for financial stability through multiple revenue streams and cash flows. The latter is critical for digital market stability, accumulation of market power necessary to dictate future pricing, supply chains and shares regulatory frameworks. Even though some studies discovered a "diversification discount" (for instance, Berger and Ofek 1995), Choi et al. (2021)

revealed that, generally, greater diversification, in terms of product and geographical markets, is related to higher company performance. Although the digital conglomerate offers exciting opportunities, it also offers complex management structures, which could potentially lead to inefficiencies and conflicts.

Moreover, it heightens regulatory scrutiny for strict compliance. Under the same line of reasoning, similarly, Witt (2022) postulated that the rise of a few dominant digital platforms with extensive global networks of interconnected services is raising substantial issues among competition agencies. Interestingly, the author (Witt 2022) opined that although the United States and United Kingdom authorities have not yet acted against any conglomerate acquisitions in practice, evidence shows that they are increasingly receptive to non-horizontal theories of harm once more. There are scarce digital entrepreneurs that bridge the gap between science, health and technology through a single platform. This may be attributed to scarce and uncontrolled resources (Zajicek and Meyers 2018). In the same vein, Lim and Anderson (2016) postulated that healthcare providers are slower when it comes to the adoption of new innovations.

The case represents the centre of interdisciplinary integration and application. This is important because, to enhance innovation diffusion, there is a need for multidisciplinary buy-in from other stakeholders (Lim and Anderson 2016). On one hand, it is the application of cardiovascular NCDs medical knowledge enabling the production and delivery of diagnostics tools, whilst promoting wellness. On the other hand, it bridges technological advancement to improve healthcare. Taken together, the former and the later are in their nature, an integration and application of scientific discovery. The case study serves as an empirical example of a triple helix model of innovation between academics, government and industry to drive healthcare service, economic growth and innovation. In support of this, Etzkowitz (2003) articulated that innovation is progressively premised upon a "triple helix" of university-industry-government connections. As an academic, the digital entrepreneur provides research-based products, whilst industry stakeholders drive its commercialisation and practical application for high impact, especially to vulnerable communities. Government provides a conducive environment for innovation and emerging markets to thrive, whilst minimising infrastructural barriers and expediting service delivery.

Lifesten provides a shared database necessary for intelligence and analytics. This enables stakeholders to access relevant healthcare data for new products, demand, forecasting and predictable healthcare plans to optimise healthcare supply chain operations. Looked at differently, healthcare supply chain partners are in a better position to collect and develop new products and services based on historic purchases, historic diagnosis, trend analysis; whilst sharing consolidated reporting across diverse business units. It is the foundation for AI-powered analytics for automated health, consumption and wellness insight that offers predictive and health consumption capabilities; whilst delivering instantaneous intelligence. This indicates that companies can build competitive intelligence through data analytics (see, for instance, Niu et al. 2021; Ranjan and Foropon 2021).

The findings of the study indicated that the digital affordance of mobile applications makes it conceivable for numerous digital products to be delivered concurrently for a transformative e-supply chain (see, for example, Wong et al. 2020; Marent et al. 2018). Also, it has been highlighted that mHealth applications should leverage their high penetration and their in-built capabilities to instantaneously diagnose and visualise NCDs. Moreover, rewards and loyalty programs can influence the behaviour of people towards positive outcome health goals and at the same time, foster client retaining for participating gyms and health stores, etc. This argument of behaviour change is supported by Marques et al. (2017) and Daryanto et al. (2010). Generally, Lifesten's supply chain and business model has a significant impact in the healthcare sector.

8.6 Conclusion

Using semi-structured interviews with the CEO for Lifesten, we analysed the implementation of AI and mobile applications to enhance the diagnostics of NCDs and promote wellness. Lifesten, a Rwandan startup, is one of the two companies in Sub-Saharan Africa that optimised the intersection of mobile applications, transdermal optical imaging AI algorithm and loyalty program to attain sustainable goal 3 of good health and well-being. The findings of the study reveal impactful mobile health applications for transdermal optical imaging, particularly in self-screening for blood pressure, improved triage and referrals to healthcare facilities and online monitoring of healthy diets. Further, the study indicates that AI-powered mHealth applications profoundly promote patient wellness and loyalty programs by highpointing the transformative effects of AI on patient wellness and loyalty programs. This case study underscores the practical applications of digital health innovations in Africa while also reflecting their broader, unintended implications for the global healthcare supply chain.

The chapter urges policymakers to adopt AI-powered application in order to enhance diagnostic tests of NCDs and promote patient wellness and loyalty programs. Also, quality criteria-based policies for sensitive data management and protocols to standardise data acquisition are required to improve performance and increase their use among patients and health care professionals. Even though the study discovered some interesting results, it can be extended in several dimensions. First, although Lifesten is the digital conglomerate that offers exciting opportunities, it also offers complex management structures, which could potentially lead to inefficiencies and conflicts. Moreover, it heightens regulatory scrutiny for strict compliance. Therefore, future studies can assess if it does not dilute focus and compromise effectiveness and efficiency. Second, future studies can explore the environmental impact of the e-supply chain model.

References

Adeoye-Olatunde OA, Olenik NL (2021) Research and scholarly methods: semi-structured interviews. Journal of the American College of Clinical Pharmacy 4(10):1358–1367

Allen LN, Pullar J, Wickramasinghe KK, Williams J, Roberts N, Mikkelsen B, Varghese C, Townsend N (2018) Evaluation of research on interventions aligned to WHO 'best buys' for NCDs in low-income and lower-middle-income countries: a systematic review from 1990 to 2015. BMJ Glob Health 3(1):e000535

Aminizadeh S, Heidari A, Dehghan M, Toumaj S, Rezaei M, Navimipour NJ, Stroppa F, Unal M (2024) Opportunities and challenges of artificial intelligence and distributed systems to improve the quality of healthcare service. Artif Intell Med 149:102779

Andrade C (2021) The inconvenient truth about convenience and purposive samples. Indian J Psychol Med 43(1):86–88

Atewologun FA, Okesanya OJ, Okon II, Kayode HH, Ukoaka BM, Olaleke NO, Ogaya JB, Okikiola LA, Manirambona E, Lucero-Prisno DE III (2024) Examining the potentials of stem cell therapy in reducing the burden of selected non-communicable diseases in Africa. Stem Cell Res Ther 15(1):253

Banatvala N, Akselrod S, Bovet P, Mendis S (2023) The WHO global action plan for the prevention and control of NCDs 2013–2030. In: Noncommunicable diseases. Routledge, pp 234–239

Belina A (2023) Semi-structured interviewing as a tool for understanding informal civil society. Voluntary Sector Review 14(2):331–347

Berger PG, Ofek E (1995) Diversification's effect on firm value. J Financ Econ 37(1):39–65

Bhatt P, Liu J, Gong Y, Wang J, Guo Y (2022) Emerging artificial intelligence–empowered mhealth: scoping review. JMIR Mhealth Uhealth 10(6):e35053

Brault N, Saxena M (2021) For a critical appraisal of artificial intelligence in healthcare: the problem of bias in mHealth. J Eval Clin Pract 27(3):513–519

Chan J (2021) Exploring digital health care: eHealth, mHealth, and librarian opportunities. J Med Libr Assoc 109(3):376–381

Chib A, Lin SH (2018) Theoretical advancements in mHealth: a systematic review of mobile apps. J Health Commun 23(10–11):909–955

Choi J, Menon A, Tabakovic H (2021) Using machine learning to revisit the diversification–performance relationship. Strateg Manag J 42(9):1632–1661

Daryanto A, de Ruyter K, Wetzels M, Patterson PG (2010) Service firms and customer loyalty programs: a regulatory fit perspective of reward preferences in a health club setting. J Acad Mark Sci 38:604–616

Deniz-Garcia A, Fabelo H, Rodriguez-Almeida AJ, Zamora-Zamorano G, Castro-Fernandez M, Alberiche Ruano MDP, Solvoll T, Granja C, Schopf TR, Callico GM, Soguero-Ruiz C (2023) Quality, usability, and effectiveness of mHealth apps and the role of artificial intelligence: current scenario and challenges. J Med Internet Res 25:e44030

Elkomy S, Jackson T (2024) WHO non-communicable diseases global monitoring framework: pandemic resilience in sub-Saharan Africa and low-income countries. Socio Econ Plan Sci 95:102043

El-Rashidy N, El-Sappagh S, Islam SMR, El-Bakry M, H., & Abdelrazek, S. (2021) Mobile health in remote patient monitoring for chronic diseases: principles, trends, and challenges. Diagnostics 11(4):607. https://doi.org/10.3390/diagnostics11040607

Etzkowitz H (2003) Innovation in innovation: the triple helix of university-industry-government relations. Soc Sci Inf 42(3):293–337. https://doi.org/10.1177/05390184030423002

Haleem A, Javaid M, Singh RP, Suman R (2022) Medical 4.0 technologies for healthcare: features, capabilities, and applications. Internet of Things and Cyber-Physical Systems 2:12–30

Holtz BE, Mitchell K (2024) Best practices for developing a diabetes mHealth app. J Diabetes Sci Technol 18(1):39–45

Johnson KB, Wei WQ, Weeraratne D, Frisse ME, Misulis K, Rhee K, Zhao J, Snowdon JL (2021) Precision medicine, AI, and the future of personalized health care. Clin Transl Sci 14(1):86–93
Lim SY, Anderson EG (2016) Institutional barriers against innovation diffusion: from the perspective of digital health startups. In 2016 49th Hawaii International Conference on System Sciences (HICSS) (pp 3328–3337). IEEE
López M (2023) The effect of sampling mode on response rate and bias in elite surveys. Qual Quant 57(2):1303–1319
Maier M (2017) Content analysis: advantages and disadvantages. In: The SAGE encyclopedia of communication research methods, vol 4. SAGE Publications, pp 240–242. https://doi.org/10.4135/9781483381411
Marent B, Henwood F, Darking M, EmERGE Consortium (2018) Ambivalence in digital health: co-designing an mHealth platform for HIV care. Soc Sci Med 215:133–141
Marques SH, Cardoso MG, Lindeza ACA (2017) Do loyalty cards enhance loyalty in the pharmaceutical sector? J Relatsh Mark 16(2):143–162
Mescher T, Hacker RL, Martinez LA, Morris CD, Mishkind MC, Garver-Apgar CE (2024) Mobile health apps: guidance for evaluation and implementation by healthcare workers. Journal of Technology in Behavioral Science 10:224. https://doi.org/10.1007/s41347-024-00441-7
Mesko B (2017) The role of artificial intelligence in precision medicine. Expert Rev Precis Med Drug Dev 2(5):239–241
Milne-Ives M, Lam C, De Cock C, Van Velthoven MH, Meinert E (2020) Mobile apps for health behavior change in physical activity, diet, drug and alcohol use, and mental health: systematic review. JMIR Mhealth Uhealth 8(3):e17046
Murray CJ, Vos T, Lozano R, Naghavi M, Flaxman AD, Michaud C, Ezzati M, Shibuya K, Salomon JA, Abdalla S, Aboyans V (2012) Disability-adjusted life years (DALYs) for 291 diseases and injuries in 21 regions, 1990–2010: a systematic analysis for the global burden of disease study 2010. Lancet 380(9859):2197–2223
Nielsen P, Sahay S (2022) A critical review of the role of technology and context in digital health research. Digital Health 8:1–10
Niu Y, Ying L, Yang J, Bao M, Sivaparthipan CB (2021) Organizational business intelligence and decision making using big data analytics. Inf Process Manag 58(6):102725
Ranjan J, Foropon C (2021) Big data analytics in building the competitive intelligence of organizations. Int J Inf Manag 56:102231
Shah SA, Anuar H, Abdul Gafor AH, Abdullah NN (2022) Poor perception of chronic kidney diseases and its influencing factors among diabetics patients. Sci Rep 12(1):5694
Tiwari M, Waoo AA (2024) Transforming healthcare: the synergistic fusion of AI and IoT for intelligent, personalized well-being. In: Revolutionizing healthcare: AI integration with IoT for enhanced patient outcomes. Springer Nature Switzerland, Cham, pp 109–149
U.S. Food and Drug Administration (2020) What is digital health? U.S. Food and Drug Administration. https://www.fda.gov/medical-devices/digital-health-center-excellence/what-digital-health
United Nations (2015) Transforming our world: the 2030 agenda for sustainable development. Resolution adopted by the General Assembly on 25 September 2015
Walton N (2014) New conglomerates and the ecosystem advantage. China-USA Business Review 13(7):431–443
Witt AC (2022) Who's afraid of conglomerate mergers? The Antitrust Bulletin 67(2):208–236. https://doi.org/10.1177/0003603X221082748
Wolf TG, Cagetti MG, Fisher JM, Seeberger GK, Campus G (2021) Non-communicable diseases and oral health: an overview. Frontiers in Oral Health 2:725460
Wong CA, Madanay F, Ozer EM, Harris SK, Moore M, Master SO, Moreno M, Weitzman ER (2020) Digital health technology to enhance adolescent and young adult clinical preventive services: affordances and challenges. J Adolesc Health 67(2):S24–S33

World Health Organization (2018) Noncommunicable diseases (NCDs): Key facts. https://www.who.int/news-room/fact-sheets/detail/noncommunicable-diseases
World Health Organization (2021) WHO 148th executive board 21 January 2021. Oral Resolution EB148.R1. https://apps.who.int/gb/ebwha/pdf_files/EB148/B148_R1-en.pdf
Zajicek H, Meyers A (2018) Digital health entrepreneurship. In: Rivas H, Wac K (eds) Digital health. Health informatics. Springer, Cham. https://doi.org/10.1007/978-3-319-61446-5_19
Zhang S, Bamakan SMH, Qu Q, Li S (2018) Learning for personalized medicine: a comprehensive review from a deep learning perspective. IEEE Rev Biomed Eng 12:194–208
Zhao Y, Chaw JK, Liu L, Chaw SH, Ang MC, Ting TT (2024) Systematic literature review on reinforcement learning in non-communicable disease interventions. Artif Intell Med 154:102901

Marcia Mkansi is the College Head of Research, Post-graduate Studies, Innovation, and Commercialisation, a Professor of Operations and Supply Chain Management and the former Head of the Department of Operations Management at the College of Economic & Management Sciences, University of South Africa. She serves as a non-executive director for Hellmann Worldwide Logistics, and an advisory board member of the Africa Resource Centre (ARC), a Bill and Melinda Gates Foundation (BMGF)-funded non-governmental organization, set up to be a resource to the public health sector in African governments. Her university-industry alliances include, but are not limited to, Kuehne Foundation, The Innovation Hub, and SAP skills Africa. She is a nominee for the Top Women Standard Bank and UN women projects, and a finalist under the research, innovation, and creative economy category of the National Science and Technology Forum (NSTF)—South32 awards.

Stephen Ogweno is a multi-award-winning global public health researcher and innovator, renowned for his pioneering work in non-communicable diseases and digital health interventions. He earned his Master's in Public Health (Global Health) from the University of Manchester, following his undergraduate studies in Population Health at Kenyatta University. His research focuses on the intersection of non-communicable diseases with health technology, health literacy, and climate change effects in low-resource settings. Ogweno serves in several key roles, including as a Steering Member at WHO NCD Labs and NCD Alliance, and as a director at the World Obesity Federation, amplifying his work in global health. With over 20 peer-reviewed publications and recognitions such as winning the WHO Hideyo Noguchi Prize for Young African Researchers in 2022, Ogweno continues to advance evidence-based public health research, developing sustainable, innovative solutions to reduce health inequities and transform healthcare outcomes globally.

Frank Ranganai Matenda is a Postdoctoral Research Fellow in the Department of Operations Management at the University of South Africa, Pretoria, South Africa. His research interests are related to credit risk, asset pricing, green finance, corporate performance and risk management, investments, corporate finance, financial markets, and small business economics. He is the Coordinator for the International Conference on Business Resilience, Continuity and Regeneration and an Editorial Board Member for the Journal of Inclusive and Innovative Practices.

Peace Iraguha is a published researcher and healthtech innovator with a strong academic focus on cardiovascular health, preventive healthcare, and digital health solutions. With a master's degree in Global Health Delivery from the University of Global Health Equity, she co-authored a groundbreaking study on cardiovascular screening in Rwanda, contributing to the advancement of early detection methodologies in low-resource settings. With over seven years of experience in healthcare research, she played a pivotal role in leading a Novartis-funded project that screened over two million Rwandans using transdermal optical imaging technology. Her research interests lie in integrating technology into healthcare systems to enhance early disease detection and improve health outcomes. Peace continues to drive innovation in digital health research. She actively participates in global academic discussions, presenting her work at leading health conferences, and remains dedicated to scaling evidence-based interventions to strengthen healthcare systems across Africa.

MIX
Papier aus verantwortungsvollen Quellen
Paper from responsible sources
FSC® C105338

If you have any concerns about our products,
you can contact us on
ProductSafety@springernature.com

In case Publisher is established outside the EU,
the EU authorized representative is:
Springer Nature Customer Service Center GmbH
Europaplatz 3, 69115 Heidelberg, Germany

Printed by Libri Plureos GmbH
in Hamburg, Germany